Urban School Chiefs under Fire

The University of
Chicago Press

Chicago and London

Larry
Cuban

URBAN SCHOOL CHIEFS UNDER FIRE

LARRY CUBAN was a teacher and administrator in
Cleveland and Washington, D.C., schools between 1956 and 1972. He received his Ph.D. in
education from Stanford University and is
superintendent of the Arlington, Virginia,
schools. He is the author of *To Make a Difference: Teaching in the Inner City;* writer and
editor of a series of textbooks, *The Promise of
America;* and editor of *Black Man in America* and
Youth as a Minority.

Epigraph is from E. B. White, *Stuart Little* (New
York: Harper & Row, 1945). Copyright 1945 by
E. B. White.

The University of Chicago Press, Chicago 60637
The University of Chicago Press, Ltd., London

Library of Congress Cataloging in Publication Data

Cuban, Larry.
  Urban school chiefs under fire.

  Bibliography: p.
  Includes index.
  1. School superintendents and principals.
I. Title.
LB2831.7.C82   371.2'011'0973   75-19509
ISBN 0-226-12314-6

Just as the sun was comin' up, Stuart saw a man seated in thought by the side of the road. Stuart steered his car alongside, stopped and put his head out.

"You're worried about something, aren't you?" asked Stuart.

"Yes, I am," said the man, who was tall and mild.

"Can I help you in any way?" asked Stuart in a friendly voice.

The man shook his head. "It's an impossible situation, I guess," he replied. "You see, I'm the superintendent of schools in this town."

"That's not an impossible situation," said Stuart. "It's bad, but not impossible."

E. B. White

For Barbara

Contents

Preface

Few people question the importance of an urban superintendent to the future of a school system. A superintendent somehow influences, directly or indirectly, the board of education, the bureaucracy he manages, and the students for whom he is ultimately responsible. Whether that influence is heavy or slight, of course, depends upon a variety of factors; but the potential is there.

I've worked for six big-city superintendents over the past seventeen years as a teacher, a field administrator, and central office director of a system-wide program. I've come to know a dozen more as colleagues on consulting jobs, on committees, and as friends. Some I liked a great deal; others I would not share a cab with. Some believed deeply in their divinity as Educators; others were just folks. While they varied in personal style, taste, and philosophy, the ones I worked for and knew believed that superintendents make a difference in the quality of education.

I, too, believe this. Perhaps, now that I have completed this study and am myself serving as a superintendent, my belief is more tempered, more modest than it was initially. But the belief remains strong, nonetheless. Perhaps, the margin of institutional change available to a schoolman is far narrower than I originally thought. But the margin remains. Perhaps a man or woman cannot single-handedly shape affairs, as I had once felt. But individual effort harnessed to intelligence and commitment still counts. With so many "perhaps" my beliefs remain only that: beliefs. This study does not elevate a belief into a fact. For those who share this belief in effective superintendents making a qualitative difference in urban education, it can become a proposition requiring repeated testing in urban school systems across the nation.

In completing this study, my debts are many. For making it possible for me to attend Stanford, for patience and advice, I owe David Tyack much. In the finest and highest sense of each word, he is a teacher, scholar, and humane being. Middle-aged professionals like myself often have difficulty adjusting to graduate school. Dave eased that adjustment for me by accepting my strengths and working with me on what I didn't know or found difficult. He blended the roles of mentor, friend, and critic into a unique combination.

For stretching my mind to consider other ways of looking at the world and life, I owe Jim March much wine, gentle conversations, and, I guess, a few poems. For a willing ear, generous accessibility, a wealth of ideas on the politics of education and constant support, I am indebted to Mike Kirst. Henry Levin's perspective and compassion I found both stimulating and rewarding. My appreciation to Hank.

I owe Barbara Cuban much. Despite her busy schedule as student, wife, and mother, she made time to proofread and type this study. We have shared many writing projects, and for all of them, as here, she supplied much encouragement and sharp insights. I thank Sondra Cuban for helping with proofreading and bolstering her father's sagging esteem when he needed it. To Janice Cuban, who also helped with proofreading, I owe at least one ice cream cone for the times I was too busy to get her one.

Debts pile up; but responsibility for what appears in this study remains mine.

Introduction

> The deaths of great men in national and political history are commemorated by song, story and memorial days. Only in secluded family circles and midst the personal friends are the works and lives of heroic schoolmasters recorded and remembered.
>
> *Aaron Gove, 1900*

Perhaps a novel, possibly a poem, and maybe a song have recorded the lives of urban superintendents. Most cities, however, prosaically remember their schoolmen either in naming a school building, dedicating an athletic field, or planting a tree. Esteemed as the position has become in the last half-century, as important as the job seems to be, the complex nature of the urban superintendency has perhaps caught the imagination of a brick mason or a gardener, but seldom a writer, poet or lyricist. For whatever the reasons, urban superintendents seem to lack the dash and glamor of businessmen, doctors, inventors, or military men.

None of this, however, stopped schoolmen from celebrating themselves as important to the growth of the nation. The *Proceedings* of the Department of Superintendence, since the 1870s, and, more currently, of the American Association of School Administrators (AASA)—professional organizations for superintendents—have resounded to the theme of the crucial role that superintendents have played in shaping the schools, and through them, the future of America. Periodically, special

The epigraph is from Denver Superintendent Aaron Gove's ''Trail of the City Superintendent,'' *NEA Addresses and Proceedings* 39 (1900): 214.

issues of annual reports have listed accomplishments of particular schoolmen. Annual necrologies in the *Proceedings* and Distinguished Service Awards for AASA have recorded achievements of noted school chiefs. In effect, a pantheon of heroic schoolmen, models for each generation of superintendents to imitate, has developed over the years. However, it is known only to those within the profession. Few non-educators have heard of William Torrey Harris, James Greenwood, Aaron Gove, William Maxwell, or Jesse Newlon.

Even if few superintendents have become household names, much has been written about how they feel and what they should do. Studies by social scientists and admirers have produced shelves of doctoral dissertations and studies documenting how superintendents perceive their boards of education, and vice-versa, or eulogistic tracts of individual schoolmen of the late nineteenth century.[1] Much literature turned out by the AASA advises schoolmen of what they can and should do, what they have done in specific aspects of their job and, more recently, what theories of administration might guide them.

However, within this large body of advice there is precious little agreement on where the superintendency has come from, where it is moving or even what its present nature is—save for the popular observation that the urban school position is "an ulcer-producing job."[2] Joseph Cronin prefaced his article on the crises experienced by urban schoolmen during the last century with a complaint about the dearth of studies on school executives. Similarly, Luvern Cunningham bemoaned the lack of intensive investigations of the position.[3] Few studies in the last decade have been undertaken to investigate how urban schoolmen functioned in the job and to explain why they functioned the way they did.[4] Our lack of in-depth knowledge about the urban school chief becomes truly awesome when we consider the AASA's assertion that the superintendent, "more than any other single person in the community, influences the shape of public education."[5]

While we know to the penny what salaries urban administrators received, what degrees they earned, and where they were born, we know very little about what they, as executives, actually do each day.[6] We can pinpoint with great accuracy the median age of urban school chiefs over the last five decades, but we have virtually no evidence on the positive (or negative) impact of university education upon schoolmen's performance on the job. Although we can detail with sophisticated statistical techniques the political behavior of superintendents, few of us can say with any degree of confidence exactly what school administrators have been doing. One authority on school administration has discussed what

he considers to be major functions of the superintendent—six score and
twelve years after the first urban school executive was appointed.[7] We
can document with a fair degree of precision that urban school administrators are, and have been, beset by conflicting cross-currents of
pressure; however, few studies have found any pattern of response to
these forces.[8]

If useful knowledge of schoolmen is ever to move beyond hunches
and folk wisdom, these researchable issues deserve serious attention
from scholars as well as from working superintendents. With the
current spasm of dismissals, forced resignations, and early retirements,
the question of urban administrators under external pressure brings into
even sharper focus the role dilemmas and problems facing big-city
schoolmen.[9] "Catastrophes, disorders, demonstrations, and strikes,"
wrote veteran Columbus schoolman Harold Eibling shortly before
retiring, "have become part of the new order of reality for the
large-city superintendent."[10]

The issue of school chiefs under pressure is the subject of this study,
which is guided by two broad questions. First, how have big-city
superintendents responded to outside pressure? Second, why have they
responded the way they have? To narrow these questions to manageable
proportions, I have examined three veteran urban schoolmen who were
highly respected by their colleagues but who came under intense
pressure from forces outside the school system in the 1960s. In each
city, two critical incidents were investigated that seemed to capture the
essence of the conflict between the superintendent and external groups.
Chapter 1 explores the context of the desegregation controversy and the
furor over an independent evaluation that faced Chicago's Benjamin C.
Willis during the 1960s. The second chapter describes Carl Hansen's
responses in Washington, D.C., to federally funded efforts to change
the public schools and sharp pressure to desegregate. San Francisco is
the focus of the third chapter, in which a curricular fracas triggered by
Sputnik and a concerted drive to desegregate the schools are examined
as two instances of pressure that confronted Harold Spears.

Chapter 4 compares and contrasts the three political contexts, school
organizations, and pressure groups. A substantial portion of this chapter
focuses on the three boards of education, the careers of the superintendents, and their bureaucracies in addition to their responses to
external pressure. In the process, the chapter also compares and contrasts these three school systems with those of other big cities.

The origin and development of the urban superintendency during the
last century is investigated in chapter 5 in an effort to determine how

big-city schoolmen have perceived their roles. Their leadership conceptions are traced from their origins to the 1960s in an effort to understand and explain why these three school chiefs believed and responded as they did. The final chapter poses several theories to further clarify the responses of these top administrators. Each explanation, plausible in itself, underscores the difficulty of using any single theory drawn either from historical analysis or the social sciences to explain data.

If the superintendent is as pivotal to the future of the urban public education as many people assert (and presumably they back up this assertion with salaries second only to the mayor's in most cities), then understanding big-city superintendents' responses to external pressure may be useful to those who are interested in improving the training and selection of school chiefs. And to those concerned about whether or not superintendent leadership can make a difference in urban education, this study may suggest some answers.

1 Chicago

In downtown Chicago, LaSalle Street is lined on both sides with tall, gray buildings. At the south end of the street is the massive, pseudo-Gothic façade of the Board of Trade. Moving northward on LaSalle one comes to the grimy granite but equally rock-like fortress of City Hall where Mayor Richard Daley has run the city since 1955. And near the Chicago River, at the north end of LaSalle, located on the site of a Jesuit Mission Post—"the earliest civilizing institution to arise on the site of this metropolis"—is the ponderous twenty-three story Builders Building. From a spacious second floor office overlooking the river, between 1953 and 1966, Benjamin Coppage Willis ran the Chicago public schools.

Buildings, growth, and controversy sum up the career of Benjamin Willis. Nicknamed Big Ben the Builder by the local press, Willis prided himself on his planting "jewels" (that is, new schools) in the crowded black South Side ghetto—buildings that even in 1973, he said, still looked "as if they were planned yesterday and just moved into." Managing the physical growth of the educational system was an enormous task at a time when the city was "piling up with people" and trainloads of southern migrants weekly spilled forth from the Twelfth Street Station of the Illinois Central.[1]

Willis planned and oversaw the details of each massive multimillion-dollar construction program, from the height of each classroom's ceiling down to the price of the nails. He drew rave notices from architects, realtors, and construction industry professionals. Spending over $700,000 a week during the mid-1950s and early 1960s, the general superintendent could point with pride in 1962 to over a hundred new buildings, an equal number of additions, and over 126,000 new classroom seats. Willis could also point with pride to the elimination of the double-shift and to the reduction of average class size from just under forty to thirty-two.[2]

Well before the furor arose over Sputnik, drop-outs, and the disadvantaged, Willis had launched programs for the gifted, had beefed up the English, science, and math curricula, and had cadged foundation grants so he could begin dealing with drop-outs and the poor.

Believing deeply in the importance of teachers, Willis managed in less than a decade to convert a low double-standard salary schedule, which paid $3000 to an elementary teacher and $3460 to a high school teacher in 1953 to a single salary schedule which paid almost double this amount. In speeches, articles, and interviews, he stressed over and over that the ''Superintendent's job was to make the job of instruction easier and more efficient for the teacher.''[3]

Thus, by the early 1960s, Willis had established a reputation as a builder, innovator, and professional. He was a man who, according to his school board president and close personal friend, ''would spit in God's face if He asked him to surrender his principles.''[4]

Most superintendents go through life hoping for an occasional article in a professional journal. Willis consistently turned up as the subject of interviews, paeans, and tirades in such diverse magazines as *Nation's Business, Look, Saturday Evening Post, Newsweek, Time, Saturday Review,* and *True.*[5]

Elected president of the American Association of School Administrators—the highest honor his colleagues could bestow upon him, appointed by President Kennedy to a national education commission, chairman of the influential Educational Policies Commission of the National Education Association, founder and chairman for a decade of the Great Cities Research Council, Willis was, in the words of a widely respected college dean, ''practically peerless as a big-city school superintendent.''[6]

Yet, in the summer and fall of 1961, civil rights groups attacked Willis on the issue of overcrowded, unequal facilities for black students. In November the Board appointed a subcommittee to consider an independent survey of the system. For the next two years criticism escalated over both these issues, eventually focusing upon Willis as the superintendent. As a friendly newspaper put it, since Willis had come to Chicago in 1953 there had been ''Eight Fine Years, Two Bitter Ones.''[7] Those two years of controversy are the central subject of this chapter.

In this chapter, Willis's style and career, especially the political and social context he operated within are sketched out in broad strokes. This is followed by a more detailed narrative of Willis's handling of the desegregation controversy. Finally, the chapter closes with a look at the furor surrounding the general superintendent's response to Dr. Robert Havighurst's independent evaluation of the school system.

Willis as Superintendent

Willis's career was stamped from the same mold that produced most of his colleagues. Raised in rural Maryland near Baltimore, he attended a one-room school and later worked his way through college. Then began his gradual climb up the professional ladder: teacher in a one-room school, principal, rural superintendent ("I took that job in the middle of the depression at a $1500 loss"); next, a matter of short jumps to superintendency of Hagerstown, Maryland; then to Yonkers, Buffalo; and finally the call to Chicago in 1953. Before he moved to Buffalo at age forty-nine, he finally completed his dissertation at Teachers College, Columbia University. "Start little and grow big"—his advice in 1973 to aspiring superintendents—summarized his career accurately.[8]

As Chicago's general superintendent, his considerable energy, single-mindedness, and towering self-confidence merged into a leadership style that bowled over staff as well as observers. Articles stressed that Willis "eats, drinks, sleeps and dreams schools." His assistant in Yonkers recalled how Willis would call him at home in the evening. "Fred," Willis would say, "I got an idea. Come over and we'll kick it around." Sardines and crackers would refuel the discussion at mid-morning and by 4:30 A.M. they would break off and go home. A decade later, he still worked sixteen-hour days like a "road runner on pep pills." Willis recalled fondly how

many times my top staff here would get a phone call to meet me at five o'clock in the conference room. This is because our office closes at 4:30. Six thirty or so I'd say let's go downstairs and get something to eat. Bacon and eggs. Pancakes or something like that. We would go back and make sure we'd adjourn at nine. Go home a few minutes after.[9]

Each day was filled. Staff meetings at breakfast, conferences with an assistant superintendent who wanted to discuss curriculum changes and a high school principal seeking a raise for his cafeteria help; quick in-and-out visits to two brand-new schools; back down to the Loop to lunch at a businessmen's club; then back to the office to study blueprints for a new high school, catch up with phone calls, and sign correspondence; now off in the late afternoon to a high school faculty meeting to discuss the up-coming revisions in the teacher salary schedule; return to the office to meet with three assistant superintendents wrestling with what to do about a series of incidents involving students at three junior high schools; more returning of phone calls and signing of letters; then another trip out to a PTA evening dinner at which he is the featured speaker on the topic "Quality Education in Chicago's Schools"; back to the office for the last time to pore over more memos, the daily mail, and phone messages; and finally, well after eleven o'clock, out go the lights, on go the coat and hat, and a half hour later his chauffeur drops him off at his North Shore apartment.[10]

Most superintendents work long hours, spin from one activity to another, and juggle a dozen different decision opportunities simultaneously. What distinguished Willis from many of his colleagues, however, was his robust, lusty embrace of the demanding routine. An associate of Willis, writing for a national journal aimed at schoolmen, described him as a "tireless executive who has dedicated virtually every waking moment to the cause of education. He has no hobbies, no free time, no moments of relaxation. He is a hard-sell salesman for education on every occasion and with every person."[11]

The penchant for detail—he knew exactly how much Worcestershire sauce was purchased annually for the schools' kitchens[12]—revealed itself in the numerous graphs and charts which he was capable of displaying at a moment's notice either to inform the uninformed, explain alternatives, or drench criticism in a cloudburst of statistics. His tight grasp of massive amounts of budget data and his eager, searching interest in everything that went on in the schools—from the cost of fuel per pupil to how many high school students could get into a Loop department store job training program—impressed both admirers and critics.

Harnessed to a strapping self-assuredness, these traits blended into a style that delighted reporters while infuriating opponents. To one reporter who shadowed him in the first months of his Buffalo superintendency, Willis was the man who "runs everything except tugboats." In an enthusiastic portrait drawn a decade later in the *Saturday Review,* he was "a man in a hurry, who knows where he wants to go and is determined to get there." And to the *Chicago Daily News* he was Ben the Boss, running a third of a billion dollar operation "with an iron fist and no gloves." But to critics, colossal self-confidence often appeared as arrogance, willful tyranny, or simply unrelenting stubborness.[13]

Willis's aggressive, brusque personal style, with its grasp of detail and its enormous drive, drew from board members and subordinates responses ranging from unqualified admiration to strong criticism. One loyal assistant superintendent proclaimed, "He leads, we follow." However, one of Willis's aides, commenting on the general superintendent's desire to stay atop the decision-making process, pointed out a problem which this personality trait produced: "Sometimes a bottleneck develops in getting things done because Dr. Willis likes to keep his finger in everything."[14]

Of the more than forty board members that served between 1961 and 1966, most were publicly enthusiastic advocates of the superintendent. Many believed along with board member R. J. Spaeth, that Benjamin Willis was "the best large city Public School administrator in the United States."[15] A few, however—notably Joseph Pois, Raymond Pasnick, Warren Bacon, and later Fairfax Cone, all of whom repeatedly clashed with the superintendent over policy matters but remained a permanent minority on the board—saw him in a different light.

Cone, a former supporter and advertising executive sensitive to public relations, once observed that Willis "gives the impression he is the only one who knows the facts and the only one who has the answers. He is so full of business he just doesn't share his decisions with other people." In the opinion of Warren Bacon, Inland Steel executive, "Willis really ran the board instead of their running him." Bacon recalled that, "one time in executive session Willis threatened to go to the press and TV if the board didn't go along with what he wanted. At my first meeting, before I was sworn in [1963], he even threatened to resign. He just bulldozed them."[16] Few observers of the eleven-member board, which was appointed by the mayor from a list of nominations submitted by a blue-ribbon panel of civic groups, could deny that by 1961 Willis dominated their policymaking.

When Superintendent William H. Johnson, tarred by scandal, was swept out of office in 1946, certain reforms were introduced to strengthen the authority of the superintendency. Far more than his predecessor Herold Hunt, Willis knew how to use this power, wielding the prerogatives of his office in a fashion that tolerated little criticism while keeping board members busy with a five-inch-thick, two-pound agenda that dealt with purchasing transactions, routine personnel matters, and contracts. Since the superintendent initiated recommendations, all information supporting these recommended actions came from Willis; moreover, he determined the length and order of the agenda. Thus, the board relied heavily upon their executive's advice. In short, the board had a strong, professional orientation, both believing in and accepting the expertise of their general superintendent.

Ex–board member Joseph Pois spent two chapters of a book on the Chicago school board analyzing their dependent relationship with the superintendent. The board itself, he concluded, failed to exercise its legitimate powers over its executive officer. Another lone dissenter for many years, Raymond Pasnick objected to renewing Willis's contract in 1961, arguing along similar lines:

There have been occasions in the past when I say that we as a Board were dangerously abdicating our policymaking responsibility. Some of my associates, perhaps because they hold our chief administrator in such high esteem, have been too eager to surrender what I consider to be important prerogatives of our office. They rarely exercise their power of disapproval . . . . Since I see little hope for change in the willingness to abdicate Board responsibility, the man we select as superintendent for the next four years will in effect have powers of a legislator and executive combined. He will, so to speak, enjoy the powers of both President and Congress in the important area of educating a half-million Chicago children.

The motion to re-elect Willis followed, carrying eight to one.[17]

It was no accident that a popular story made the rounds in newspapers during the Willis years. An unnamed school board member, the story went, was quoted as saying, "I'm not against the superintendent one single tiny, little bit even when he accuses us of making policy."[18]

If this steamroller style found vigorous acceptance among most board members, it also gained him a high reputation with the business community. Often mistaken for a businessman both in dress and demeanor, Willis cultivated contacts within Chicago business circles. He joined the influential Commercial Club, dined at numerous businessmen's clubs, and counted bankers, industrialists, and realtors as friends. "When Willis came [1953]," a Loop banker recalled, "he approached people individually; he picked up the contacts Hunt [the previous superintendent] had. He made a point of going to the Association of Commerce and Manufacturer Association; any group that would have him, he would go to." In one researcher's interview with a representative sample of influential business leaders, out of twenty-two, twelve said they were "close personal friends" of Willis, and nearly all claimed they were "good friends."[19] During the crises that occurred over de facto segregation, these businessmen openly and informally supported the superintendent, at least until 1965. After that, business support for Willis significantly dropped off.

And what of the larger political arena? Where did Willis stand? Technically, school board matters were inviolate from mayoral or city council interference, save for board appointments. Through these appointees, the Mayor's influence was felt indirectly but powerfully; and most appointees were consistent supporters of Willis's policies. When crises developed, direct political influence by the mayor upon the school system was minimal (this limitation was the result of the series of scandals that rocked the city in the 1930s and 1940s). But when things got especially messy, certain clear-cut patterns of influence would emerge. They did so because of the past history of municipal interference and the way Chicago city government was organized.

A word about this system is perhaps in order. Because Chicago is governmentally decentralized (that is, with separate and independent city council, city treasurer, schools, transit authority, public housing, and scores of other agencies), the mayor can only make policy and implement it if he can informally centralize these fragments of governmental authority. The tool to do this was (and still is) the Democratic political machine. Slates of candidates, significant patronage in exchange for support, and dozens of other benefits glued the fragments together into a viable, powerful lever of informal government.

Often the machine works in subtle, patient ways. Chicago contains myriad civic and ethnic groups, each with fundamentally different interests. Seldom will there be unanimity; more often, disagreement is the norm. When disagreement escalates into controversy and the usual political strategies of bargaining, compromise, and clout fail, the mayor usually does nothing. Edward Banfield, who studied Chicago in the late 1950s, described this pattern. "Watchful waiting will offend no one, and to be negative when one does not have to be is bad politics."[20] Thus, the mayor usually would let a civic controversy develop without any interference from his office and would wait for the opinion of the press and civic leaders (or "public opinion") to turn one way or the other before he stepped in.

The mayor followed this route in 1963 when controversy over empty classrooms, de facto segregation, and Willis's policies mushroomed into a full-blown crisis. To civil rights leaders' demands to get rid of Willis, Daley replied: "I won't inject politics into school matters." At another time he said the "people of Chicago look to the Board for the development of policies which govern our fine school system. Since I have been Mayor, I have adhered strictly that there should be no interference of any kind."[21]

Willis's domain was the school system. Daley could exercise indirect influence, and did, as later events will show, but only when a controversy reached crisis proportions. Short of that, Willis had little to worry about from City Hall.

By 1961 few informed observers questioned that Benjamin Coppage Willis dominated policymaking and the administration of school affairs in the first decade of his tenure. Negative criticism of the general superintendent's leadership and domination of the board had increased somewhat, yet it was still muted and isolated. In July the board granted Willis a new four-year contract and substantial raise that made him the third highest paid public official in the United States. He was at that time President of the American Association of School Administrators and a recent recipient of a Harvard honorary degree that touted him as a "determined defender of the proposition that American cities deserve good schools." And when the superintendency of New York, the largest school system in the country, fell vacant, he was offered the job. Turning it down, he was applauded by Chicago admirers.[22] At age sixty, Willis seemingly was at the peak of both his personal and professional prestige.

Vacant Seats, Segregation, Protest, and Willis's Response

The very familiar urban pattern of the poor, black population remaining in the inner city while middle-income white families flee to the suburbs made itself known again in Chicago following World War II. The South Side—already black and itself a product of earlier waves of migrants—ballooned in population, pushing at the edges of surrounding white, ethnic communities. In one decade alone (1950–60) Chicago's black population almost doubled.[23] As thousands of migrants from Appalachia and the Mississippi Delta left the Illinois Central depot for South Side and near West Side tenements, other, more affluent, migrants trekked out to the North Shore and West Side into high rises and suburban tracts. The shift in population left Chicago with fewer people in 1960 than it had in 1950—but not in the black ghetto or its schools.[24]

Migration within the city combined with a high birth rate to swell the South Side, further burdening already packed schools, parks, and other public services. Between 1953 and 1963, while Chicago's population dropped by 70,000, school attendance increased by over 100,000 and most of these were black children.[25] Every chart produced by the school system and demographers showed heavy dark lines climbing from the late 1940s at an angle of 45 degrees or more.[26]

But these statistics represented people. With school construction taking anywhere from three to five years from blueprint to ribbon-cutting, where were the children to be put? On a temporary basis, double shifts and rental of space in churches, synagogues, and other community buildings were used. Successful bond issues in 1951, 1955, 1957, and 1959 provided the dollars to build roofs and buy desks. Of twenty-two schools planned for the 1958 budget, eleven were located in all-black areas. Yet, all the new schools and additions never quite caught up with the growing student population. By 1960 over 33,000 school children remained on double shifts, and classes were large. Both conditions occurred in black neighborhoods.[27]

The general superintendent's priorities were clearly stated: reduction and elimination of double shifts, and the relief of overcrowding, with an average class size of thirty pupils.[28] Nonetheless, all the new additions and mobile classrooms that dotted the South Side were insufficient in numbers to satisfy increasingly critical parents and civil rights groups, for although double shifts and over-sized classes had been reduced, they had not been eliminated.

While the problem of attaining ''quality'' schools had been initially defined by Willis and the board in terms of enough space in which to educate children, a gradual redefinition of the problem was underway—one not managed and influenced by professional opinion. The problem which increasingly faced school critics was no longer that of whether or not there was a seat for every child, but rather where the school was located and who went there. These priorities, according to the growing public voice, determined ''quality''—not how many windows would be in the building or what type of plaster was to be used in the walls.

From questions on things (in effect, questions which professionals were accustomed to asking) there was a shift to questions on neighborhood school policy (questions which professionals seldom raised). Schoolmen's old ways of defining school problems were becoming less acceptable to emerging groups of activist parents and to civil rights groups.

By the late 1950s a number of concerned citizens—blacks and whites —centering first in the NAACP education committee and the Urban League and later in CORE, had gathered sufficient evidence to charge that the Chicago schools were segregated as early as 1956.[29] They surfaced a number of issues that concentrated upon double shifts, unequal facilities, and overcrowding (more than forty students to a class in some black neighborhoods). Through presentations to the board of education, lobbying with particular board members, and repeated requests that the board act, citizen demands sparked occasional responses from particular members of the board (especially Joseph Pois and, later, Raymond Pasnick) and occasional articles in the local press. But until 1961 nothing much else happend.

In June of that year the NAACP blasted Willis for permitting "overcrowded schools where helpless teachers are forced to do the best they can with forty-five and fifty in a classroom." Three months later, the local chapter of the NAACP sponsored an Operation Transfer in which black parents tried to register over 200 children in predominately white, single-shift under-capacity schools. Parents were refused entry by school officials. Within two weeks the NAACP had filed *Webb v Board of Education,* charging that the board had purposely gerrymandered districts to create all-black schools. Furthermore, they asserted, the board and Dr. Willis discriminated against blacks in classroom size, and cited classes as large as sixty, inferior instruction, and unfit facilities. (Paul Zuber, who had just won the New Rochelle case, was hired by the plaintiffs.) In a fact-packed affidavit, Dr. Willis vigorously denied all charges. "I know of no attendance area in the city of Chicago," Willis said, "that has been gerrymandered for the purpose of maintaining a 'racially segregated' school."[30]

In early September, in a strongly worded editorial, the Chicago *Defender* berated the superintendent for not sharing with the public "accurate facts about the capacity and use of the public schools." Not doing this "is an admission of his incompetence as well as an insult to the intelligence of the people . . . . His scheme is to postpone as long as possible genuine integration in our public schools" Shortly after this, the Urban League submitted a resolution to the board of education raising questions about what was to be done about double shifts and under-capacity white schools. The league asked the board to admit the "inequities of segregated education as it now exists in Chicago." For the board to claim that residence patterns and community beliefs were responsible and beyond its power would be, according to the league, "unjustifiable."[31]

The board naturally did not want to admit that segregation existed for fear that in doing so it might incriminate itself for any pending and future litigation; it was understandable why a board would be reluctant to confess its responsibility. Pressed by a growing crescendo of protest from the NAACP, the Urban League, and community groups, and by persistent efforts of board member Raymond Pasnick, Willis investigated the situation. In November he reported to the board that there was a "surplus of 14 rooms" in the entire school system.[32]

Willis's estimate triggered a rash of investigations by the Urban League and community groups which were then followed by a series of rebuttals from Willis. How many unused rooms were there? The Urban League's claim of 380? Or fourteen, as the superintendent claimed? Confidence in the technical competence and impartiality of the general superintendent eroded, at least in the eyes of civil rights activists, with the squabbling over exactly what was defined as a "classroom." The black newspaper, the *Daily Defender,* summed up a growing feeling among activists.

Mr. Willis is the highest paid public school superintendent in the United States. . . . For this amount of money, the city of Chicago should have no difficulty getting a school head of high professional calibre and integrity, and broad social vision and convictions; one who would not equate sound administrative procedures with politics.[33]

The exact amount of available space, as John Coons stressed in his 1962 report to the Commission on Civil Rights, was crucial.[34] If there was no space, black children in overcrowded schools could not transfer to white schools. But if there was sufficient space, then existing no-transfer policies, double shifts, and mobile classrooms meant that the board and administration consciously discriminated against black children.

Since few members of the board or administration, save Raymond Pasnick, saw board or superintendent actions as discriminatory, the controversy eventually boiled down to a matter of who had lost confidence in Willis and attacked the neighborhood school policy, and who trusted the general superintendent and supported this board policy.

Superintendent reports reaffirmed that policy. "There is no question," Willis said in December 1961, "but that an elementary school which serves pupils who live in the immediate area around the school is best able to involve community and parents in a quality program of education for their children." Ten months later he publicly stated, "The life and comprehension of the small child focus close to home. Centering the life of the child within its known and explorable neighborhood provides the emotional security required for his wholesome development."[35]

And in April 1963, after 1,000 black parents petitioned the State Superintendent of Instruction to investigate whether or not the policy was a cover-up for segregation, Willis testified at the hearings. "There are 525,000 children in Chicago schools," Willis said. "Without a neighborhood school policy, I just don't understand how you'd organize the schools." When a panel of five experts was appointed to investigate racial imbalance in Chicago, the president of the school board assured the city that "by no means does the appointment of the panel indicate abandonment of the neighborhood school policy."[36]

By the summer of 1962, when there was a slight relaxation of the no-transfer rule in order to adopt a "permissive transfer" policy, it was done in the context of preserving neighborhood schools.[37] As an emergency measure (those are Willis's words), permissive transfer allowed interested parents to transport their children at their own cost and enroll them in selected under-capacity elementary schools provided—and here was a proviso that sorely irritated civil rights advocates—that the transferring children came from schools in which there were more than forty students in their class and the receiving schools had classes with less than thirty.[38] Less than a year later, when Willis submitted another permissive transfer plan (this time for high school students), demonstrations, picketing, and sit-ins erupted.

Thus, in the spring of 1963 civil rights groups that initially had seen the issue of overcrowding as the predominant issue became convinced that the basic problem was the neighborhood school policy, which produced de facto segregation, and its chief defender, Benjamin C. Willis. As the controversy grew, the groups' usual strategy of gathering facts and making presentations to the board of education increasingly gave way—in the face of apparent official intransigence—to both legal and direct action strategies—lawsuits, picketing, sit-ins, and boycotts.

None of these approaches was mutually exclusive. The Urban League seldom involved itself in direct action but did make repeated requests to the board for action and worked behind the scenes for its goals. CORE, on the other hand, tried each strategy, turning finally to civil disobedience. The organizational rivalry and struggle for leadership with the civil rights movement in the early 1960s virtually guaranteed that each of these approaches would be used at any given time.

The Urban League—and the NAACP, though much less so after late 1962—dominated the protest scene until the spring of 1963. In one statement to the board, Urban League President H. B. Law noted that his organization "isn't happy about the fact that . . . some people have cast us in the role of villain in the Chicago school situation. The fact is, we'd much rather negotiate than fight. We don't want to live in the trenches forever.''[39]

By June 1963 CORE, bolstered by an aggressive national civil rights campaign, had captured headlines by using direct action tactics. Much smaller in membership than its sister groups, CORE became the radical activists within the movement goading the NAACP and Urban League to take more aggressive positions. The Chicago CORE chapter had experienced ups and downs in its organizational history. Active in the mid-1940s, the chapter lapsed into inactivity around 1947. Revived in 1960 by a dozen members, its early activities were aimed at integrating five-and-dime lunch counters. When the first mobile classrooms were erected, CORE, which was mostly white in membership, picketed those. The organization's leadership shifted often, especially where factional struggles erupted over tactics.[40]

Also on the scene was the Coordinating Council of Community Organizations (CCCO), an umbrella organization of seventeen civil rights groups. Initially established as an informal group to share information and general strategies, the CCCO was pushed by a series of CORE sit-ins at the board during the summer of 1963 into a more assertive and dominant position under the leadership of Al Raby, a Chicago school teacher. In addition to these citywide organizations, there were numerous active community groups that shared the same interests and were affiliated loosely (or actively as the case demanded) with CCCO.

The largest and most aggressive, as well as influential, of these community groups was The Woodlawn Organization (TWO), a coalition of churches, businesses, block clubs, and neighborhood associations in the area near the University of Chicago. Organized in 1960, TWO was built upon both the organizational principles and tactics of Saul Alinsky and directed its efforts to rent strikes, consumer direct action, and demonstrations over school and civil rights issues. The Truth Squads mentioned earlier (see note 37), the picketing of Inland Steel (the socially conscious employer of Board President William Caples) over segregated schools, and other dramatic maneuvers quickly moved TWO and its chairman, the Rev. Arthur Brazier, into a prominent leadership position within CCCO during that summer.[41]

As the tempo of protest stepped up and racial consciousness within the black community surfaced, more and more local groups, ad hoc associations, and previously dormant organizations moved from the usual approach of making requests of the board of education to laying out demands and even marching, picketing, and lying down in front of bulldozers. Rivalries between civil rights leaders and organizations, among other things, produced sharp militancy as each tried to outdo the other in becoming spokesmen for the black community.[42]

While it is tempting to describe these events as a product of local conditions, one event simply causing another, the explosive summer of 1963 must be placed in the context of the two previous years of growing protest, the organizational rivalries among local groups, the narrowing of issues to one man—Benjamin Willis—and, finally, what was happening in the nation at the time.

The Summer of 1963

How easily forgotten are yesterday's names and places. From the summer of 1963: Medgar Evers; Cambridge, Maryland, and Gloria Richardson; Mississippi and James Meredith; Bull Connor's dogs unleashed on marchers during Birmingham demonstrations. After two years of sit-ins, "freedom rides," and demonstrations, with plans underway for an enormous march on Washington, the social consciousness of Northern liberal whites and blacks was raised and sensitive in many communities across the nation, including Chicago.

That was also the summer when Mayor Daley was booed from the speakers' stand during the June NAACP national convention when he said Chicago had no ghettos. July saw almost daily marches, picketing, and demonstrations in the Loop by both black and white protesters. Television and newspapers showered viewers and readers with minute details of arrests and violence.[43] Even the conservative *Tribune,* notorious in Chicago for its hostile reporting on racial affairs, devoted its usual 72-point-type, heavy black headlines to news of Willis's home being picketed, riots in Cambridge, bombs in Birmingham, and civil rights groups seeking a school boycott. And the consequences of these tactics were visible: Loop traffic was constantly being rerouted; in the Builders Building a partition was erected to prevent protestors from entering the school board's second-floor offices. In short, it was a summer of peak civil rights activities meshing legal strategies of an earlier period with the frenetic pitch of direct action tactics and culminating in a massive school boycott. It was Chicago's first—but by no means last—summer of racial crisis over the public schools.

On July 7 the board speedily approved school boundary changes recommended by the general superintendent. Without any mention of how many students would be involved or how other schools would be affected, Willis ran through a series of charts explaining what was to occur. Raymond Pasnick's objections were heard and ignored. When the meeting ended, twenty clapping and singing blacks and whites, CORE activists, took over President Claire Roddewig's office. They demanded an immediate revoking of the boundary changes, immediate plans for integration to begin by September (seven weeks away), and, finally, the calling of a special board meeting to implement these demands. To a reporter Roddewig said, "I told them this is not the way you get a public body to act by sitting in and laying down demands."[44]

For the next ten days the sit-ins continued. Sporadic melees with police over attempts by additional CORE members to get into the board offices led to arrests, more picketing, increased threats, and some physical injuries. "Our members," one activist said, "will walk into the classrooms of all white high schools, sit in the classrooms and demand an education."[45]

The sit-ins dominated the news. But at a cost. One CORE spokesman said, "Everyday it becomes necessary to do something a little stronger so that the group obtains the publicity that it needs to make the public aware of what the Board of Education needs." Sam Riley, Chapter chairman, apologized for the violence and resigned his post. "I believe," he said, "there should be more discipline among the demonstrators."[46]

Finally, on July 19, Roddewig ordered the police to remove the protestors from his offices. Subsequently, CORE representatives, four board members, and Dr. Willis met to discuss the issues. Charges of gerrymandering were aired, but no resolution occurred. Willis said nothing.[47]

Within two weeks, civil rights activists shifted their attention to sites where mobile classrooms were being constructed at 73d and Lowe on the South Side. CORE and neighborhood groups picketed the sites. Pickets carrying signs such as "We Want Buildings, Not Boxcars" and "Wagons Are For Loading, Not Learning," marched around the construction machinery. On August 2, in the midst of a driving early morning thundershower which turned the dirt lot into mud, the pickets lay down in front of bulldozers and graders to prevent their use. Arrests were made. Within a few days the demonstrations turned ugly. When police moved in to arrest pickets who were "lying-in," a flurry of rocks struck them. A number of officers were injured; some demonstrators were subsequently beaten into the mud. By this time, more than 170 pickets had been arrested.[48]

While picketing at the construction sites continued, pressure expanded to demonstrations at the homes of Board President Roddewig and Mayor Daley. At its next meeting, the board refused to stop construction of the mobile classrooms. Willis, however, finally made a public statement on the issue.

To accomplish our task of providing quality education for all children, overcrowded conditions in schools must be eliminated. This is accomplished in part by the use of mobile classrooms, which are the most modern and efficient type of classroom available until a new school building is constructed.

The next day, twenty-five pickets marched for two hours in front of the Edgewater Beach apartments where Dr. Willis and board member Frank Whiston lived. That evening a number of mobiles were set afire.[49]

Pressure increased on Mayor Daley to do something. Claire Roddewig's home was picketed and the board president pleaded with the protestors to leave since his wife was very ill. They refused to do so. Daley blasted the pickets. "When a man's wife is ill," he said, "people should have the decency not to cause a disturbance in front of their home." What irritated the mayor even more was "a few irresponsible people . . . . from all over town and some from out of town. Some of them don't even represent organizations." Nevertheless, the mayor met with civil rights representatives. Presenting him with a 1300-signature petition objecting to mobiles, neighborhood protest leaders urged the mayor to get Willis fired. As he always had, Daley pointed out that he, as Mayor, could not intervene in school affairs but would bring this to the attention of the Board.[50]

What halted the construction of the classrooms, of course, was not the petition. NAACP lawyers on the *Webb* case offered to settle out of court if the board would make some concessions. The superintendent and board informally agreed to have a panel of five experts determine whether or not de facto segregation existed in Chicago. Moreover, the board agreed to halt the violently contested construction of mobiles at 73d and Lowe.[51]

Protest marches and picketing, however, burst out anew a few days later when the board took the mobiles from the 73d Street location and placed them at Guggenheim School on 71st. Pickets appeared almost immediately; boycott threats were made; and delegations of parents from Guggenheim and four other schools met Mayor Daley. He promised, as usual, to arrange a meeting with the board.

On top of all this, not only were black parents from the South Side complaining about Willis's policies, but over 2,000 white parents were picketing Bogan High School, protesting what they thought would be the imminent transfer of a handful of gifted black students to their already crowded school.[52]

Worse yet for the Mayor, in the midst of these other demonstrations, 4,000 white homeowners, mostly housewives pushing baby buggies, protesting a city council open-housing ordinance supported by the mayor, marched through the Loop singing (to the tune of "Won't You Come Home, Bill Bailey"):

> I'll pick my own neighbors and sell to whom I choose
> The politicians didn't buy my home.
>
> We know you're to blame, ain't you ashamed?
>
> Dick Daley, won't you please get lost?[53]

After the marchers finished at City Hall, about 500 parents from Bogan broke off and walked a few blocks to the Builders Building, where they marched back and forth protesting the transfer of any students to their school. In an unusual move, Superintendent Willis met for almost an hour with a delegation of these parents; he had not previously met with any civil rights delegations who had demonstrated at board offices.

Willis Resigns for the First Time

At the July board meeting in which Dr. Willis charted the new boundary changes that sparked the CORE sit-ins, he had also recommended a permissive transfer plan for talented high school students. On August 28 the board authorized Willis to transfer students from fourteen over-crowded schools to twenty-four under-capacity schools. Fewer than 500 students were involved; eventually only 105 took part in the transfer.[54]

As described earlier, protests mushroomed, especially from white parent groups at the receiving schools such as Bogan High School. On September 18, after consulting with only the board president, Willis reduced the number of receiving schools from twenty-four to nine. Cut from the list was Bogan, a school that, ironically, no black student had chosen to attend.[55] The rationale for the change was to exclude over-capacity schools, ones that had branches in elementary schools, and schools not yet on a four-year basis. A plausible rationale, it would have gained acceptance within civil rights groups had it accompanied the original recommendations rather than come on the heels of protests from white parents.

Civil rights groups howled. Twenty-four Hirsch High School students, most of whom were black, wished to attend two schools dropped from the list. Complaints from all civil rights groups poured into the board. On September 25, in an extraordinary action, the board directed the superintendent—in a 9–0 vote—to issue transfers for the Hirsch students. Two days later, Willis stated that he would not issue the transfers until "further study of enrollment figures" at the receiving schools had been made.[56]

Community groups from where the students lived telegrammed Roddewig. "The blatant defiance of the Board by the superintendent indicates that the Board has no control over the school system." Willis had interpreted the board's decision as a suggestion. He felt any board member could make a motion to reconsider the situation and the board could even reverse itself. But board member Warren Bacon said, "the Board's decision [to transfer students] was a direct order to Willis and not a 'suggestion.' "[57]

Parents of four Hirsch students filed suit in Cook County Superior Court asking for an injunction ordering Dr. Willis to issue the transfers. On October 3, Judge Arthur Sullivan ordered the superintendent to carry out the board's directive or an injunction would be served. After a great deal of trouble in locating Willis to serve the order, the deputy sheriff delivered the court order to him the following morning.[58]

The next day, after a last-minute effort by board lawyers to get the Illinois Appellate Court to grant a stay of the order, at a press conference where, according to one report, "no one shed a tear, . . . no one applauded, no one jeered," Benjamin C. Willis announced his resignation.[59]

The superintendent said his reasons were personal "although the cause is professional."

A circumstance has arisen over the central issue in which Board and superintendency relationships operate and only by which their separate responsibilities can be discharged with integrity . . . .

Over the period of more than a year we have had in Chicago a series of events, each small in itself and affecting singly only limited numbers of people, which in the aggregate indicate a pattern of administrative activity on the part of the Board. [He is referring here to the Havighurst Survey, which is discussed in the final section of this chapter.] The latest of these occurred on September 25th when without requesting a report on the status of the permissive transfer plan or prior notice to me, the President of the Board suggested an administrative action and directed its adoption. Members of the Board will recall previous, comparable incidents.

I can no longer continue to discharge my responsibilities under such circumstances since the present practice is counter to all the fundamentals of good board-staff relationships in public education and elsewhere.

In a later letter to the board and in a radio interview, Willis said, "I cannot be a party to this discriminatory action," that is, transferring Hirsch students to certain schools; it "violates my basic principles and professional integrity."[60]

The issue quickly boiled down to whether or not the board would accept Willis's resignation. A special board meeting for the 7th was called. Willis went fishing.

Public response was immediate and, as expected, divided. For the most part, civil rights groups rejoiced. CCCO chairman, Charles A. Davis, spoke for almost twenty groups when he said:

It is unfortunate that the difficulties in the school system deteriorated to a personal campaign against Dr. Willis . . . . However, it has become clear during this campaign for improved educational opportunity for Negroes that the stumbling block in this direction was the Superintendent's office if not the superintendent in person. Clearly, in the past year, Dr. Willis was a man functioning out of harmony with the community and his own board at the same time. His position was untenable.

Urban League director Bill Berry was equally as candid: "The removal of Superintendent Willis may prove to be the initial step in correcting the basic weaknesses of our school system."[61]

Opposition to Dr. Willis's departure came from home-owners' associations and west side community groups (both of which were from heavily white areas), as well as from teacher and principal groups, bankers, realtors, and businessmen. One telegram, in particular, among the thousands, was signed by twenty-three businessmen—a virtual roster of Chicago's Who's Who in the business community. Authored by Virgil Martin, president of Carson, Pirie Scott and Company and a very close personal friend of the superintendent, the telegram gave Willis unequivocal support for his achievements and policies.[62]

Pressure to retain Willis also came in the form of a letter from the state chairman of the North Central Association of Secondary Schools, who threatened that unless the board and superintendent worked out their differences in Willis's favor, accreditation of every single Chicago school would be withdrawn. Moreover, two members of the recently selected blue-ribbon panel to investigate de facto segregation said they would not serve if Willis's resignation was accepted.[63]

Telegrams and letters running strongly in favor of retaining the superintendent poured into Roddewig's and Daley's offices. The mayor—still beset by demonstrations and an aroused and increasingly divided citizenry—said again that he could not interfere. "I realize Dr. Willis has made a great contribution to the city and I regret that he has taken this action." Publicly he could say little more.[64]

On October 7, with Willis off fishing, the board met. On a 6–2 vote they refused the superintendent's resignation. A board subcommittee was appointed to negotiate with the superintendent ground rules for future board-administration relationships. Two days later, the board voted to rescind their earlier action directing the superintendent to transfer the students. Thus, the immediate reason for Willis's resignation was now eliminated.

That sharp pressure was brought to bear on individual board members is clear. While some may see as coincidental Fairfax Cone's resignation to accept another post prior to the crucial votes, most informed observers sensed the strings that had been pulled on this matter. But who the pressure was from, how much of it had been applied, and what its nature was, is less clear.

Shock, then anger, resonated throughout civil rights and active community groups. "We knew the meeting was coming up," recalled Harold Baron.

We expected the Board to accept his resignation. What Board would stand for that crap? As bad off as we knew this Board was, damn if they didn't plead for him to come back. We were shocked. I was at that meeting. Bill Berry [Urban League director] had invited every one from CCCO over to his house for a victory party.... You know, we went down to the Board; we were finally running this son-of-a-bitch out of town and we were going to have a big party that night. Chunk! It happened. We were stunned.[65]

At that premature victory party CORE's Lawrence Landry came with plans for a school boycott. What began in shock produced three weeks later the first massive school boycott in a major city.

On October 16—with the boycott less than ten days off, with the reopening of the *Webb* case imminent, with a major survey just getting underway to investigate the system, with new sit-ins already in progress at board offices, and with the daily arrival of telegrams from groups protesting his return—Benjamin Willis, accompanied by a police body guard, entered the board room and walked to his cushioned swivel chair. He was "received by spectators as a conquering hero." Applause lasted for a full minute.[66]

The Havighurst Report

In September 1961 when black and white parents were protesting over-crowded classes and the first *Webb* case was being filed, the board authorized the first survey of the Chicago school system in thirty years. Shortly afterward, a board subcommittee headed by Fairfax Cone was chosen to narrow the focus of the survey and choose a director. For the following year, $100,000 was appropriated. Dr. Willis commented on the survey.

I would like the record to show at this time . . . that I not only have no objection, but I, in fact, welcome an exhaustive clear-cut study by responsible people of any and all aspects of this school system. I welcome a carefully designed, all-inclusive study, not to satisfy any individual or group but to insure in the years ahead that the public schools in this city may make the maximum contribution.[67]

At that time Chicago PTAs, civil rights groups, and the Citizens Schools Committee (CSC), a powerful watchdog organization that spearheaded the clean-up of the corrupt school system in the 1940s, applauded the move. The CSC and civil rights groups had campaigned for an independent survey of the whole system. Committed to the belief that the impartial collection and analysis of data provides the best basis for intelligent action, the CSC, composed of over 200 constituent groups, unrelentingly pushed for speedy action. And civil rights groups supported this move since they believed that an impartial study would reveal the truth of the charges made by the NAACP and Urban League about the overcrowding and de facto segregation. Both urged the board to move quickly.

Little movement occurred. For a year and a half the board subcommittee searched for a survey goal and a director. Former Harvard president and author of *Slums and Suburbs,* James Conant, former Indiana University president Herman B. Wells., Harvard Graduate School dean Francis Keppel, and thirty other prominent educators turned down the offer to head-up the survey.[68] Finally, on January 9, 1963 Dean Eldridge R. McSwain of Northwestern's School of Education agreed to lead the effort.

By this time, Cone and the subcommittee had narrowed the purpose of the survey to an investigation of curriculum. In his report to the board in January, 1963, Cone said that "overcrowding is markedly diminished. The double-shift is all but ended; and we have [loosened] the tight . . . neighborhood school policy. No survey," he concluded, " is necessary in these areas." The subcommittee recommended examining the curriculum, neighborhood school policy, and administration of the schools. McSwain, an avowed supporter of the superintendent, accepted this assignment probably because he wanted to avoid a large-scale, critical investigation of the schools. "A survey is an outside organization employed to tell you the pluses and minuses. Chicago has a very fine school system and for someone to think there has to be a survey which will put more emphasis on the minuses than on the pluses is not a constructive approach." For the nominated head of a supposedly impartial survey to announce the results before the study began was, to be charitable, injudicious.[69]

What complicated matters even more and drew a barrage of criticism from the CSC, PTAs, and civil rights organizations was Willis's acceptance (with board approval) of an offer to direct a survey of Massachusetts schools. The change in purpose for the survey, the appointment of a seemingly uncritical survey director who already had telegraphed his conclusions, and the imminent departure of the superintendent for a $32,000 part-time consulting assignment angered many. In a letter to Board President Roddewig, the CSC mentioned its disappointment, chiding that the board's subcommittee had fallen "far short of fulfilling [its] original purpose." As to the subcommittee's failure to obtain an independent group to survey the system, Edward Keener, head of CSC, remarked: "it is unfortunate that they havé been unable to find such an agency although the State of Massachusetts . . . succeeded."[70]

Understandable were the screams of outrage from civil rights activists who pointed to Willis's combined salary of $80,000 and his absence from the system at a time when he should be especially responsive to Chicago's needs, not those of the Bay State. Hostile press and television editorials over the leadership and direction of the survey and the board's approval of Willis's consulting job stung Cone and the board.[71]

By early April, 1963, McSwain had withdrawn himself from consideration for the post. On April 22 Cone surprised critics, Dr. Willis, and the city by announcing that Professor Robert Havighurst of the University of Chicago had been persuaded to head the survey. Havighurst had been one of the early advisers to Cone's subcommittee and had originally recommended McSwain. More important, however, was Havighurst's record as persistent but constructive critic of the public schools and an advocate of integration and of the schools' playing an active role in revitalizing the city.[72] A member of CSC's Board of Directors and consistent fighter for human rights, within the liberal community his credentials were impeccable.

At the next board meeting, however, confirmation of his appointment was deferred. It was subsequently postponed for two meetings. Clearly, deferral was a move by those board members opposed to Havighurst in order to gain time to build a case against the professor.[73] For the next month the city was treated to an exchange of charges and counter-charges about Havighurst's integrity, his past record as a supporter of "leftist" causes, and the usefulness of a survey.

The attack on Havighurst came from various directions. From one corner came American Legion and John Birch Society accusations that the professor was a "pinko." They pointed to his support of recognition for "Red China," his earlier position with UNESCO, and his signing of petitions for organizations which turned up on the U.S. Attorney General list of subversive groups. From yet another corner, board member Raymond Spaeth, presumably voicing the superintendent's opinions, wrote to his colleagues a long letter detailing his objections to the survey and proposing, in its stead, a self-study chaired by the general superintendent. "It is no secret," he argued, "that the Superintendent opposes the suggested survey." If the survey is undertaken, he argued, conflict will inevitably surface. And if the survey ends up critical of Dr. Willis, "then we must face up to the possibility of his resigning as a result."[74]

Willis cared little for Havighurst personally, much less for his directing the survey. A number of sources document that the superintendent railed against the professor in executive meetings.[75] At the May 22 meeting in which Havighurst was to be confirmed as survey director, Willis in an effort to block the appointment, redefined the issue in two ways. First, he argued that independent surveys designed by outsiders are ineffective compared to self-studies, a point which board member Spaeth had stressed the previous month.

If any study or survey of this school system . . . or of any business is to be fruitful . . . in moving the enterprise forward, it should be discussed and planned and designed by the people who desire the survey, who have been and are responsible for the enterprise. . . . In this case, the persons involved in the planning and design are the total Board of Education as trustees for the public and the General Superintendent and staff of the school system.[76]

Secondly, he accused the board of changing the neighborhood school policy "without asking for data from the administration or its analysis." Some board members, according to Willis, had commented to reporters that they agreed with some of Havighurst's speeches concerning integration and the creation of regional high schools rather than districted ones. From these comments in the newspaper Willis inferred the end of the neighborhood school policy.[77]

In effect, Willis had converted the issue into a board-superintendent confrontation over policymaking. The superintendent pointed out:

The relationship of a superintendent with the Board and of the Board with the superintendent requires the greatest openness on administrative recommendations. This I have always tried to do. . . . Similarly, the Board should tender openness on policy matters to the superintendent. It has been a matter of concern to me that, in this instance, openness has appeared to be lacking. One might feel such instance to be an accident. . . . Were such lack of openness to be a reflection of the judgment of the total board, it would be a reflection of their attitude toward me.

Vice-president Thomas Murray, a loyal supporter of the superintendent, responded,

I am a member of the School Survey Committee and I want to assure Dr. Willis that at no time did the . . . Committee . . . even indicate that the creation of a School Survey and the selection of a director would mean that we abandon the neighborhood school policy.

Agreeing with Murray, other Board members denied Willis's charge. The local press supported the board and jabbed at the superintendent for raising a false issue. The *Defender,* a long-time caustic critic of Dr. Willis, called his charge a "strategem . . . to create a schism in the school board." Moreover, an editorial stressed, "to advance the argument that Dr. Willis was not consulted in this matter is tantamount to saying that the Board should take orders from the Superintendent."[78]

Nonetheless, on May 28, after a long, heated debate in executive session, Willis threatened to resign and go on WGN-TV unless he played a larger role in planning the survey.[79] Roddewig negotiated a compromise formula in which a *troika* of Havighurst, Willis and a mutually-agreed-upon third person would serve as a committee overseeing the Survey. (Alonzo Grace, Dean of Education at the University of Illinois, was subsequently named.)

Even with Havighurst acting as chairman of the committee and in charge of the budget, TWO's Rev. Arthur Brazier remarked that it was as if "a bank teller was named to investigate his own records." Board President Roddewig, however, thought "we could get a better report this way and better acceptance of the report." Much skepticism was expressed as to whether or not an impartial survey could be mounted.[80]

Both Willis and Havighurst left town for the summer. Havighurst had made a prior commitment to be in Brazil. Willis commuted back and forth between Massachusetts and Chicago to fulfill his consulting contract. Recall that, meanwhile, CORE sit-ins, demonstrations over placement of mobile classrooms ("Willis Wagons"), and marches were occurring weekly—often with Willis out of town or being hastily recalled. Thus, both principal investigators were out of town during a crucial summer that shaped the direction the survey was to take.

By the end of summer the Hauser Panel, appointed as part of an out-of-court settlement of the first *Webb* case, began investigating racial imbalance in the public schools. Initially de facto segregation was to have been a major area for examination in the Havighurst survey. While it would still be part of the overall design submitted in November, clearly the subject had been preempted by the Hauser Panel. Furthermore, the hot summer led to the resignation of Willis, further endangering the whole effort. When Willis withdrew his resignation, matters resumed their course, but Willis's hand with the board was much strengthened.

Professor Havighurst, of course, was in a tight spot. Two days after he was appointed survey director, he wrote Edward Keener, president of CSC, asking for a leave of absence from his duties as a member of the CSC board of directors, a group that persistently criticized the superintendent's policies. On the same day, he wrote Keener again, describing candidly the taut line he would have to tip-toe along. "As Director of the Survey," Havighurst wrote, "I must change my role from that of a critic of the school administration to that of a judge who hears and weighs evidence and eventually states his own opinion." Moreover, he would have to function as investigator to collect evidence. Admitting that the shift in roles was difficult for him, Havighurst reminded Keener that already "I have made several speeches in which the two roles of critic and judge were somehow mixed up." As for working with Willis, the professor did not want to antagonize him. "I do not want him to believe that I have been critical of him or I am opposing him on matters where I have not been critical and am not in opposition." Finally, Havighurst expressed his desire that the survey not be done in "the mood of a war." The survey should aim at improving the schools, "not at arriving at judgment upon the past record of the Superintendent."[81]

By late November Havighurst had assembled a staff, recruited consultants, and presented a survey design to the board. The board approved the design and authorized a budget of $190,000. But, once underway, the troika just didn't work. Between January and September 1964 not one committee meeting was attended by Willis. Dr. Arthur Lehne, his assistant for educational extension, did attend as his nonvoting representative. Asked why he couldn't attend one particular meeting with Havighurst and Grace in May, Willis replied that "the real estate committee takes precedence over everything else." The superintendent selected twelve committees from his staff to collect data for the survey staff. Havighurst, however, was not allowed to meet with these committees. Instead, data came via reports filtered through Dr. Lehne, with final approval from one of Willis's other lieutenants. In effect, Professor Havighurst, who depended upon the administration for much of his basic information, could only get what Willis wanted him to have. On one occasion the superintendent refused to authorize a questionnaire for teachers because he objected to certain items in it on race, marital status, and teacher opinions. The survey director deleted the offensive items while revising others. It was then sent out.[82]

When Havighurst submitted to Willis a draft report on higher education, the superintendent made some suggestions which were then incorporated in the report. Yet when the professor and Alonzo Grace went to the board with the revised report, Dr. Willis bitterly attacked the report in open session, shocking both the board and his fellow committee members.[83]

What little doubt the survey committee and staff might have had about Willis's response to the effort was removed when the 500-page report was finally released in November 1964. At the meeting where it was presented, Willis did not look once at Havighurst during the director's presentation to the board. At its completion, no word was spoken by either, and Willis left the room without giving the professor any sign of recognition.[84]

The report itself is written in sober, restrained prose. No exhortation or anger characterize the text. Nonetheless, the report points clearly to the school crisis facing Chicago. It calls for aggressive action by the board. The report characterizes two opposing ideologies among schoolmen on how best to run a big-city system. The "four walls" approach is

to do the best possible job of educating every boy and girl who comes into the school, whoever he is, whatever his color, nationality, I.Q. or handicap. This means building good school buildings, equipping them well and staffing them with well trained teachers. At its best, it means being courteous and friendly to parents and to citizens ... but making it quite clear to them that the schools are run by professionals who know their business and do not need advice from other people .... It means keeping the school 'out of local politics.' Staff appointments are to be made on the basis of merit alone ....

The four walls type of school system works for efficiency and economy and attempts to free the creative teacher to do the best possible job of teaching under good conditions. The community outside of the school is regarded as a source of complexity and of tension arousal if the boundary between community and school is not clearly defined and respected.

The other ideology Havighurst called the "urban community school." Schoolmen who believe in this see the city as being in grave trouble; what is required is the "active participation of schools in making and practicing of policy for social urban renewal."

The urban community school attempts to act constructively in the crisis by involving parents and citizens in the decisions about school policy and practice. The educator accepts the frustration of working with people who themselves are confused and uncertain about the schools, believing that the only way to solve the problems of the city is to work on a give and take basis with citizens and community organizations.[85]

Alert readers knew full well which ideology described Willis's and which Havighurst favored. Survey recommendations revealed clearly both intentions and preferences.

Havighurst stressed that fifteen of the twenty-two recommendations could be put into effect within months through board action without any dollar cost to the system. Others would involve increases in subsequent budgets. Three recommendations, in particular, he felt were "most important." One involved different ways to further integration of Chicago through the elementary schools. Another was improving the education of the poor. The third important one was reorganizing administration to place more decision-making authority into the hands of principals and teachers.[86]

Within a week Willis presented to the board his analysis of the survey recommendations. He agreed with sixteen of the twenty-two, disagreed with three, and on two—in Havighurst's careful phrase—Willis "has not spoken clearly."[87] Of the three which the survey director thought "most important," Willis either disagreed with or spoke ambiguously about two. The one with which Willis agreed was one he already prided himself on: compensatory programs and services for the disadvantaged.

However, neither concerted efforts by CSC to get the board to take action on these no-cost recommendations nor extensive press support for speedy action carried the impact that advocates had hoped for. By February 1965 Havighurst's speeches to PTAs and community groups took on a hard edge. In one he strongly criticized the superintendent for not once speaking out in support of integration even after the board accepted the Hauser Panel's recommendations on integration in April 1964.[88]

Two years after the survey was completed, and just a few weeks after Willis had resigned for good, Havighurst totaled up the score and found that only six of twenty-two recommendations had been acted upon, and those were, ironically, the most expensive (though, significantly, least controversial) recommendations. The no-cost ones were the most disputed. Nothing had happened on those. "It's amusing, in a way," Havighurst said.

When we gave the report to the Board everybody said, 'Well, we can't possibly get all the money these programs would cost.' So they never really considered them. But in a few months Congress passed the Elementary and Secondary Education Act. That meant Chicago could get all the money it needed for our programs and more.

Then the board didn't know what to do with it.[89]

After lawsuits, sit-ins, violent demonstrations, two boycotts, and a blue-ribbon panel inquiry on de facto segregation, civil rights groups had apparently failed to budge Willis from his embrace with the neighborhood school policy (save for a slight relaxation in permissive transfers). Nor had they persuaded the superintendent to recognize integration as a valid school goal. Even a threatened cut-off of federal funds engineered by CCCO in the fall of 1965, narrowly averted by Mayor Daley's influence at the White House, had little apparent impact on Willis's policies. Would, then, the Havighurst Report achieve that which litigation, direct action, and federal threats could not gain? Clearly, it couldn't and didn't.

Willis Resigns for the Last Time

In the spring of 1965 Willis's contract came up for renewal. CCCO marched on City Hall, urging Mayor Daley to pressure the board not to rehire Willis. An open letter signed by 125 professors from eight Chicago universities urged the board to replace Willis. Pickets and counterpickets marched through the Loop to City Hall and the board. Other protests erupted, both for and against his continuation as general superintendent. On May 28, 1965, the board, after a heated debate, voted 7–4 to renew Willis's contract. But the board extracted from Dr. Willis his promise to retire at age 65, a year hence.[90]

It almost seemed as if the civil rights movement, insofar as its emphasis on schools was concerned, was back where it began five years before. But things had changed. Willis no longer had the uncritical, enthusiastic support of the business community. Stubbornness and his refusal to deal openly with civil rights groups had cut deeply into his support. Yet, as in 1963 when Willis had resigned, a telegram, authored again by Willis's close friend, Virgil Martin, and signed by prominent businessmen (but missing many men who had signed the one in 1963) was sent to the board asking that Willis be rehired. Their support, however, was polite, insubstantial. "I think at one time," a banker and close friend of the superintendent said, "he probably had the support of 90 percent or more of the business community; by the time he left he only had about half." Another friend, who was a president of a utility company, felt that the superintendent was "a high grade educational administrator but he is a completely inflexible person; he made no effort to make a public image acceptable to the community." Stephen London, who has examined the details of Willis's departure, concluded that by the summer of 1965, the school board, mayor, and businessmen agreed that a new superintendent should be hired.[91]

The 7–4 vote mirrored some of the changes that had taken place within the board. The board that humbly took the superintendent back in 1963 had been beaten publicly on a number of issues since then and now linked their difficulties to the intractibility of their executive officer. One civil rights activist characterized the superintendent as "the man who organized the movement for us. His arrogance, stubbornness made it easy for us to get supporters." A board employee who knew him well remarked, "he was his own worst enemy." The board had slowly arrived at a similar conclusion.[92] No board majority existed to bump the superintendent, but sufficient concern for change was there to make demands upon Dr. Willis. The eleven-member board was divided into four pro-Willis, four anti-Willis, and three swing votes. As in most divided boards, issues were resolved less on their merits and more on what position the superintendent took. Superintendents seldom last long with such split boards.

Still, the board did not want to force Willis out in disgrace; thus, a face-saving formula for both board and superintendent emerged. With the board determined to ease him out, there were no more strategies that Dr. Willis could use to defy, defuse, and deflect pressure. On August 31, 1966, he left.

2 Washington, D.C.

John F. Kennedy had been president for two years. A nuclear show-down over Russian missiles in Cuba had been nervously averted. James Meredith had finally been admitted to the University of Mississippi. Mobilization for Youth, a multi-million dollar effort to crack the poverty cycle on New York's lower east side, was underway. A handful of American advisers was assisting the South Vietnamese stave off Vietcong advances. Unemployment figures had dipped, but wages were rising. So were prices, although few knew it and even fewer seemed to care. It was 1963. And Washington, D.C. was poised on the threshold of a major battle for change in its public schools.

Within half a decade, Kennedy would be murdered; James Meredith would leave Mississippi, only to return and get shot; Mobilization for Youth would be a tiny limping organization competing for survival amongst the thicket of antipoverty organizations; and a half-million GIs would be poured into Vietnam. Wages would continue to rise, but prices would outdistance them. To the surprise of economists, unemployment figures would also climb upwards. And in Washington, the battle between Carl Hansen and groups pressuring for school change would have been joined, fought, and ended.

In 1963 there were 136,000 children in Washington public schools, of whom 86 percent were black. The staff was 75 percent black, and on the appointed board of education there were five white and four black members.[1] The board had the authority to hire and fire the superintendent and to make policy for the system, but it answered to city government and, ultimately, Congress. With no elected government—the President appointed major city officials—Congress reviewed local affairs carefully as well as controlling purse strings. What local political life there was revolved around influencing members of the Senate and House District Committees to move in desired directions. Political parties existed but lived on the ebb and flow of congressional favor and executive appointment. In short, the federal presence dominated the scene.

Within this context, Superintendent Carl Hansen had directed the school system since 1958 and had gained a two-fold national reputation. First, he had played a major part in desegregating the District schools in 1953–55 and, later, had defended what had happened before a hostile congressional investigation. Second, he had instituted throughout the system by 1963 the Track System and the Amidon Plan.

Carl Hansen as Superintendent

To insiders and outsiders alike, Carl Hansen, the Amidon Plan, and tracking were synonymous with the D.C. schools. To understand the school system prior to the struggle for reform, one must reckon with who Carl Hansen was and what he stood for.

A native small-town Nebraskan and former principal of an Omaha high school, Hansen came to Washington in 1947 as executive assistant to Superintendent Hobart Corning. The nation's capital was a rigidly segregated city then, more akin to Baton Rouge, Louisiana, than to Boston, Massachusetts. Its dual school system prevented teachers, principals, and administrators from sharing experiences and working together on common problems. The line of racial etiquette was drawn taut.

Hansen had no knowledge of segregation. On the train eastward, he recalled, he found on the seat next to him a magazine which described pictorially the color line in Washington. "For the first time," he said, "I became aware of the degree to which racial segregation was practiced in the nation's capital."

Within the white division of the system, Hansen swiftly moved up the ladder. After being executive assistant, he directed all elementary schools, then moved to a similar position for secondary schools, and finally, in 1958, to the superintendency. His quick ascent in the bureaucracy was tied to the prominent role he played in carefully shepherding desegregation through a board of education that adhered to the separate-but-equal letter of the law. "Whenever we moved to contravert existing segregating practices," Hansen said, "we had to do so in such a manner that the board of education would not be forced to make an adverse ruling on what had been done."

The pamphlets Hansen wrote, and his statements to the press on the need for desegregation, often angered both superiors and influential Southern Congressmen while endearing him to local liberals. But he seldom took an ideologically liberal or conservative position. In describing how administrators responded to desegregation, Hansen observed that:

Many felt that everything that could be done to weaken the evil effects of such a system should be done. Others, of course, believed intensely in the correctness of racial segregation by schools. The extremists at either end were the ones who got us into trouble. The best work was done by the reasonable people who felt they could do more for children if they did less for special ideologies.[2]

Dr. Hansen considered himself one of those reasonable people. But on the Amidon Plan and tracking, the superintendent was seldom moderate; he often dug in his heels and refused to budge.

The Amidon Plan (named after a new elementary school built in an urban renewal site) was a "return to the sanity of order and logic in curriculum organization and to the wisdom of teaching subject matter to children in direct and effective manner, using with judgment what is known about how we learn." Stressing phonics, order, and discipline in tightly prescribed periods of instruction, the plan was teacher-centered. Under it, the teacher moves to center stage and orchestrates the class. "She returns to the front of the room," he wrote, "with

chalk in hand to explain, discuss, reinforce learning by immediate check on class responses . . . . From the wealth of her own scholarship she helps her class to see connections between the known and the unknown, giving meaning to what otherwise may be missed by the pupil and taken for granted by the teacher.[3]

Tracking, or the "variable curriculum," was introduced into the high schools in 1956 and into the junior high and elementary schools in 1958.[4] Children were assigned to tracks according to their ability as revealed by intelligence and achievement tests, teacher recommendations, and so forth. Such ability grouping attempted to tailor curriculum and instruction to individual differences. If tests masked a student's ability or if a student demonstrated marked improvement in one track, then, theoretically, movement into the next higher track was possible. Downward movement, of course, could occur also.

Hansen's pedagogical convictions were strengthened by the belief that professional educators possessed the training and experience to guide local school affairs. When he was attacked by critics, Hansen lashed back at "those who demand innovations and new and imaginative ideas yet, speak in the thin voice of dilettantes ... of benchwarmers."[5]

By 1963 Carl Hansen's educational philosophy and program dominated the system. It did so because Hansen dominated* the decision-making. The superintendent and his staff defined the policy issues, produced the alternatives and the research to support each alternative, drew up the formal agenda for each meeting, and recommended specific policy choices. The board of education complied. What Carl Hansen wanted from the board, he got; what he didn't want, the board seldom saw on the agenda. Hansen made sure the budget reflected his priorities. The superintendent's commitments to tracking and the Amidon Plan permeated the system. As he said, a "good administrator makes sure everything is planned."[6] And he tried.

By 1963, Carl Hansen—a man respected by associates for his integrity, admired (and hated) for his fearless and snappy decisions, and recognized by both friend and critic as the man who runs the D.C. schools—was confronted by ambitious reformers.

Professional Reformers at Work

In the late 1950s, when few major social changes could be initiated with a conservative president and divided Congress, social critics in American life had begun to agree upon a focus for reform: revitalize the dying city; transform urban decay into growth; take deteriorating "grey area" institutions and invest them with the breath of life; convert citizen apathy into hope and, in the process, preserve social stability.

The Ford Foundation was on the cutting edge of this movement. Ford grants to ten school systems (Washington was one) in the early 60s—the Great Cities Projects—produced a multitude of team teaching, prekindergarten, remedial reading, and community school projects. These initial educational grants were, in the words of Paul Ylvisaker, the director of Ford's Public Affairs Program, "a stepping stone to larger grants that would stimulate broader and more coherent community approaches to the physical and human problems of the grey areas."[7]

But the professional reformers in foundations, universities, and government didn't have the next stone to step to. They felt that the school

---

*Hansen read an earlier version of this chapter and objected to the word "dominated." He defined the word in terms of arbitrariness and dogmatism—traits which he rejected. He preferred "heavily influenced."

system, or, for that matter, any single, established urban institution, could not implement a creative approach combining public and private services to solve the problems of the city. A new kind of agency unburdened by narrow vested interests or political constituency was needed. Not public, not private, yet possessing the capacity to coordinate both domains this new entity would catalyze the total community into taking action in its behalf.

The development and growth of Mobilization for Youth (MFY), a nonprofit corporation established by both public and private agencies and working on the lower east side of New York City, offered a model of an agency for community action. Reformers at Ford were captivated. They invested in MFY. They spread the MFY word in reform-minded circles. By December 1961, the first of six grants to similar quasi-public corporations to reform grey areas was made to Oakland, California. Ford money would come to Washington within two years.

With the election of John F. Kennedy, New Frontiersmen turned to an attack on urban problems, the most compelling, and very political, of which was youth crime, or the "social dynamite" of the slums. The President's Committee on Juvenile Delinquency and Youth Crime (PCJD) was established in May 1961.

Vigorous intellectual traffic between Ford and PCJD staff often resulted in similar information and assumptions about urban problems and the strategies to solve them. And as events moved swiftly, joint grants were made to cities. As Ford had moved from solo grants to big city school systems to a search for another instrument, preferably a planning and coordinating one, PCJD moved from a primary focus on delinquency to an attack on poverty through a similar instrument. To attack poverty, reform urban institutions, and thereby reduce delinquency, PCJD believed deeply in a rational analysis of problems. Their strategy was to secure commitments to change from institutional leaders and carefully plan demonstration projects in selected cities. Washington received one such project.[8]

Beginnings of a Subsystem: WAY vs. DCPS 1963–1964

In early 1963 Washington Action for Youth (WAY)—a planning organization funded by the PCJD—rented offices in a drab gray building two blocks from the White House. By the time cherry blossoms were blooming on the Tidal Basin, Carl Hansen and WAY had locked horns.

In one sense such a confrontation was predictable. The new director of WAY was Jack Goldberg, who, in the words of the *Washington Post,* was both "dynamic and abrasive."[9] Younger than Hansen, used to working with sleeves rolled up and using pungent language, Goldberg was trained as a social worker and therapist. Experienced in New York settlement-house work, Goldberg fervently believed that institutions, especially schools, needed changing and must be shoved off dead center. Hansen, a man who seldom loosened his tie, took off his suitcoat in public, or dropped a four-letter word, was the opposite in style. Equally as frank, Hansen nonetheless chose words and situations carefully in expressing himself.

In a larger sense, the clash was inevitable. Given WAY's analysis of school problems, their proposed strategies, and their belief in controlling the reform process—as contrasted with Hansen's beliefs that the system was making substantial progress in dealing with problems and that schoolmen, not outsiders, should manage the process of change—a collision course was predictable.

Funded by PCJD, and sharing most of its assumptions about delinquency and poverty, WAY concluded that "parents and youth in low-income neighborhoods do not lack knowledge of the 'good life' and its benefits, but ... opportunity channels for fulfilling their aspirations are blocked." WAY programs were "geared toward changing institutional systems to make them more relevant to the needs of persons in (poor areas) and more understanding and accepting of these persons." And the schools? The WAY report was unequivocal.

> One institution requiring modification ... is the school system.
> This is the basic agency to which all youth are exposed and which can prepare them for entry into an increasingly complex society. The school must take over additional functions and it must strengthen existing ones.[10]

More than the superintendent's expertise was at issue. There was more to this struggle than professionals resenting outside interference. Power to control the reform process was at stake. "Goldberg," the superintendent said, "openly was after the Track system."[11] Discrediting school professionals would inevitably lead to the superintendent's losing his grip on the school decision-making machinery; Amidon and tracking would be endangered. Thus, Hansen and Goldberg symbolized a power struggle between professionals and lay reformers that had periodically marked attempts to change urban school systems since the late nineteenth century.

Shortly after Goldberg's arrival, a target area for WAY pilot programs was chosen. The Cardozo area was selected, Goldberg said, because it represented a cross-section of district problems, "not because it was a jungle."[12] There was, however, much left unsaid. Although the Cardozo area, a brisk walk from the White House, contained, as most black ghetto areas do, a substantial portion of home-owning, middle-class Negroes who deeply resented the slum label that tagged the area, Cardozo also contained all the depressing indices of poverty in full measure.

What angered the superintendent, however, about the choice of Cardozo over a half-dozen other similar impoverished areas, was that he hadn't made the decision. Hansen knew that the principal of Cardozo High School, Dr. Bennetta B. Washington, was a close personal friend of Goldberg and one of the early critics of his administration. Her ties in the affluent black community were substantial and not to be ignored. Goldberg wanted Cardozo for precisely those reasons. And Hansen didn't.

WAY's intervention and Goldberg's style led to a series of turbulent meetings between him and the superintendent. Goldberg recalls those early meetings.

We had a few face-to-face confrontations. We talked about the track system. . . . He had the attitude of who the hell are you guys to tell me what to do. You know, the professional educator idea. What also bothered him was the Cardozo-WAY alliance [that is Bennetta B. Washington, principal of the high school and close friend of Goldberg]. Bennetta was strictly on his shit list. So, you see, we tried to go through this process with him and as we didn't, it heightened the differences between him as a professional administrator and us. Here was federal intervention of a professional administrator in the Cardozo area. He said he didn't like Cardozo to begin with, "and now with you people I even like it less." He said, "I would do anything I could to defend myself from you." And he did.[13]

After WAY had launched some summer pilot programs in teacher training, employment, and delinquency prevention, the simmering conflict erupted in October, when WAY submitted to Hansen twenty proposals to reform schooling in the Cardozo area. Included in this package was a series of federally funded programs, including teacher, principal, and counselor training, parent involvement, increased emphasis on vocational education, and ungraded primaries in the elementary schools—all of which were to be lumped together into an experimental subsystem located in the Cardozo area.

At the Franklin Building, an old elementary building converted into administrative headquarters, fury greeted the proposals. School officials said the WAY proposals were "usurping" powers of the board of education and superintendent.[14] Yet within two months (in January 1964) Hansen had recommended to the board a substantially revised WAY package; it was clear that Hansen had whipped WAY.

What saved the superintendent, permitting him to brush aside the first attack upon his control over policymaking, was the assassination of President Kennedy. The director of WAY recalled:

I went to the attorney general and told him that, in my judgment, I didn't think that this guy [Hansen] was movable. The attorney general accepted our perception of the situation. Then the assassination came along. On the day of the assassination we had set up a meeting between Hansen, the attorney general, some school people, and others to discuss the possibilities of change. We had this meeting scheduled; it was D-Day for Hansen. The game plan was set for that very day to see if Hansen could be budged. The message to Hansen was going to be: Look, Mac, either you pick up your marbles and get out or you stay here and do it the way we want you to do it.

Hansen didn't have to pick up his marbles. Less than two months after Dallas, the superintendent recommended to the board a compromise plan costing almost one and a half million dollars to establish an "Inner-City Target Area." Incorporating some of the WAY proposals along with those of his staff, Hansen recommended a series of compensatory programs that supported the existing structure, making no major changes. The programs included efforts aimed at preschoolers and high-school dropouts—focusing, as most programs across the nation did, on the "culturally-deprived" child, not the system. Even had the assassination not occurred, Hansen felt that "Jack could not have touched me with a ten-foot pole. I had," he said, "the board, community and staff solidly behind me."

At the January board meeting, the director of WAY, powerless even to see the compromise document prior to the meeting, agreed that the "content of the program would be clearly the responsibility of the superintendent and board of education." To a board member's question, Goldberg said, "I think we are moving in the correct direction. If we can move as quickly as we can to implement the total program—and assuming we are going to come up with top echelon people, I think we have a good ball game going.'' Privately, Goldberg felt differently.

What came out of it was not a fundamental change . . . . Some partial stuff came out but Hansen was sitting on top of the goddam bag . . . . After the assassination, we were dead ducks. He knew it . . . . I had no more power base. Whatever compromises and changes that were worked out came as a result of internal pressures and accommodation with the black community.

Within six months, Goldberg had resigned and returned to New York. Hansen brushed aside this first direct thrust at his grip over policymaking. "I think Jack Goldberg," the superintendent concluded, "handled us in the schools the wrong way . . . . His approach was negative. Change in the schools was his chief cure for juvenile delinquency. Schools were mainly the cause of youth crime. If he had come at us more constructively, we might have been easier to work with."[15]

The Model School Division Is Created

To a degree the superintendent was right. Two other governmental agencies, eager to reform the D.C. schools, did approach him "constructively" in 1964 and did find he was easier "to work with." Before this encounter is discussed, however, a few words about the times are necessary.

Submitted to a Congress and country still reeling from the impact of President Kennedy's murder, Johnson's poverty and civil rights legislation swept through committee hearings and ended up in legislation with little public debate. An irresistible flood of rhetoric poured forth. "We can win the War Against Poverty," declared Sargent Shriver, director-designate of the Office of Economic Opportunity, "because we have the tools, we have the know-how, and we have the will."[16] Optimism spilled over with the passage of the Civil Rights Act. Racial discrimination was solved, many believed. Within this national context—because of its location Washington resonated vibrantly to federal interests—the President's Panel on Educational Research and Development and the United Planning Organization negotiated with Carl Hansen for reform.

The panel (one member of which was Benjamin C. Willis) was an advisory unit created by the President's Science Advisory Committee. Having no operational function or funds, the panel was appointed chiefly to suggest possible directions which government agencies involved in education could pursue. Throughout 1963 and early 1964 the panel held a series of education seminars, one being devoted to the "Deprived and Segregated." All of these meetings were attended by either Hansen or his executive assistant, Norman Nickens.[17]

At one of these meetings, in September 1963—or, roughly, at the same time that the Cardozo target area had been identified and the Goldberg-Hansen polarization had already occurred—a new idea for organizing change in urban school systems was proposed. Said Joseph Turner, staff assistant for the panel, and its chief advocate, "The idea of establishing an autonomous, experimental subsystem within a big city school system grew out of [the] two-week seminar." At this meeting, according to Turner, the District was suggested as a site for such an experiment. A number of panelists from Washington warmly pushed the idea.[18] The District schools looked like a sound choice. But a sound choice for what? What would this subsystem do that was not being done by the overall system? According to the panel report, a different reform strategy was necessary since overcentralization and excessive bureaucracy stifled innovation.

With [a subsystem in a big city] as an unobstructed testing-ground new programs can be developed, not in isolation, but in concert and on a proper scale, with provision for rapid feedback and rapid exploitation of new opportunities as they occur....

The subsystem would have its own lay advisory council or "board," including members of the school staff, members of academic faculties of universities, and artists, musicians, writers, lawyers, etc.[19]

Turner and others met with Hansen and Nickens, encouraging them to broaden the initial target area idea into the model subsystem concept of the panel. Implicit promises of substantial funding were made to school officials. And with developing antipoverty legislation, more funds would be coming into the District. Conditions seemed to support movement toward broader, comprehensive action. On June 11, 1964, Hansen recommended to the board the establishment of a "model school subsystem" and advisory council within the Washington public schools. Joseph Turner, who drafted the superintendent's recommendation, testified in its behalf. One week later, the board approved the plan.[20]

Had Hansen embraced the reform ideology? No. Yet to read the document submitted to the board, one would think so. The report to the board details the creation of the target area but points out "that our original concept began to grow and to change until we began to ask ourselves if this plan were bold enough, imaginative enough and flexible enough to accomplish our goals.'' The superintendent concluded that the concept of a model subsystem ''has created greater potential for total impact in conjunction with a community action program than the original concept.'' In effect, Turner had drafted for Hansen the panel's chief recommendations.[21]

Yet, Hansen said he had motives other than reform in mind when he recommended the plan to the board.

Help from any source was what I wanted.... The White House, which seemed to offer now a new means of support [i.e. model subsystem] I wanted to tap for all it was worth. I doubt that I have the instinct of a highway-man, but I was rapacious to a fault where the schools were concerned. We hoped for money for the schools from this kind of White House interest.... I proposed to the Board of Education that it set up a model subsystem with Cardozo.[22]

The Politics of Getting Started: The First Year, 1964–1965

Whatever motives or pressures there were, a model subsystem was born. That it would be under the control of Hansen had been determined by the struggle with WAY and the manner in which Turner and panel members approached the superintendent. In August 1964, when the superintendent chose a black man, Norman Nickens, his trusted executive assistant, to become the acting assistant superintendent of the infant Model School Division (MSD), any uncertainty was removed.

While real control of the scope, character, and direction of the reform would never be more than a few doors away from Nickens's office in the Franklin Building, the magic optimism of the times swept early pronouncements to the heights of reform hopes. The new assistant superintendent called the MSD ''revolutionary.'' Within the first year the direction of the MSD was shaped for the next five years—but not necessarily in a revolutionary fashion.[23]

Shortly after the board approved the MSD in June, Hansen met with the Director of UPO to line up consultants to draft an administrative structure for the new subsystem. Some flesh had to be put on the bones served up by the panel report. At the initial meeting of consultants, school officials, and UPO staff, Nickens presented his guidelines, agreed to by the superintendent, for the consultants to use in framing their recommendations. The key ones were:

The ''model school system'' remains an integral part of the regular school system.

The Assistant Superintendent will have autonomy in the
introduction of new programs; curriculum materials;
supportive services, etc., with the approval of the
Superintendent and Board of Education.

The Assistant Superintendent will have autonomy in re-
commending the appointment of personnel beyond the
regular budgetary staffing . . . .

Existing school programs . . . will be implemented and
expanded in the "model school system." We will use
the best of existing school programs and not innovate
for the sake of innovation or for change alone.[24]

The resulting consultant document, hereafter called the Harvard Report, accepted these guidelines as a framework for their conclusions.

The consultants' report, in effect, then, retreated from the panel
recommendations in two significant directions. First, it accepted and
strengthened Nickens's guidelines that MSD should remain an integral
part of the larger system, and thereby rejected the panel's stress that the
subsystem be nearly totally autonomous in order to assure innovation.
Second, the panel's recommendation that the main task of the lay advisory council was to provide "cooperative *direction* of a comprehensive
experiment" was rejected by the consultants in favor of a board that
reviewed and advised but did not determine policy for the subsystem.[25]
Both recommendations of the consultants were satisfactory to the
superintendent and assistant superintendent.

Advisory Council

The presence of a prestigious thirteen-member blue-ribbon citizens'
committee anxious to get started and begin implementing the June 11th
action of the board proved troublesome to Hansen. Would the citizens
committee end up determining the direction of the Model School Division? After wrestling with WAY and winning, Hansen was not about to
let the policymaking power over an infant experiment slip into another
group's hands.

Six weeks after the board approved the advisory council, yet one
month before the consultants submitted their preliminary report, Hansen
wrote to the president of the board:

The Committee, in my opinion, will serve as advisor in the main. It
will meet perhaps no more than once a month to react to ideas having
to do with the development of the model school system and to submit

suggestions for consideration by the school staff and the Board of Education.[26]

The Harvard Report, unsurprisingly, reached the same conclusion.

In November the board approved Hansen's recommendations on the advisory council; it could only advise, nothing else. Or, as the council's executive assistant concluded, board action left the committee "without any useful function." Power and authority were, of course, at the heart of the matter. School officials were not about to surrender policymaking power to a citizens' group, particularly after the scars WAY had left.[27]

After Hansen had submitted his recommendations on the advisory committee and they were reported in the press, Judge David Bazelon, chairman of the committee, wrote to Board President Wesley Williams.

If the Committee is not to exercise independent judgment in planning for the Model School Sub-system I would question whether it has any useful function to serve or whether it would merely be window dressing aimed at obtaining additional funds for District of Columbia Schools.

Except for the energetic activities of its executive assistant, the advisory council was little more than "window dressing."[28]

By mid-1966, the advisory council had stopped meeting; it slid slowly into oblivion. Nickens must have breathed a sigh of relief, for he was a man knocked back and forth between loyalty to his boss and advocacy of reform. Looking back, he could say "fortunately, it didn't last long."[29]

First Education Proposals Submitted to UPO

As early as the mid-June recommendation to the board for a model subsystem, Hansen and Nickens knew that new federal money would be probably coming into the District through the United Planning Organization. Meetings between Hansen, Nickens, and James Banks, executive director of UPO, had been going on since early spring. The employment of consultants to design administrative machinery for the MSD had been cleared with and financed by UPO. Rumors and criticisms of the proposal's content and the infant experiment led Hansen and Banks to issue a joint news release a few days after the board received the proposal. Both organizations desperately wished to avoid a repeat of the earlier WAY-public schools scrap.

The school system's initial package for the subsystem stressed that it was UPO's educational weapon in the war on poverty. The program would develop an "across-the-board experiment in areas of curriculum development, utilization of teachers and the management of the system itself, with provision for rapid feedback of results and rapid exploitation of new opportunities." The model system would experiment with:

a. the recruitment, selection and training of teachers.

b. team-teaching, non-graded organization, teacher resource rooms.

c. part-time assistants and volunteers in tutoring programs including housewives, and professional persons such as artists, musicians, scientists and engineers.

d. use of school facilities in afternoons, evenings, weekends, summers for less formal types of study such as library, art, drama, music, laboratory, and shop.

e. conversion of parts of existing buildings, not presently schools, for use as preschool centers.

f. selection of textbooks, teachers' guides and other instructional materials.

g. development of new curriculums and materials where no existing materials are found suitable.[30]

In late November UPO announced the grant of $650,000 to the MSD. Unfortunately, bureaucratic problems with D.C. government stalled the program. In March 1965, or four months before school closed, Nickens officially launched the model subsystem.

By June, experimental reading programs (Words in Color, Science Research Associates, Initial Teaching Alphabet, etc.) were in planning, developmental, or installation stages. Longer school day, remedial reading programs, tutoring by college students and adults, cultural field trips, and some teacher training were at various points of implementation. By summer's end, about 6,000 of the 17,000 students in the MSD were involved in the experiment.[31]

By early spring 1965 the infant experiment was underway. Under the watchful eyes of Carl Hansen, Norman Nickens had been named the permanent assistant superintendent of the reform effort. He had helped to maneuver the advisory committee into a position of powerlessness, had established a beginning framework for the MSD, and had learned to negotiate the byzantine corridors of federal bureaucracies to gain the first half-million dollars to operate the subsystem. Still, criticism continued to focus upon the issue of autonomy. How could MSD really do anything, critics said, unless the umbilical cord to the system were cut?

More Autonomy

"What we have," said Herman Branson, Howard University professor and member of the advisory committee, "could not be called a model subsystem by any means."[32] Just two months after MSD programs were launched and almost a year after board approval, he described the subsystem as a collection of isolated experiments grafted onto the old school structure. The problem seemed to be a lack of real independence.

As a result of the local press's sharp criticism of the reform and growing criticism from UPO and OEO, Hansen moved to redefine autonomy. In late August 1965 Hansen announced he would recommend to the board that all nineteen schools in the division be under the direct control of Nickens. The reform was now to be a decentralized administrative unit reporting directly to the superintendent. Offices would no longer be in the Franklin Building. "The primary change will be that the staff will look to Mr. Nickens as the man in charge," the superintendent said. There will be "greater autonomy to proceed with new ideas."[33]

On September 22, 1965, the board of education approved the creation of an "autonomous geographical district." When a board member asked for a more precise definition of autonomy, the superintendent replied:

Autonomy means, for the purpose of this organization, independence of administrative control and supervision, choice of personnel within the rules of the Board and the legislative controls set by Congress, the management of funds for special programs, the assignment of teachers within the division . . . .

We cannot, nor would I recommend it, and I hope that the Board would not approve it if I did, set up a division of the school system which is not responsive to the rules and regulations of this Board or to the legal requirements set forth by Congress on the operation of the school system.[34]

In effect, the MSD would now have more operational control over teaching, personnel, curriculum, instruction, and supervision. It would, however, still depend upon the regular system for its budget, assignment of principals, and purchasing. The guidelines that Nickens gave the Harvard consultants in the previous year remained a firm principle;

MSD's tie with the regular system still remained intact. It would remain so because Hansen wanted it that way.

While Hansen candidly admitted that his initial attraction to the subsystem was the lure of badly needed cash, he grew increasingly cold to the concept and its ramifications. When, he wrote, "I asked the Board of Education to accept a grant of $6,131.99 from . . . the United Planning Organization, . . . I should have known that any agency that would propose a grant short of one cent to round out the dollar would be a difficult Santa Claus to deal with."[35] Such government-subsidized changes, he felt, could be dangerous to the existing school structure, a structure that Hansen found sound. The superintendent needed to keep close watch on its operation, yet not too close to be accused of strangling reform. Hansen maintained control through policymaking in three areas: delegation of authority, choice of personnel, and funding decisions.

Delegation of Authority: Autonomy of MSD and the Advisory Committee

WAY, UPO, PERD, and the Advisory Committee wanted complete independence for the subsystem. Hansen interpreted autonomy differently. The 1964 initial guidelines for the subsystem clearly stated the limits on independence. After extensive external pressure, Hansen bent, extending slightly more authority but still maintaining budgetary and supervisory control. Not until early 1967 when Hansen was under heavy attack and struggling for survival, did MSD get the sort of authority its early well-wishers had hoped for.

While the advisory committee wanted governing power, or at least a sharing of authority with the board of education, the question of what authority the committee would have was again answered by Hansen. Citing legal requirements established by Congress that made the board solely responsible for operation of the system, he also used the device of a Harvard consultants' report to frame an advisory role for the committee; he chose not to support independent funding for the group and, wherever possible kept the committee uninformed. So when the advisory committee would send recommendations to the board, one member recalled, the "Board would say the hell with it."[36] In disgust, the committee gave up.

Personnel and Funding Decisions

In every instance where a key position was to be filled, Hansen's man was selected. In April 1964 Dr. Paul Cooke was appointed over Jack

Goldberg's candidate, Bennetta Washington, as the first director of the Inner City Target Area Project. After this project was shelved, Norman Nickens was tapped acting head of the subsystem experiment in the summer of 1964. After the formal announcement requesting applications for assistant superintendent of the Model School Division was circulated, a few months later, to no one's surprise, Norman Nickens was again selected.

Twice during the early years of the MSD, federal funds with few strings attached were available. School officials had great flexibility in allocating these federal dollars. One would assume that if the MSD had the real priority that official rhetoric indicated, more than a token sum would have been allocated for the experiment. But Hansen's priorities were elsewhere. In December 1964, $2.5 million in Impact Aid funds became available; not until two years later was even a fraction of these funds spent on MSD. In November 1965 Title I of the Elementary and Secondary Education Act, aimed specifically at poor children, gave the District $6.3 million. Of that amount, $500,000, or less than 10 percent, went into the Cardozo subsystem although it had over 20 percent of all poor children in Washington. Finally, certain kinds of budgetary rearrangements in delegating authority and administratively reorganizing could have been made without spending one penny had Hansen wished to. No such funding decisions were made.[37] The superintendent's control of policymaking in these areas guaranteed that the MSD would move no faster or further than he wished it to.

By October 1965 the MSD had more independence than when it was approved; what it had was satisfactory to the superintendent. Norman Nickens, who firmly believed that nothing meaningful could be done unless "Hansen is fully behind us," felt that he now had "all the autonomy" he needed. But UPO was now having misgivings about the Model School Division as the education component of a community organization.[38]

United Planning Organization and Model School Division, 1964–1967

UPO began as a Ford Foundation invention using President's Committee on Juvenile Delinquency funds and ended up coordinating Washington's war on poverty. Beginning in August 1963 with a handful of employees, a year and a half later UPO had 16 million dollars in federal grants and over 500 employees.[39]

Around UPO Executive Director James Banks swirled the forces that created and shaped a federally subsidized new institution committed to action on behalf of the poor. Like Nickens, Banks was a native Washingtonian.[40] After graduation from Howard University, Banks climbed slowly upward through federal and District bureaucracies as a professional civil servant. Gaining most of his experience in public housing and slum clearance agencies, Banks captured respect in both black and white professional communities. Quiet and calm, Banks counted upon persuasion and negotiation to achieve his goals. To white professional reformers eager to underwrite change in Washington, D.C., James Banks was an ideal choice for leadership.

As executive director, Banks had great leverage. The thirty-member, predominantly white board of trustees chaired by a corporation executive seldom countermanded Banks. Outside of the constraints of grant regulations and local and federal politics, Banks had a free hand.

That suited the superintendent of schools just fine. After abrasive Jack Goldberg, the calm, pipe-smoking, conservatively dressed James Banks was most welcome. "My strategy," Banks once said, "was to see if I can get him [Hansen] to agree to do things that he didn't want to do. He had been through one ordeal with Jack and he would welcome my approach." Banks and Hansen had, according to the UPO executive, "friendly relations—we would go to the Cosmos Club [prestigious Washington private club] and be very charming." To further encourage closeness, Banks hired as his top educational advisor Dr. Irene Hypps, who was recently retired from the school system. Dr. Hypps believed that UPO "should be very innnovative and firmly critical of the school system in a constructive manner." Dr. Hansen wrote a warm recommendation for his former associate.[41] Moreover, Banks and Nickens, graduates of the same high school, were old friends. Such a setup yielded harmonious relations between the two agencies. A bumper crop of press releases, mutual praise and pats on the back were harvested the first year of the experiment (June, 1964–June, 1965). But at a cost.

Increasing skepticism of Banks's leadership style and substance from within UPO top staff, and growing criticism outside the agency over the direction and operation of the subsystem, drove Banks to reassess his approach. After a year's work with MSD, Banks reluctantly arrived at the conclusion that cordial relations with the superintendent and Nickens were superficial and yielded precious little in tangible reforms. The heat Banks was getting from OEO and inside his own organization was intense enough to make him shift positions. Within a year an internal position paper concluded: "The first responsibility of UPO should be to help organize poor people in the greater Washington area so that they can act collectively to achieve economic self-sufficiency and full parti-cipation in the community.'' All UPO efforts, the paper said, should be evaluated against this criterion. MSD failed by this criterion; the con-clusion was obvious.[42]

Ironically, precisely at the point that UPO officially divorced itself from MSD, Hansen, who was reeling from a barrage of criticism and a hostile board of education, was no longer able to monitor his assistant. As UPO passed from the scene and as Hansen bucked enormous crit-icism, MSD expanded operations and gained stature within the school system. On June 26, 1967, the board voted MSD an extra $100,000, additional authority, and increased autonomy. Board approval gave the MSD the most authority and autonomy it had had in its three years. This occurred just a few weeks before the board refused Hansen's request to appeal the recent *Hobson v. Hansen* court decision. The superintendent, reluctant father of the subsystem, resigned.

Desegregation

Hansen's resignation came at the end of four years of growing, increas-ingly bitter criticism of his policies and programs. When he said that 1963 was the end of a ''golden age in Washington education'' he was correct insofar as he was concerned.[43]

In 1963 he had solid board support. His three-year contract was renewed early the following year by a 7–1 vote. The Track System and Amidon Plan had attracted national recognition, increasing his local reputation.[44] The influential Washington *Post* and especially the *Eve-ning Star* supported him consistently. He had successfully maneuvered desegregation through dangerous terrain, protecting it from critics' ar-rows and friends' embraces.

But in 1963, with WAY's stinging attack, the taboo against open criticism of the superintendent and public schools broke apart. As it splintered, so did Hansen's support. While Hansen skillfully coopted WAY's pressure for change, there was little he could do to manage spreading criticism of his programs. Board members Euphemia Haynes, a retired D.C. Teachers College math professor, and Mordecai Johnson, former president of Howard University, attacked tracking and inequi-table allocation of resources to black and white schools. Though still in the minority, their persistent criticism at board meetings combined with

WAY's aggressive actions, found a platform in the local press, especially in the *Post*. Such assaults attracted others discontented with Hansen's leadership.

By early 1964 WAY had died. Yet what had been unleashed—in particular, criticism of tracking—still faced the superintendent. Two days before Dr. Hansen victoriously presented his version of WAY proposals, he was forced to review the track system at a special board meeting in response to Haynes's and Johnson's vigorous questions. Criticism of tracking snowballed throughout 1964 and 1965, culminating in another special board meeting to debate the topic. At that meeting, the motion to abolish tracking—the first such move to face Hansen—lost 6–2. But on the subsequent motion for the board to "reconfirm its support" of tracking, the vote was only 5–3 in favor.[45] Later that year Hansen agreed to contract for an independent evaluation of the entire system. Even with his board majority, Hansen was in trouble.

Simultaneous with this gathering storm over tracking came another attack on both superintendent and board from a seemingly separate direction. The desegregation controversy raging in other big cities finally touched Washington. Between June 1964 and March 1965 Hansen tangled with the Urban League over their desegregation proposals; it was also the year that tracking opposition consolidated. Deeply committed to his views of desegregation—a distasteful word to the superintendent, who preferred "racial imbalance,"—and having taken many lumps over his positions from die-hard segregationists in the late 1950s, Dr. Hansen felt that the two issues of race and tracking were somehow linked. "I always thought," he said, "there was a connection between the thrust toward ending the track system and desegregation. Mixing children on the basis of race would lead to an end of ability grouping. Also the same people were behind both efforts."[46]

When the Urban League first submitted to the board their June 1964 analysis of segregation in the District schools, few cities could claim that they had already desegregated their schools as Washington had done a decade earlier.

One week after the historic Supreme Court decision in May 1954 the board voted unanimously to pursue a policy of:

> Appointing, transferring, promoting all Board
> employees on the basis of merit, not race.

> Pupils attending schools in their neighborhoods, except
> for emergency reasons "and in no event for reasons
> related to the racial character of the school within
> the boundaries in which the pupil resides."[47]

By September 1955 two separate school systems had merged. A neighborhood school policy had been instituted. Save for some noticeable exceptions, which will be dealt with later, all children were to attend school in their district. Teachers were permitted to stay where they taught or they could apply for transfer through usual channels and for the usual reasons excluding, of course, race. No longer were black children forced to walk past a white school to attend an all-black one three blocks away. No longer were teachers of one race compelled to teach in schools with children of the same race.

Between 1955 and 1962 Dr. Hansen led desegregation forces within the city, creating, in his words, "a miracle of social adjustment."[48] Attacked in 1956 by a Southern-dominated congressional investigating committee, Hansen, then head of secondary schools, aggressively defended desegregation before the Davis Committee. He wrote, for no fee, two best selling pamphlets on desegregation for the Anti-Defamation League. In them he proudly pointed to the increase in black academic achievement and the improvement of interracial contacts.

After 1958, when he became superintendent and introduced first the four-track organization and later the Amidon Plan, Hansen's prestige as an educational leader peaked. Appearing often at national human relations workshops, in demand as a national speaker on school desegregation, the superintendent was seen as an aggressive, no-nonsense schoolman. *Time* did two articles on him within six months. He had "begun turning the wreck of Washington's schools into a model that less beleagured cities may envy." *Saturday Review* featured him as one of the nation's "movers and shapers of education." These and other articles stressed his achievements in avoiding the worst excess of desegregating schools that appeared to have befallen other cities.[49] If there had been an educational Hall of Fame in the 1960s, Washingtonians, white and black, would surely have installed Hansen in it for his desegregation efforts.

Yet in 1966, after four days of Dr. Hansen's testifying in court and 8,000 pages of testimony from scores of witnesses, Judge Skelly Wright concluded in the *Hobson v. Hansen* decision (1967) that what had happened between 1955 and 1962 was no miracle of social adjustment but a debacle of resegregation.

When in 1958–59 there were about 75 elementary schools that were predominantly black (that is, 85 percent or more black), five years later there were 94, and by 1966–67 there were 109 schools. Where in 1958–59 there were 13 elementary schools that were physically integrated (that is, between 20 percent and 70 percent black), five years later there were less than 10. Where in 1958–59, there were 19 predominantly white schools, five years later there were the same number.

Teacher assignments and principal selection policies produced by 1962–63 either all-white or all-black staffs in 40 percent of the elementary schools. Referring to the fact that 15 of 17 white schools had 100 percent white faculties, Judge Wright concluded that the "mathematical possibility of this concentration of the relatively few white teachers in the school system's relatively few white schools happening by chance defies calculation by methods available to mere laymen." As for principals, black teachers were often promoted to administrative posts. In fact, of all school administrators, 56 percent were black. Yet in 1962–63 no Negro principal or assistant principal served in a predominately white school.

On the basis of such evidence, Judge Wright concluded that administrative policies such as the use of optional zones by which clots of white population within black neighborhoods slipped into predominately white schools, and teacher and principal assignment which as late as 1963 produced all-black staffs for all-black schools—such policies, regardless of their nonracial intent, resulted in a segregated school system.

Of even more importance was the fact that the court found the track system—itself an admittedly sincere effort to cope with large numbers of low-achieving black children—"insulated the more academically developed white student from the less fortunate black schoolmate."

Hansen, the Court believed, was no segregationist. He was "personally . . . then and is now motivated by a desire to respond—according to his own philosophy—to an educational crisis. . . ." Neither tracking nor optional zones or teacher assignment policies were intentionally discriminatory acts. Yet over all of them, considering their unforeseen consequences, hung "the taint of segregation."[50]

The point of the foregoing is not to dispute Dr. Hansen's claim that 1955–62 were indeed "golden years" or to deny Wright's conclusion that the administration deprived black children of an equal education. It is to underscore the simple truism that climate of opinions and perceptions had changed. Applause from liberals in 1960 had become boos by 1965 and abusive name-calling by the time Wright issued his 1967 decree.

The Urban League proposals of 1964–65 demonstrate clearly how pressure for change had shifted from Southern foes of integration to civil rights activists, and how the superintendent responded to this shift in perception and pressure.

Urban League Proposals, 1964

By 1964 the D.C. Urban League was on the right wing of the local civil rights spectrum insofar as direct action was concerned. Criticized by the *Afro-American* for not participating with CORE, NAACP, and other civil rights groups in a mass march protesting discrimination, Sterling Tucker, executive director of the league, defended the organization's role. "We believe," he said, "that licking postage stamps, digging out facts and engaging in showdown confrontation can be as important to the struggle for equal opportunity as joining a picket line, marching in a demonstration or going to jail." Informed activists knew that the league funding came from the local welfare council and militant tactics could kill the organization. They also knew and agreed with Urban League President Grayson McGuire that the "Urban League is in the unique position to polish off the jagged points after the demonstrations are over as well as to participate in knocking down the walls [of discrimination]." Still, the criticism had a telling effect. The March on Washington, and vigorous action by other Urban League chapters pushed Tucker into a more aggressive posture.[51]

Contacts with school leadership up to this point had been cordial. "Future for Jimmy," an ambitious volunteer tutor program enrolling black and white middle-class men and women to work with disadvantaged children gained both board and superintendent support. Activists on the League Education Committee, however, generated a flurry of critical position papers on tracking, de facto segregation, the Model School Division, and similar topics. In June 1964, with Tucker's assent, the education committee presented "Integration and the Public Schools" to the board of education.

The aim of the document was to "excite thought and set forth some of the directions in which solutions may be found." Realizing that 85 percent of the school population was black and that only one of every ten black children was in schools with whites, the league proposal recognized that it is "patently impossible and undesirable to spread white children around." What the recommendations sought, then, was for the board to reaffirm integration as its goal and to act modestly but determinedly in dealing with segregation.

For those areas where neighborhoods were mixed, predominately white or mostly black but adjacent to integrated ones, the league proposed a color-conscious site-selection policy, redrawing attendance areas, bussing at public cost, educational parks, and expanded use of under-capacity schools. For those areas untouched by these proposals—and the plan acknowledged that these schools were the majority—more compensatory education and experimentation along the lines of the newly established Model School Division were recommended. Finally, the league proposed establishing a permanent Advisory Council on Integration.[52]

After the presentation, the superintendent thanked the league's representatives, saying the organization had made "great contributions." He had no objections, he continued, to the board reaffirming integration as a goal, since the board's position in 1954 was clear on this point. But the proposal for an advisory committee, he said, might well become "a second board of education."[53] He promised to have a full response to the league proposals by September.

Superintendent and Board Response

At the September meeting Hansen presented his views. Appreciative to the Urban League for forcing him to rigorously analyze the system, the superintendent launched immediately into the meaning of the phrase *de facto segregation*. Citing recent court decisions, he rejected the assumption underlying the phrase as implying a school system's culpability. Racial imbalance and cultural isolation—phrases he preferred—came from economic and social forces, not school policies. "Is it not misleading and productive of error in treatment," he asked, "to use the term *de facto* segregation to name a condition not produced by law?"

Admitting that 79 percent of the schools were imbalanced in 1963, Dr. Hansen pointed out that "white and colored pupils were going to school together" in 152 out of a total of 179 schools. Conceding that in many of these schools only a few white or black pupils were involved, "nevertheless," Hansen stated, "the complete separation that exists in the ghetto-like schools does not, for the most part, exist."

On the main league recommendations, Hansen scored the proposals for dealing with symptoms rather than causes—that is, white flight to suburbs dating back to 1945 and the influx of black migrants since 1950. Consequently such solutions as, for example,

the arbitrary moving of children to achieve a better racial balance in schools offered, at best, only temporary benefits. Plans to reduce *de facto* segregation that do not get at the basic causes are destined to fail or even worse create greater confusion and loss of educational advancement than if they were not undertaken.

The superintendent defended school policies. He stressed previous board statements on integration and the freedom of choice black parents had to send their children to a neighborhood school or if it were overcrowded to transport them to another school. Contrasted to pre-1954 conditions, when black children had to walk past a white school down the street to attend a black one over a mile away, such choice in 1964 denied the phrase *de facto* segregation.

On teacher placement, administrative promotion, and instruction—Hansen rejected the charge of discrimination and aggressively pointed to recent board policies and actions. Taking up bussing, boundary changes and site selection, the superintendent again rejected making color-conscious decisions as being inherently discriminatory and probably unconstitutional. To redraw boundaries on the basis of race, for example, "that will deny a child admission to a school in his neighborhood . . . even if done to reduce the level of segregation in a school is evil in principle and dangerous in the precedent it sets."[54] Color-blind decisions, he felt, were needed, not color-conscious ones.

The neighborhood school, the superintendent stressed, is a principle that "puts people first." In view of the District's history of *de jure* segregation, this policy was seen as fundamental to quality education.

It would be extremely unfortunate if the community should be panicked into abandonment of the neighborhood school as an illusory means of eliminating *de facto* segregation, particularly since to do so has nowhere achieved this purpose.[55]

In the final section of the report, Hansen recommended various ways to improve schooling and diminish the impact of cultural isolation. His last point dismissed the league recommendation for a permanent Advisory Committee on Integration in lieu of an expanded superintendent's advisory committee on human relations and direct dealings with the board.

The board accepted the superintendent's response without any major objection. They deferred action until the league reported back. Later, Hansen recalled lunching with Tucker. Driving back to the Franklin Building, Tucker pressed Hansen for support of the league proposals. "At least," Tucker insisted, "you could recommend . . . the city-wide advisory committee on Integration. Surely you can't be unwilling to listen to advice?" Dr. Hansen replied that his files were loaded with citizen committee reports. They say that schools "ought to be racially balanced, that school boards ought to get whites into Negro schools and vice versa. I don't see that anything comes of pushing around the same old ideas."[56]

Even with Hansen's negative response, the league made a concerted push for an advisory committee. In December the league presented to the board a thirty-six-page report calling for a five-man fact-finding citizen group responsible to the board "to advise the Board with regard to the racial implications of different aspects of educational planning and to develop recommendations designed to foster high quality integrated education."[57]

No response from Hansen. At the February meeting Dr. Herman Stamps of the league education committee read another statement on the proposed advisory committee. The board voted to devote an hour of discussion at the next meeting.[58] At the March meeting, after desultory discussion, Hansen recommended that the proposed advisory committee not be created. The board voted 6–3 in favor of the superintendent's recommendation.

Hansen's patience, rational arguments, and a reliable board majority,[59] combined with the league's clear lack of mass support, made it possible to deflect and ultimately ignore league pressure. "My view, an admittedly sociologically unsophisticated one," Dr. Hansen concluded,

is simply that children are in school to be taught. Though they come in assorted sizes, shapes, and colors, they have one thing in common, the hope to mean something not only to themselves but also to others. What then does race really have to do with the children in our schools? Or anywhere else, for that matter? What we should ask for them each is freedom to come and go, regardless . . . of the shade of skin . . . . I believe race will not be the telling factor as time goes on and the current babble about Negro rights will soon be judged as sounding brass with no truth in its voice.[60]

With the Urban League proposals dead, criticism of Hansen escalated. Increasing attacks on tracking from the Urban League and other groups, personal abuse from liberals who had supported him loyally a half-decade earlier,[61] the gradual replacement of supportive board members with ones less congenial to the superintendent's policies, and, finally, the court suit, all laid the basis for Hansen's departure. The Wright decision in 1967 abolished tracking, ordered bussing of black children to under-used white schools, and directed the administration to begin a color-conscious teacher and principal assignment. Hansen asked the board to appeal the decision. They refused. "Maybe the Wright decision offered me a suitable platform to leave,'' he recalled. ''I knew it was all over by then.'' He resigned.

Father of the track system and reluctant parent of the Model School Division, Dr. Hansen saw one abolished by court order, the other incorporated into the system. Though he had been a skillful politician, by 1967 his string had run out. ''An irresistible tide,'' he called it. ''It was too great to overcome.''[62]

San Francisco

The day of sentimentality for the *poor superintendent* is past. He doesn't need sympathy; he needs only respect for his position, his professional ability and leadership—respect that he must earn, just as other business and professional workers in the American enterprise system earn their position.... It is a compliment for us as we take positions that are tough. Certainly if we keep talking about the superintendency that way, somebody will write in the magazines that we can't handle the job and we will go back to the day when the business manager ran the school system and not the educator.

My friends see me on the street and say, "Won't you be glad to get out of it?"

I say "No, I won't be glad to get out of it. That is my life. That is my profession."

Harold Spears, 1967*

Arching bridges and green velvet hills. Silent, billowing fog and clear, breezy days. Ocean beaches and wharfs. Opera and symphony. Bottomless go-go dancers and hard-core pornography flicks. Chinatown, North Beach, Fillmore, Pacific Heights, the Mission, and Haight-Ashbury. Black, yellow, and brown people—a rainbow of humanity. A cosmopolitan and liberal flavor to the city. Cable-cars, cabarets, and Golden Gate Park adding to the charm attracting annual swarms of tourists.

*American Association of School Administrators Convention Report, 1967–1968 (Washington, D.C.: AASA, 1968), p. 160.

Even though it has the highest suicide rate in the nation, even though critics rail at the Manhattanization of the city, opinion polls say it is still the place that most Americans would like to live. Closer to home, one disillusioned native called the city a "wormy Eden but... the only Nirvana around."[1] Few of those judging San Francisco, however, know much else about the place. Consider local government.

Where Chicago is dominated by the Democratic machine and Washington by the politics of congressional favor, San Francisco is, in Frederick Wirt's phrase, "government by indecision."[2]

To prevent widespread corruption, a 1932 city charter divided governing power amongst numerous boards, commissions, and administrative officers. Theft of city coffers was avoided and citizen participation was encouraged. But at a cost. A part-time board of supervisors, for example, elected at-large on off years, makes law but cannot intervene directly with the mayor or tamper with appointed commissions. Similarly, the mayor is hedged in by numerous boards to which he appoints members, yet he cannot determine their policies. Moreover, civil service effectively shelters most city departments from mayoral patronage. The mayor who wishes to leave more than a trace on historical record must be a persuader and negotiator par excellence.

While this description applies to many big cities, what's missing from San Francisco is a party machine. Turbulent politics built upon ethnic and economic differences within a heavily unionized city have produced partyless politics. Temporary coalitions elect candidates and ultimately splinter, only to reemerge at a subsequent election. No party discipline, then, exists to keep officeholders accountable to voters. Yet this brand of politics is responsive to a bewildering range of constituencies, since candidates must meet with and gain each one's support. Thus, an intricately structured charter joined to partyless politics have created a pluralistic, fragmented local government sensitive to citizen participation but at the price of having much policy made by civil servants.

Within this context, the appointed board of education operates independently of city government. No mayor, board of supervisors, or city commission dictates to it. Serving the entire city and county, the seven-member board[3] sets the school tax rate and approves, without review from the city administration, a budget drawn up by its chief executive officer.

Since 1923 the school board has appointed its superintendent (prior to that, the position was an elected one). Of all the superintendents who served during the past half-century, Harold Spears served the longest tenure. A native of Indiana, Spears came to San Francisco to direct its curriculum department in 1947. Within eight years, he had reached the top.

Like most of his colleagues, Harold Spears climbed a familiar career ladder. Teacher, principal, and curriculum director in Evansville, Indiana, he moved to Illinois to superintend a small district. By this time, he had earned a Columbia doctorate. After three years in Illinois, he traveled eastward to head the department of education at Montclair Teachers College in New Jersey. In 1947 he accepted the San Francisco offer. During his second year in the district, he was promoted to assistant superintendent for elementary schools. Finally, when Harold Clish resigned in 1955, the board appointed Spears superintendent.

What distinguished Spears' rise through the ranks was his prolific writing and involvement in international education. Interested in journalism, he authored a number of books on the high school and curriculum. (In fact he often did cartoons to accompany articles he wrote. His cartoon skills and his dry, puckish wit often entertained colleagues and friends at AASA conventions.) By 1947 Spears was already a nationally known specialist in these areas. Moreover, in 1944 he had been appointed a U.S. adviser to the Chilean Ministry of Education and a decade later was selected to represent the United States on a UNESCO curriculum advisory group. Few superintendents have written or traveled as much.

At the 1957 UNESCO meeting in Paris news of Soviet Russia's October 4th launching of Sputnik shocked the assembled representatives. Many members, Spears recalled, pressed him for a guess at what the American response would be. What impact on education would the Russian accomplishment have? The moment remained vivid in Spears' memory a decade and a half later.[4] Also vivid was his anticipation of Sputnik's effect on his school system.

The Barrage Begins, 1957–1958

Less than two months later, with "Sputnik" already a household word, the *Call-Bulletin* ran a cartoon which depicted Uncle Sam at the chalk board writing "Readin', Riting, Rithmetic and Rockets."[5] It was the opening shot of a sporadic cannonade that would last for months.

During the fall and winter of 1957–58 such nationally known critics of public schools as historian Arthur Bestor, chemistry professor Joel Hildebrand, and Vice-Admiral Hyman Rickover came to San Francisco.

Here they blasted "progressive"* education, weak science and math programs, and the overall deterioration of quality in American schools. Generally, the response from their San Francisco audiences was favorable, although critic Mortimer Adler did run into trouble when he spoke to 500 Explorer Scouts and called for more school homework as a necessity in catching up with Russia. He was booed loudly.[6]

During these months all four local newpapers ran front-page news articles, editorials, and weekly series, with titles such as "U.S. Schools—Can They Win the Science Race?" and "What's Wrong With Our Schools." *Examiner* editor William Randolph Hearst, Jr., traveled to Russia to see and report on their schools firsthand. Reprints of Bestor and Rickover criticisms appeared. Breast-beating editorials like "The Blame Rests on All of Us" were common. Between November 1957 and February 1958 at least two to five news articles on either U.S. or Russian education appeared daily in the local newspapers.[7]

Until February, in the press's fascination with Russian and U.S. education, there was little mention of the local schools. In these interim months, Spears reported to the public on beefed-up science courses, the high standards in the city's high schools, and, at one high school, even the addition of Russian and Mandarin Chinese courses. A few times, he spoke out against "unreasonable" criticism of national education. Answering specifically the Bestor and Rickover critiques, he pointed out that "12% of the Russian budget goes to education while only 3% of ours does." Moreover, he said, these critics ignore that the current curriculum, now under heavy attack is what parents demand. They want typing, vocational training, physical education, and driver training. Critics think "every student can take a strict academic course. This isn't so." Bestor, Rickover, and the rest, concluded Spears, just don't "know enough about our schools."[8]

In February direct denunciation of the San Francisco schools erupted with a vengeance. In their monthly bulletin, the Teacher Association of San Francisco (TASF), independent group comprising about half of the city's classroom teachers, blasted Spears for the excesses of "progressive" education. These teachers were concerned about what they considered to be the erosion of standards and a superintendent whom they

*Quotation marks are used here to indicate that the word, in the hands of critics, had become synonymous with life-adjustment curriculum, permissiveness in discipline, anti-intellectualism, and anything associated with the influence of John Dewey, Columbia Teachers College, and the like. Used as an epithet, it described little that existed. See Lawrence A. Cremin, *The Transformation of the School* (New York: Random House, 1964), pp. 338–47.

saw as soft on academic subjects while pushing mushy life adjustment courses. It was not a new charge. They had, in Spears' words, "tried to light a fire under me many times in the past."[9] This time, with Sputnik, the charges stuck.

Picked up by the local press, the group's indictment detailed a hodge-podge of charges. Consider:

> promoting children without regard to achievement;
>
> "instruction in social living takes precedence over the vital subjects";
>
> large classes;
>
> too much clerical and extracurricular work;
>
> paternalistic attitudes of administration toward teachers.[10]

Shortly afterward, the local chapter of the American Federation of Teachers issued a similar broadside.

Taken aback, Spears did not immediately respond to the criticism. Instead he asked to meet with all teacher groups in order to iron out their grievances. Before these sessions took place, however, at a standing-room-only board meeting in March, Spears took the offensive. He delivered a report (one the board had not yet seen) asking for "a crackdown on educational laggards and a stepped up program for those who can assimilate a heavier program."[11] Spears' fifteen-point program, as it came to be known, caught critical teachers off guard. Both board members and teachers at the meeting ended up applauding his presentation. His "toughening up" program skillfully beat his critics to the punch.

What the superintendent presented was a melding of programs which had already been put underway within the system to answer critics' demands for new directions. Emphasis was placed on more science and English instruction and counseling services. Unnecessary classroom interruptions were to be eliminated. A cadre of classroom teachers would be recruited to work on developing new math and science curriculum materials.

Approved by the board in May, the fifteen-point program demonstrated that, with his solid board support, Spears could move quickly to outflank critics. The superintendent had "passed the peace pipe . . . to the two teacher organizations which had gone on the warpath for school reform."[12]

Teacher representatives began meeting with Dr. Spears. And their organizations continued issuing condemnations as well as position papers blending grievances with demands for more of the 3R's* and tighter discipline. Talks with Spears broke off at one point. Elizabeth Murphy, spokesman for TASF, scored the superintendent for believing in "long-range studies, ponderous surveys," and in going from school to school for his answers. The association believed that these methods "could drag out for months and eventually result in the curriculum being talked to death."[13]

Spears' position on initiating system-wide changes remained steadfast throughout this ink-slinging debate: no new change or program would be "handed down from the central office."[14] His professional career was based on the principle that classroom teachers must be involved in curricular change. Much time, therefore, would be required for any substantial revision.

3R's Faction on Board Moves

All the criticism about the superintendent being too "progressive," about insufficient science and math in the curriculum, and a de-emphasis on the basic subjects drew favorable responses from a three-member bloc on the board. John Levison, Adolfo de Urioste, and Elmer Skinner repeatedly read into the record articles by Hildebrand, Bestor, and anyone else pointing out the abandonment of high standards. To a proposal that any curriculum study be done carefully and slowly and that no special meeting of the board on the topic was necessary, board member de Urioste answered:

I don't think we can afford to stall on the change of curriculum . . . . I think that is the final answer to school work, isn't it? That's the only reason we have teachers, the only reason we have school buildings, the only reason we have boards of education and superintendents and so forth. . . . Now, there are too many complaints. I don't know whether they are justified or not, but there are just too many complaints that most of us hear regarding the type of education the children are getting.

If we are going to examine the curriculum in the schools

*Like the word "progressive," 3R's was a shorthand term—this time for emphasis on basic skills, academic subjects (no frills such as driver education, big gyms, etc.) and hard-nosed discipline; to child-centered educators and laymen, 3R's was an epithet they hurled at reactionary, neanderthal critics of current schools.

with a critical eye, whoever examines it, whether it is the Superintendent, whether it is outside consultants . . . . I think that it is
the number one problem and I don't think with the temper of the public as it is today we will be doing [them] a good service if we stall on
curriculum.[15]

But the 3R's faction's criticism was softened by its deep respect for their
superintendent's professional expertise. To move for a rigorous examination of the curriculum by either the board or outside experts would
implicitly condemn Spears' leadership. For a minority bloc on a professionally oriented board, achieving the former without suffering the latter
would be extremely tricky. The potential messiness of it all was clearly
present in June 1958, when the entire board, on its own initiative, raised
Dr. Spears' salary $1500 and gave him a new four-year contract—after
three months of a steady tattoo of knuckle raps on curriculum from
teachers and board members.[16]

Spears remembered these months after Sputnik as difficult but manageable ones.

The TASF was a conservative group . . . . They were giving me the
needle. I played the game, but it never kept me from going to parties
and speaking to those gals who were getting up at board meetings and
bugging me. There was something about it that you just don't mark
people off.

When the AASA Executive Committee, meeting in San Francisco at
this time, called him to ask if he needed any help, Spears recalled:

Well, this Committee believed all the stuff in the newspapers and
wanted to help me. I told them, if you want to bury me in that job,
you could come over and talk to my Board as if I'm in trouble. But, I
said, that would be the kiss of death for you fellows to put your arms
around me now . . . . They wanted to come to my rescue. I was playing
the game a certain way . . . with a straight face; it's a poker game at
times.[17]

Over the summer and into the fall of 1958, public criticism of the San
Francisco schools mounted. Mortimer Smith, the founder of the Council
for Basic Education, wrote an article for *Atlantic* which caustically
ripped schooling in California, singling out Harold Spears for his
"anti-intellectual bias and life-adjustment orientation." Quoting from
Spears' *High School for Today,* Smith condemned the superintendent's
"general permissiveness."[18]

The *Examiner* hardened its editorial position and slapped the superintendent for being a "gradualist in all things." The San Francisco *Progress,* a neighborhood newspaper, proved to be the most scaulding of the local papers. A September editorial claimed that citizens were unwilling "to spend a plugged penny for a school superintendent who deals in vague burblings." A month later, the *Progress* asked for "a clean sweep of the slate." The city "needs not only a Superintendent with respect for learning but a replacement of the entire roster of progressive educationists who have been mouldering in the school department."[19]

At the October board meeting,[20] John Levison again proposed that a board committee be appointed to investigate whether faculties at Bay Area universities could be tapped to "visit our schools and see whether they [professors] got any constructive suggestions in any directions." The next hour was taken up debating Levison's motion. When asked to clarify why professors should be invited, Levison answered that they would "look into this whole problem with us." Board President Joseph Moore asked "which problem?" "The problem," Levison replied, "of if we are going in the right direction and if we are on the right track in this whole curriculum improvement program." Such fuzzy definition of the task persisted throughout the controversy.

Opposition to the motion came from board member Mary Draper, who argued that university scholars "are not trained to evaluate an educational program in different areas, different locations and different types of problems." Furthermore, she had confidence in the superintendent, who was especially qualified in curriculum. "I just think," she said, "that he is doing a splendid job."

De Urioste replied that the superintendent is only one person and

we are letting one man's ideology here decide what is right or wrong. It may be very good. I don't question whther he has the ability. He certainly has written many books, he certainly has certain methods as to how the educational system should perform and it may be fine but we, as Board members, have the responsibility ... to look into curriculum, and I am amazed that there should be any objection to a committee of the Board sitting down with those who are willing to give us their time to discuss their ideas of what might be done.

The motion to have a board committee contact Bay Area professors to discuss the school curriculum was tabled on a 4–3 vote. At the November meeting de Urioste, Skinner, and Levison pushed to hire Stanford and Berkeley professors to evaluate the curriculum and for the board to establish a special curriculum committee. Both motions lost 4–3.

Now the battle lines were clearly drawn. Pressed by teacher groups, increasingly feisty newspaper censure, and a free-floating anxiety about the job schools were doing, the three-member bloc could no longer tolerate Spears' fifteen-point program as a sufficient response to what they saw as a crisis.

At a February 1959 meeting, after Spears had presented a report entitled "Steps Taken to Strengthen the Curriculum," de Urioste thundered that the superintendent's "toughening up" program was really a "piecemeal super-structure imposed on a shaky foundation which remains essentially unchanged." The fifteen-point program and Spears' progress report on its implementation was, in de Urioste's words, "a recapitulation of standard practices. . . . Much that is trite and obvious is described in the report with an air of discovery, as if it were new."

The minority bloc felt strongly that things were awry with the curriculum but found it difficult to crystalize their concerns into specifics that could be evaluated. Moreover, they were the first to admit that they were laymen trespassing on professional turf. How could laymen get an accurate assessment of the curriculum without destroying confidence in the superintendent? A dilemma.

Board Minority Becomes a Majority

Knowing that the majority and the superintendent were opposed to bringing in outsiders to survey the curriculum in the general terms they proposed, the three-member bloc pressed to establish a number of standing committees, one of which would deal with curriculum. This committee could become a platform for publicizing the 3R's position. Even though board committees had been abandoned fifteen years earlier because of their constant meddling in administration and even with vigorous press resistance to this move, the board bloc picked up a vital fourth vote in Charles Foehn, who was in favor of a particular committee. Spears tried to avert this move by offering the board a counterproposal to hold a series of committee-of-the-whole sessions. Each meeting would focus upon particular segments of the school program. The proposal was brushed aside. Spears tried again by meeting privately with Foehn to persuade him not to vote for standing committees.[21] This, too, failed.

A curriculum committee convened shortly afterwards and held a series of open meetings throughout the spring of 1959 at which teachers, administrators, and community representatives testified. Spears did not appear before the committee. After ten meetings in which scores of specific proposals and hundreds of transcript pages threatened to drown the committee in a sea of curriculum change, the majority bloc faced the enormous task of digesting it all. Worse yet, no clear-cut support for or against the 3R's emerged from the open meetings. What to do? To turn to Spears, their professional adviser, wouldn't advance their cause. After all, they knew where he stood. On the other hand, they could hardly judge which proposals were sound or silly; each board member was on record numerous times as to their lack of expertise in such technical areas as curriculum. Why not, then, secure outside assistance?

What the board had wanted earlier but had not voted for now seemed as an entirely logical choice. Thus, in June 1959, almost a year and a half after the idea was first suggested, the board voted 4–1 to spend $10,000 to hire eight professors from the University of California at Berkeley and Stanford to conduct "a survey of curriculum needs."[22]

Professors' Survey

The blurred aim of the study was never cleared up. With the prevailing climate opposed to anti-intellectualism, no education professors at either institution were contacted—only those teaching academic courses. They were, de Urioste reasoned, "in a better position to point up any deficiencies which our students may have when they arrive at the university campus."[23] Was the study aimed at those students entering college? Perhaps. Co-chairman of the survey, Henry Rapoport, also had his views on the purpose of the study.

> We were hired as curriculum consultants, not investigators. We assume the Board wants our expert knowledge and opinions of subject matter, particularly as it prepares students to get into our hands or those of any employer.[24]

Fuzzy aims given to eight academic professors, many of whom were highly critical of public schools, plus the requirement that they complete the job in ten months (without any release from their university obligations) hardly guaranteed an objective appraisal of a system with over 100 schools, 4,000 teachers, and 95,000 children. Hired by a board majority extremely critical and vocal about the evils of "progressive " education, could anyone doubt the conclusions of the report?

Just in case someone might, Curriculum Committee chairman Elmer

Skinner produced a sixty-page report summarizing the conclusions—as he interpreted them—of the hearings before his committee. Entitled "Back to the 3R's" the report roasted the superintendent's fifteen-point program and his subsequent efforts to strengthen the curriculum. Board member Claire Matzger refused to sign Skinner's report. "I don't see how those professors can do an independent and objective survey when this report means to prejudice their conclusions," she said. At a different level, Matzger felt that the professors were men of distinction and integrity. "Yet I found it hard to believe that they could have any sense of the realities of the public school system." She doubted that they could propose anything "either reasonable, practical or desirable for the schools."[25]

Meanwhile, something else happened which would be far more important to the final outcome of the Professors' Survey: Mayor Christopher replaced retiring John Levison with a moderate who was uncommitted to the 3R's. Such a shift meant that Spears' majority (Foehn usually supported the Superintendent) was again intact.

Released in April 1960, the Professors' Survey came as no surprise to informed citizens. The academicians evaluated the San Francisco curriculum against a "suitably high educational standard" (one which they never defined). Searing language scored the schools for a widespread "attitude of indifference if not exactly hostility to intellect."[26]

They then proceeded to make 186 recommendations on the organization and content of curriculum, reading, English, foreign languages, mathematics, science, and social studies. Recommendations ran from a call for more tracking in the high schools, to advice on the number of periods there should be in the school day, to the suggestion that phonics be used in teaching reading. The aim of these recommendations reaffirmed that "the purpose of education . . . is to inform the mind and develop the intelligence."

The professors saw the San Francisco schools as being imprisoned by the theory that schools should prepare children to live in a democracy; such a theory, they said, was "profoundly hostile to excellence in education." More specifically, the professors called for the abolition of social studies in the first two grades of elementary school. The content—Home, School, and Neighborhood—"is little more than a string of platitudes; the time can be better used in teaching the basic skills of reading, writing, and arithmetic." Although not asked to make recommendations in foreign language ("nor are we specially qualified in this field"), the academicians offered thirteen recommendations for more instruction in French, German, and Russian. As for science, it should be dropped from the curriculum of the first three grades because of its inferior quality. Furthermore, science in the primary years "divert teacher and pupil alike from the really important job before them, that of equipping the students with the basic skills." In short, here was a tract for a rigorous academic education.

The board accepted the report, turning it over to Dr. Spears for his analysis of the professors' recommendations. This in itself was a significant move, illustrating, perhaps, that the adversary relationship between board and superintendent had been replaced by the usual cooperation.

Six weeks later, the superintendent presented his "Preliminary Reactions to the Report of the San Francisco Curriculum Survey Committee." Spears recalled those weeks vividly.

They were eager to get after us because they had a point of view they wanted to present and here was the launching pad for it. When the time came and they listed all these recommendations, . . . they itemized everything.

My job, then, was to see which of these I could take. It wasn't to fight what they said. I just marked off all the elementary division suggestions on the grounds that none of them had been trained in that field . . . . We came up with twenty-three points we could take from them without hurting us.[27]

Of course, within his official response the superintendent was more circumspect. He indicated which recommendations could not be adopted due to state regulations. Others required large sums of money, and he called attention to that. Many, however, were simply ignored. The twenty-three recommendations acceptable to the superintendent were either a reinforcement of the earlier fifteen-point program or a logical extension of earlier suggestions. In no way could the response be seen as an embrace of the rationale or spirit of the professors' survey.

Yet the tone of the preliminary reactions was conciliatory, blurring any difference between the superintendent and the academicians. Quoting from earlier reports, Spears pointed out repeatedly the similarity in aims stated in the professors' survey and his own program. On a number of occasions, the superintendent agreed with the conclusions of the survey.[28]

The seven professors present at the board meeting held to consider Dr. Spears' response, however, saw basic differences. Stanford's Dr. William Bark remarked:

Although Dr. Spears expresses pleasure that our report has placed emphasis upon excellence in education, there is in reality a considerable gap between his basic view and ours. What I mean by that is that Dr. Spears does not, as far as I recall, distinctly and clearly disavow devotion to life adjustment.[29]

On each of the twenty-three recommendaitons, Bark and his colleagues grilled Spears on why he didn't go further or didn't include other points or why he omitted particular suggestions. Spears resolutely maintained with seldom any anger or sarcasm that he would not command curricular changes. Nor could the professors urge otherwise, given their stated commitment to teachers as the key to improved schooling.

The board approved Spears' "Preliminary Reactions" in June. At that time, the superintendent underscored the point that sufficient time would be needed to implement the twenty-three recommendations.[30]

Criticism from the TASF, Mayor Christopher, and other groups came throughout the fall and winter of 1960 over the superintendent's slow response. Although he replied to critics that he needed time, he needn't have bothered. The "Preliminary Reactions" in fact turned out to be the final reactions to curriculum improvement. After a voluminous six-volume progress report was submitted and approved by a tired board in June 1961, nothing more officially was done. Backed by the board, exhausted from hassling over curriculum, and with Foehn and Levison gone (and Skinner about to leave), the superintendent's expertise was solidly entrenched.

Spears recalled clearly the moves and countermoves over the professors' survey.

Those fellows, . . . went hog-wild on what they recommended . . . . They were going to save the nation. It became a cat-and mouse game. We opened the doors to them, but we kept book on them. We told the principals to keep track of how much time these professors spent visiting.

So later, when they came out with this thing, I had book on them. I could say it was too bad, I was sorry that they didn't have enough money or the help, and I was sorry they'd spent only so many hours in the schools, seeing so little of what was actually going on in the schools. I didn't criticize them for it, because the fellows were a little bit stupid for making a year-long study and only being given $10,000 for the whole group of them. I didn't think they had too much business sense about them to begin with . . . .

Now, I went in at that big meeting, with a straight face and praised them for what they had done with the little amount of time and help they'd had. We didn't let them bother our school system at all. It was a cat-and-mouse game, getting through that one.

You didn't want somebody to inject into a school system practices in education that had no foundation whatsoever. That was the issue. The board adopted what I recommended. The board followed my suggestions.[31]

The curriculum controversy ended.

Desegregation Controversy

As the curriculum fray whimpered to a close—in fact, on the very day that a chamber of commerce member publicly castigated Spears for issuing a much too weighty and complex curriculum progress report—a group of lawyers filed charges of de facto segregation against the San Francisco schools. Spears remembered this with a smile. "One issue passed the other. And I went from one fire into another."[32] By mid-1961, when the National Lawyers Guild leveled their charge, race had already become a national issue. While Southern Freedom Riders and sit-ins made headlines, other Northern cities with much larger percentages of black population than San Francisco had already become entangled in controversy over de facto segregation.

San Francisco in 1960 was a multi-ethnic community:[33] white 81.6 percent; black 10.1 percent; Chinese 4.9 percent; Filipino 1.7 percent; Japanese 1.3 percent; other 0.4 percent. Blacks were concentrated in Hunters Point and the Western Addition (or Fillmore District). The Ingleside area was a transition district that middle-income black families were rapidly moving into.

Yet the racial imbalance within public schools was much less in San Francisco than either Chicago or Washington. In 1964 not one high school was completely segregated (using a maximum of 85 percent for any one group). Six of the fifteen junior high schools had between 61 and 86 percent of a minorty group attending. At the elementary level, one-third of the elementary schools had over 90 percent minority students enrolled. Of these, nine schools (or 10 percent of the one-third figure) were predominately black. In other words, there was a racial imbalance but not the gross sort reported elsewhere. In fact, San Francisco, more than most large cities, had one of the highest percentages of its black students attending desegregated schools (70 percent attending schools which were at least 10 percent white).[34]

These figures underscore a simple, often overlooked, statement: there is no necessary relationship between the percentage of blacks in a community, or the level of racial imbalance in schools, and the eruption, development, or resolution of de facto segregation. Nor do minority populations figures explain the level or direction of civil rights activity—a point that will be explored later.

"Integration No Problem Here," ran the lead for a newpaper story in September 1957. At the height of the Little Rock crisis, Dr. Spears assured one reporter that "everyone living within a certain area, regardless of race, goes to the school in that area." Moreover, he continued: "We have all races in our schools . . . . You can ask a teacher who has had classes of mixed races how many of such and such a race he has. He will just scratch his head and be unable to say, for it doesn't really matter."[35]

However, the president of the American Federation of Teachers (AFT), along with parents from middle-income Ingleside, accused the administration of abetting de facto segregation through inaction. "There's absolutely no policy," the superintendent replied, " to put Negroes in one school and whites in another." Boundary changes are based on school capacity only. If there is overcrowding "we have to relieve it." Redistricting "will continue as long as we have dynamic and changing communities." When the leader of the parents, Asa Davis, a black minister persisted in his demands, Spears answered that when a particular group "tends to pile up in a certain section than the school population will reflect that group." He denied any charge "that this results from a school policy." Board President Burt Levit reaffirmed the primacy of the neighborhood school policy. Editorials clearly supported the board and administration. "To introduce 'ethnic'—a fancy word for racial—considerations," a *Call-Bulletin* editorial argued, "would be to stir up a hornet's nest of trouble."[36]

In each subsequent school year, as in 1957, newspaper articles on desegregation in the South and in Northern cities would appear. Invariably, an ad hoc community group, the American Federation of Teachers, the American Civil Liberties Union, or a similar group would write a letter to the board or meet with the superintendent to ask for an investigation of the schools. And invariably, in September or October, the board or superintendent would deny that any de facto segregation or racial policy existed. Usually this was joined to paeans to the neighborhood school. Such was the case between 1957 and 1961.

In the winter of 1961 a number of issues surfaced that injected race into schooling as nothing before had ever done in San Francisco. First, Mayor Christopher appointed a black man to the board of education. James Stratten, director of a black settlement house, was not the black community's leading candidate. But he was a Republican willing to support the mayor's bid for a higher office. In the black community, Republicans were tough to uncover.[37]

Second, Lowell, the historic academic high school that San Franciscans pointed to with pride, was to move to new quarters. The question of whether it should be converted into another comprehensive, districted school like other high schools or remain academic and open to the city's best students had to be answered. Spears compromised and tried to mix the two. Howls of outrage, especially from Lowell alumni and, for the first time, members of the black community, greeted Spears' proposal. U.S. Attorney Cecil Poole, representing the NAACP, pointed out that an undistricted school avoided ''the evils of residential segregation'' and a ''blind insistence upon neighborhood'' attendance zones, thereby being most fair to blacks and other minorities.[38] Numerous other civil rights groups, such as the American Jewish Congress and the recently organized CORE chapter, testified before the board in behalf of retaining Lowell's open enrollment policy at the new site. The board reversed the superintendent and kept Lowell an academic, undistricted high school.

Third, CORE met privately with Dr. Spears to protest de facto segregation. They asked for a board policy statement recognizing the problem; they also asked for a board resolution pledging to eliminate the situation. Shortly afterward, the Bay Area Human Relations Clearinghouse—an umbrella civil rights group—persuaded CORE to withdraw its demands. Few facts were known, they argued, and what was needed was a citizens commission to investigate the problem. CORE agreed.[39]

On January 23, 1962, the board heard for the first time a coordinated series of requests from civil rights groups for official action on de facto segregation.[40] Beverly Axelrod, a lawyer representing CORE, described the results of a CORE survey taken at three schools, in various parts of the city, that were either predominately black, white, or Chinese. With such clear evidence of de facto segregation, maintained Ms. Axelrod, the ''Board cannot refuse to assume responsibility for school segregation merely because the Board itself did not foster it.'' CORE asked the board to acknowledge officially the existence of de facto segregated schools, declare that such schools are ''educationally undesirable,'' and finally begin an effort to abolish them. Frank Quinn, representing the Bay Area Human Relations Clearinghouse, appeared next. Seconding CORE's conclusions, he urged that the board ''create a commission . . . with citizen participation . . . to study the extent of the problem . . . and to formulate a plan of action.''

The board voted to refer these requests to the superintendent for analysis and recommendations. Dr. Spears pointed out that while he was in sympathy with what he heard presented, he didn't want the board or any group to "feel we are starting from scratch. There has been progress in San Francisco on this problem since World War II." Moreover, he continued, "I think the public schools have been the greatest integrating force in this city and I will match them against any other portion of the City for getting people to live together."

Of far more importance to what eventually happened was Spears' quietly calling the board's attention to what he felt was the central issue. He said, "the Board would have to come around to the issue of whether neighborhood schools in the present plan are undesirable."

Six weeks later, Spears reported back to the board on the ethnic population and their location in the city as detailed in the 1960 census. Opposed to any racial head count, the superintendent repeated again that teachers were "not conscious of racial distribution. I'm sure of that," he said, because they were "too busy teaching school to be thinking about something else."[41]

As weeks slipped by, few civil rights groups were pleased with the superintendent's slow, deliberate response to requests made in January. NAACP representatives, both local and national, lashed out at "foot-dragging" and "stalling" by the administration.[42] If they were disappointed in May, Dr. Spears' report to the board in June totally dismayed them.

In "The Proper Recognition of a Pupil's Racial Background," Spears spoke frankly.[43] After reviewing the ethnic diversity and shifting city population patterns, he stressed the importance of the neighborhood school policy. Adopted by the board in 1936, the "neighborhood centered school is popular with parents, . . . [and] we find it most efficient both educationally and fiscally." Yet even with this policy, when population shifted and overcrowding occurred, district lines were changed and children were bused to relieve the situation. (More than 200 mobile classrooms were also used. However, unlike the case in Chicago, no uproar occurred over these units.) "Both Chinese children and Negro children have been transported to schools in practically all white neighborhoods," he noted. The point, he asserted, was that efficient building use, not racial balance, dictated the move, even though desegregation resulted.

Were the board to change its policy, the superintendent warned, there would be difficulties ahead. Consider that the Chinese community had "already expressed its desire to keep their children in the schools close to their homes." Consider, too, the cultural handicaps of language that black children bring to school. Skilled teachers, he said, working with pupils in their respective neighborhoods where there is a homogeneity of language and culture can build this into the curriculum.

Furthermore, Spears noted, the school system was already doing a great deal in properly recognizing the student's racial background. Programs had been tailored to each group's needs. Mentioned were human relations programs, teacher-training efforts aimed at those staff members working with black children, vocational programs, and compensatory projects growing out of a quarter-million dollar Ford Great Cities grant in 1961.

A final section of the report warned the board on the "Dangers in the Present Period." During his professional career Spears had witnessed changes in American education such as homogeneous grouping, standardized testing, and special classes. He felt that the "pendulum invariably [swings] too far in one of these drives after another." So, too, he feared would be the case with the emphasis on color differences. Why, Spears asked, put a racial tag on a child's school? Why take a racial census?

If we were preparing to ship these children to various schools, in predetermined racial allotments, then such brands would serve the purpose they have been put to in handling livestock. But until somebody comes up with an educationally sound plan . . . then this racial accounting serves nothing but the dangers of putting it to ill use.

Sensing that the purpose of the school was being distorted, Spears acknowledged that the school is "an instrument through which society both preserves the culture and brings out social change" but warned that "children are not to be used as tools."

His final recommendation came as no surprise. "I have no educationally sound program," he said, "to suggest to the Board to eliminate the schools in which the children are predominately of one race."

The board accepted the report and set a September date to give the community more time to consider de facto segregation and the superintendent's response. They recessed, but not before dumping into Dr. Spears' lap a fiery issue raised that very evening.

Central Junior High School

Central Junior High School, Spears recalled, "provided different elements in the civil rights movement with something to get their teeth into. It's one thing to talk theoretical to a board; now here was a chance to do something."[44] The old Lowell building had been closed. Short on space, the administration converted it into a junior high and readied it to open in September of 1961. In April of that year, however, in the midst of the ballooning de facto segregation issue, white parents of sixth-graders reassigned from Grattan Elementary (in Haight-Ashbury) to Central discovered that the school would open up with an estimated 60-percent black population. This percentage was significantly less than that at the overcrowded, nearly all-black Benjamin Franklin Junior High which Central was to relieve; but the Haight-Ashbury area, which would also be served by Central was "in transition," (a euphemism for blockbusters and sprouting "For Sale" signs on lawns), and opening a school with a black majority population would probably further panic the neighborhood. So the Haight-Ashbury parents claimed. They began pressing the board and superintendent to redraw boundaries to decrease the black majority to a figure closer to their numbers in the entire city—that is, 10 percent black.[45]

In early June, representatives of Grattan parents, the Haight-Ashbury Neighborhood Council, NAACP, CORE, and area PTAs met with Spears to discuss racial balance at Central. They asked for redistricting. Spears replied, "you are asking me to do exactly what I have recommended the Board of Education against doing. If we deliberately set up a school district according to race, I will have to have direction from the Board to do it." A subsequent meeting resulted in further confusing the issue. Grattan parents felt that Spears had conceded to their wishes and promised action. Spears denied both. "They are going further than I said."[46]

The July meeting of the board produced threats from Terry Francois, NAACP president. Unless the administration took action to prevent Central's opening as "a ghettoized school," picketing, a lawsuit, and even a boycott would take place. Two weeks later, angry partisans and opponents crowded into the board room to press for action on Central. Earlier that day, after meeting with CORE representatives on the Central matter, Mayor Christopher had wired the board to please consider race in making boundary changes. With this in hand, the board listened to a succession of twenty speakers rail passionately for or against correcting racial imbalance at Central. After five hours, board member de Urioste pleaded with the audience to "give this poor unfortunate Central Junior High a fair chance to operate. Don't let's go into boycotts. Don't let's go into lawsuits. Let's just try."[47] After warm debate, the board declined to act on the Central boundaries.[48]

Rapidly splitting the community, Central had become a symbol.

Sit-ins at the superintendent's office and pickets around board offices were matched by outpourings of support for Dr. Spears and the board from taxpayer and civic action groups located in white areas. Leon Markel, chairman of the newly organized Citizens Committee for Neighborhood Schools, felt that "CORE and NAACP are fighting to reduce the number of Negroes at Central. What they are saying is whites will love the Negroes if there are only 10% of them but not if they are 40% of the students."[49]

Both the *Chronicle* and *Examiner* criticized the board and superintendent for inaction. A *Chronicle* cartoon had the board around a table with a roaring fire engulfing them. The fire was labeled "Growing Segregation Problem" and one member was asking: "Are We *Sure* We Don't Smell Smoke?" One Urban League official called for Spears' resignation. All the while picketing of the board continued. To no one's surprise, the NAACP brought suit in behalf of nine Grattan children due to enter Central. They asked for an injunction to halt the school's opening.[50]

At the August 21 meeting, the largest crowd ever turned out. Spears, at this point, felt that nothing could be done that would satisfy all parties. He then asked that the board close the school. They agreed.

"The board was helpless," Spears recalled. "Here they had the community on their backs. And I got them out of it." What's more, he continued, "I think they respected my leadership on this. They had no way of getting out of it. And if we didn't close the school we'd had a running fight all fall. We'd had that school picketed. We'd run the danger of kids getting hurt. We avoided that situation." It wasn't an easy decision to close the school.

I had to struggle with myself. Does it look like you're backing out of something after you had said something. Didn't take me long to come to the conclusion that this was the only sensible thing to do. I didn't at all feel guilt about proposing something and then withdrawing my proposal. That's the only time I ever did that.[51]

For two years, children who were to attend Central were bussed to mostly white schools, overcrowding some classes. Civil rights groups were satisfied to have made the administration and board back down. Grattan parents were pleased. Those fearful that pressure groups who had forced the board to kneel on this issue would do so on other issues were displeased.

Closing the school that had never opened (the chapter on Central in Spears' autobiography is called "The Never-Never School") destroyed a symbol which partisans for or against could rally around. It shut off a boycott and picketing and terminated a lawsuit. An *Examiner* cartoon had Central Junior High with a "Closed" sign across the door. Two figures with hammers in their pockets were labeled "School Board" and "Pressure Groups" were running off in separate directions. The caption: "The *Problem* Wasn't Boarded Up."[52] In short, the issue was defused—at least for a couple of months.

Ad Hoc Committee

At the September meeting emotions already strained over the Central fray again spilled over at a six-hour board session in which one speaker after another either defended or attacked the administration, the neighborhood school policy, and the board's inaction on the requests made at the January board meeting. With Central gone as a focus, the heat generated by the speakers touched many areas. Again civic groups, PTAs, and individuals praised the superintendent and board for their independence and wisdom. From the NAACP, CORE, and the Council on Civic Unity came another series of requests, demands, and compromise proposals.

Running through the civil rights groups' presentations was an insistence that the board officially recognize the existence of de facto segregation and then act on it—that is, appoint a citizens' committee, bus students, change boundaries, and so forth.

The board chose none of these. Their counsel, Irving Breyer, had warned that to concede the existence of de facto segregation and then state that the board favors maximum integration would be "like saying we are a little bit pregnant." From a legal viewpoint, Breyer contended, such an affirmative statement would be used to haul the board into court when "somebody decided that we're not going as far as we should in regard to that statement."[53] Taking Breyer's advice not to make any policy statements on this issue, the board moved carefully. James Stratten moved that a special board committee be appointed to analyze the issue and to judge—with the advice of the superintendent—all recommendations made before the board, reporting back no later than April 1963.

Board President Samuel Ladar summed up his colleague's opinions when he said that a board committee is preferable to a citizens' committee. The board, he reasoned, "is a group of citizens. They are charged by law with the responsibility to govern the school district." More important, he continued, were the different backgrounds, faiths, and races of the members and their years of experience in school matters.

Furthermore, there would be the aid of an experienced professional staff. He concluded that "trained, objective appraisal . . . is needed more than piling up the emotional outbreaks and outbursts which are on a high pitch and higher level every time I hear the subject discussed." The board agreed. A three-member Ad Hoc Committee to Study Ethnic Factors was created to study the problem further.[54]

When the board meeting adjourned at 2:30 a.m., angry CORE activists staged a sit-in until 7:00 a.m. Two weeks later the NAACP, acting in behalf of 159 black and white students, filed suit against the superintendent and board. The NAACP charged that the neighborhood school policy led to segregation and thereby deprived students of full equal protection under the Fourteenth Amendment.[55]

After this outburst of protest against the board's decision to study the issue further, the next six months were relatively quiet. A virtual moratorium on protest descended on the city, broken only by the NAACP suit (which was finally dropped by the NAACP in December 1964) and mild criticism of the hearings held by the Ad Hoc Committee.

Ten meetings were held by the committee between November 1962 and March 1963. Central office administrators compiled the bulk of the presentations covering attendance zones, student transfer policies, human relations programs, dropouts, and class size. Committee chairwoman Claire Matzger wrote the final report. "I sat at home and wrote sections," she recalled. "Then I would meet with the board president and Dr. Spears to revise if necessary." There were few changes, according to her. Adopted unanimously by the board, the report was well received—and, to her surprise, Mrs. Matzger became a frequent dinner guest at homes of prominent liberal members of the black community.[56]

Thanks to the Ad Hoc Committee's report, for the first time since the issue had surfaced fifteen months earlier, the board of education went on record in support of racially balanced schools. As in other cities, however, the report denied that de facto segregation existed. The term, they said, was a "misnomer," for "segregation is an overt act that has not occurred in San Francisco." To confuse "local racial concentration" with segregation "is a disservice to the city and its schools." Nonetheless, the report directed the administration to now consider race as a criterion in establishing and changing attendance zones. Similarly, race must be considered in selecting sites for new schools. How much relief this would bring to imbalanced schools was admittedly small. And the committee opposed busing employed "for the sole purpose of relieving imbalance."[57]

Throughout the report there was a vigorous commitment to compensatory education. The report admiringly pointed to the previous efforts undertaken by the superintendent in this area. It called for more funds and more effort. Similarly, the committee saw the need for more intergroup education and recommended that a new central office position be created to administer human relations policies and compensatory education. Given the warm support expressed in the report for superintendent policies, this was a significant step away from the seemingly inflexible resistance of an administration that had no sound educational plan to offer. But even with unanimous board approval and warm community response, the move seemed only a tiny step to civil rights activists.

Criticizing the Ad Hoc Committee, the education chairman of the NAACP felt that it had tried to do a fair job but seemed "desperately committed to extracting from the administration [the assurance] that the . . . [system] does not discriminate against minority groups." By doing so, they had missed the central issue: what to do about nonracial policies that produce minority ghettos in schools.[58]

A persuasive argument could be made for this point. Yet the Ad Hoc Committee had wrestled with it by asking questions that most civil rights groups either chose not to ask or assumed were answered. Candidly, the committee asked whether racial composition and pupil achievement were positively related. Did busing influence student behavior and achievement? What impact did class size and ability grouping have on performance? Reliable, unambiguous answers to those and other questions might have driven the committee into investigating the impact of racial imbalance more vigorously. But no answers existed then, nor do they now.

The Ad Hoc Committee's report satisfied, for the time being, the demand for a positive board response to racial imbalance. However, no citizen advisory committee—the chief demand that had kicked off the dispute in January 1962—was convened during Spears' tenure. Spears did eventually concede on a number of other issues, ordering a racial census and releasing the results. This he did reluctantly in August 1965 after being the target of three official investigations of discrimination within the system.[59]

Periodically, between April 1963 and July 1965 there were eruptions of civil rights demands, sit-ins, picketing, and threatened boycotts, accompanied by conciliatory responses from the board and Spears. The superintendent, however, escaped much of the personal abuse that was dumped upon many of his colleagues elsewhere, because in July 1965 he announced that he would retire in 1967. Unlike Hansen and Willis, who were symbols around which civil rights opposition could organize, Spears, both in personality and style—and with an announced retirement—could not be cast as a stubborn, imperious racist. Moreover, his board support remained strong and vigorous until mid–1965, at which point new board appointments and erosion of personal authority owing to his frequent absence for AASA business (he had been elected president) combined to make him a caretaker during the last year and a half of his superintendency.

4 Comparisons and Contrasts

The Cities

Few American cities could differ more than Washington, D.C., Chicago, and San Francisco. The nation's capital, the "I will" city, and the Golden Gate city possess diverse historical traditions, populations, political structures, and school systems.

Consider where people lived. In D.C., whites were a rapidly diminishing minority in the 1960s. The bulk of white neighborhoods were located in the far northwest area with occasional mixed areas scattered throughout the city. Whole sections of the city were predominately black, and these were further subdivided into wealthy, middle-income, and poor neighborhoods. In Chicago, where racist tradition locked blacks into the South Side, successive waves of Southern migrants since World War I had piled up into densely packed tenements. Pushing outward at the edges of the ghetto, blacks faced bombings, riots, and rough harassment. By 1960, the swollen South Side was a textbook version of a ghetto, containing wealthy, middle-income, and poor blacks surrounded on three sides (with Lake Michigan on the east) by hostile white communities. By contrast, San Francisco had Chinese, Filipino, Japanese, Spanish, and black neighborhoods dispersed throughout the city. White ethnic areas, as such, were distinct, but color was present in many areas of the city.

Now consider political structure. While Chicago and San Francisco both had the familiar elected mayor-city council arrangement, the two cities differed widely in how the mayor's relationship to the council (or board of supervisors in San Francisco) had developed over the past half-century. The Daley machine, for example, with its stable of reliable aldermen, had no San Francisco counterpart. In D.C., a citizenry lacking the right to vote in presidential elections until 1961 and without locally elected officials until 1968 depended upon a Southern-dominated House District Committee; it was governed by a city administration funded by Congress and managed by civil servants. The whole official structure was topped, like a bizarre ice-cream concoction, by commissioners serving at the President's pleasure.

Table 1   Socioeconomic Comparisons of Populations in Three Cities, 1960

	Population	Percentage				
		Minority	Foreign-born or mixed parentage	Manu-facturing	White-collar	Unem-ployed
Chicago	3,550,404	24	36	33.5	42	5.4
Washington	763,956	55	13	6.2	50	4.1
San Francisco	740,316	18	46	16	52	6.2

SOURCE: U.S. Department of Commerce, Bureau of the Census, *Population: 1960* (Washington, D.C.: Government Printing Office, 1961), part 10, D.C., p. 10-45, 10-27; part 6, California, p. 6-224; part 13, Illinois, p. 13-237.

Unlike those in her sister cities, Washington's citizens were especially unprepared, even reluctant, to play partisan politics. Where political activity existed, it focused upon lobbying for favors from the Senate and House District Committees and the White House. Independent, partisan campaigns were frowned upon since they invited congressional or executive reprisals. In a town that depended upon the federal presence, local political activity was primitive, little more than shadow boxing with phantoms.

San Francisco politics, on the other hand, gyrated frenetically. Rooted in a rich variety of ethnic, civic, and socioeconomic groupings and a historic tradition of kaleidoscopic politics, ever-changing splinter groups combined and recombined into a loose party structure. Party discipline was fragmentary. And without tight discipline based upon party loyalty, no dependable machine could be built. Personal politics dominated the city. The mayoral metaphor was Bargainer and Negotiator.

In Chicago the metaphor was Mayor as Boss. Since 1955, Richard Daley had dominated Chicago politics. His power to deliver Chicago's votes made him Mr. Democrat, a power within the national party. His patronage extended from local to federal positions. Getting on the Democratic city or state-wide ticket meant winning the Mayor's blessing—and virtual election.

Related to political structure was the pattern of community decision-making. No single dominant elite decided major issues facing Chicago or San Francisco. Various elites did, indeed, exist, and in particular choices they brought influence to bear upon the agency or person charged to make the decision. Numerous investigators have documented the pluralist structure in the two cities and its varying impact upon decision-making.[1]

Washington, however, was another case. Local business and commercial interests and the House District Committee, imperiously presided over by Representative John McMillan of Florence, South Carolina (population 25,000), made critical policy decisions for the city. Labeled a colony by the liberal press, Washington was closer to Florence in its decision-making structure than it was to Chicago or San Francisco.[2] It had no electorate. Congress had the power to slap down, fulfill, or ignore vital civic interests; real estate and commercial elites saw to their own vested interests, which often overlapped the political concerns of the Southern congressmen who dominated the District Committee—all of this in a nonunion city. In short, Washington resembled a Southern mill town more than the large, cosmopolitan city it appeared to be.

Given these differences, what similarities existed in the three cities? Consider, first, the enormous pressures confronting these cities. Between 1950 and 1960 most cities got blacker and poorer. Physically and fiscally, cities were crumbling. White flight and black arrivals sent shock waves through city halls. Shopping plazas and suburban tracts sucked profits and tax dollars outward to garden communities ringing each city, inevitably shrinking the downtown core of the city. Middle-income whites seeking greener and more spacious surroundings abandoned older neighborhoods to recently arrived, poor families who were unprepared to halt the decay that invariably followed such an exodus. Mounting demands for more schools, police protection, housing, and jobs came in the early 1960s at precisely the time that tax dollars hemorrhaged the heart of the city. Such changes struck with varying intensity in each city, and city officials were pressed for action.

School officials soon felt the jolt of these demographic changes. While predominately white schools in some neighborhoods declined in population, schools in minority neighborhoods bulged at the seams.

Children sat in overcrowded classrooms and attended double-shift schools. Inevitably, demands from outraged parents fell upon three boards of education and their administrators. The influx of blacks and the white exodus illustrate one instance of demographic pressure generating demands which were common to the three cities.

What heightened white perceptions of black numbers was the growing militancy of the civil rights movement in the 1960s. Rooted in the South and spurred on by beatings and jailings, the movement's moral fervor was welded to direct-action strategies which eventually were tested in front-line combat with Southern police chiefs and mayors. Accompanied by constant publicity from the media, both fervor and strategies spilled over the Mason-Dixon line into northern and western cities. Regardless of the percentage of blacks in a city, the benign calm in the North and West was soon ruptured by sit-ins, freedom riders, and martyrs. Inevitably, political demands fell upon the schools.

Table 2	Changes in Three Cities, 1950–1960				
City	Percentage black		Percentage decrease in population 1950–1960	Daily school membership (in thousands)	
	1950	1960		1950	1960
Chicago	14	24	1.9	342	440
Washington	35	55	4.8	113	139
San Francisco	6	10	4.5	74	91

SOURCES: U.S. Department of Commerce, Bureau of the Census, *County and City Data Book,* 1952, pp. 442, 450; ibid., 1962, pp. 450, 486.

Other political pressures triggered similar demands upon the schools in these three cities. Soviet Russia's launching of Sputnik in 1957, for example, fed a growing public clamor for improved public schools. One barrage of charges after another burst over urban school systems. Demands for change were hurled with varying velocity at each of the three systems. Regardless of the differences in the cities, Sputnik triggered scathing indictments from critics and spirited defenses from schoolmen.

In the late 1950s and early 1960s, then, municipal governments and school systems lacked command of their environment. Both were very vulnerable systems, pierced continually by demographic, political, and socioeconomic forces with which they were unable to cope. Common to all three cities were insistent demands for change that were often aimed at municipal and school officials. Among the three cities there existed a rough-hewn political separation of the school system from city officials and partisan politics that somewhat diminished this vulnerability. But, although the Chicago and San Francisco boards of education levied taxes and prepared their budgets apart from the mayor's office (Washington did not[3]), all at some point had to obtain approval from their mayor or council. Some sort of municipal review, usually pro forma, existed, regardless of whether the school district was financially dependent or independent.

Still, the operating climate in the three cities was one of noninterference. Mayors Richard Daley and George Christopher appointed board members but stressed almost ritualistically the independence of the public schools from partisan politics or direct intervention from their offices. Similarly, the three district commissioners followed a general hands-off policy. Clearly, when school crises affecting the entire city erupted, pressure was often placed on the mayor's office to do something. During the de facto segregation fracas, for example, community groups pressed Daley to dump Willis. Mayor Christophor received angry letters from teachers outraged at Spears' supposedly soft "progressivism," wanting the mayor to push the board toward the 3R's. District commissioners often received requests to do something about Hansen and tracking. Seldom did they intervene.

None of this, of course, is to imply that the commissioners, Daley, or Christopher never exercised their influence informally upon board members and school officials. They did. The point is, however, that the taboo against direct political intervention into school operations remained strong throughout this decade in the three cities.[4] Thus, a cocoon of political independence insulated school officials from the larger governmental arena. Willis, Spears, and Hansen, for all the problems they faced in these years, seldom had to worry about direct interference from City Hall.

School systems in these three dissimilar cities, then, possessed at least two key common traits. First, their vulnerability to outside forces produced familiar dynamics in each city that triggered off parallel demands for change. Second, the political segregation of schools from municipal operations established a protective perimeter which encouraged the development of an organizational environment highly sensitive to professional concerns. Political insulation, then, nourished a professional homogeneity among the three cities.

Men, Boards, and Bureaucracies

Over coffee and Danish pastry in a suburban garden apartment, former Superintendent Carl Hansen and I made small talk.

"Who else have you interviewed?" he asked.

"Ben Willis and Harold Spears," was my reply.

"Why," he asked, "do you want to study dinosaurs like us?"[5]

Dinosaurs!—a familiar enough epithet which critics had hurled at the three during the turbulent 1960s. Three superintendents as dinosaurs? Through my mind flashed images of hulking beasts, with pea-sized brains, mucking about in a world which was changing so rapidly that they could not adapt to it. There was no self-pity in the word; as Hansen said it, there was a crusty, almost defiant ring to it as if to say, "we went through those tough times together—and survived."

Benjamin Willis, Harold Spears, and Carl Hansen did, indeed, have much in common. Consider, for example, their career patterns shown in table 3. All three had been born at the turn of the century and reared in rural areas; they had taught and principaled in small rural districts for over a decade, returning to graduate school to earn doctorates which enabled them to reach the top rung of the ladder—an urban superintendency. Arriving at this peak in the 50s, each had already established a reputation among his colleagues. Willis and Spears had already begun their trek upward in their professional association. Both would ultimately serve as presidents of the American Association of School Administrators. Author and speaker Carl Hansen was highly respected for his instructional leadership.

But were the three very different from the rest of the big-city superintendents serving at the same time? Were they unique among educational professionals in their backgrounds and careers?

When compared with their big city colleagues (see table 4), our trio proved slightly different in some categories, but by and large their backgrounds and careers remarkably converged. Beyond being more schooled, serving slightly longer, and being a bit older at the time of their superintendencies, Hansen, Willis, and Spears mirrored well the general social background and upward trek through the ranks that marked the careers of most city superintendents. Respected by colleagues, having risen to the top of their profession—dinosaurs or not—they were pure casts from the mold.

Predictably, their executive styles were similar. Each drew on considerable reservoirs of personal energy to see him through the frenetic pace of daily affairs during the crises described in the previous chapters.

Table 3   Career Patterns of Three Superintendents, 1963

	Place of birth	Number years teacher or principal	Age at advanced degree/university	Age at first superintendency	Age in 1963	Number of years in current post (1963)	Total number years as superintendent
Willis	Baltimore, Maryland	12	49/Columbia, Ed.D.	33	62	10	13
Hansen	Wolbach, Nebraska	20	38/University Southern California, Ed.D.	52	57	5	9
Spears	Swayzee, Indiana	17	37/Columbia, Ed.D.	39	61	8	12

SOURCE: Compiled from interviews with the three superintendents, and from autobiographical accounts and biographies prefacing articles about each.

Table 4	Three Superintendents Compared with Big-City Colleagues		
	Three superintendents	Twenty urban school chiefs[a]	AASA[b]
Percentage raised in small town or rural area	100	60	66
Percentage taking first teaching job in small town or rural area	67	55	—
Percentage who served as teachers	100	82	88
Percentage who served as principals	100	80	82
Median age at first superintendency	41.3[c]	43.0	40.0
Median age in 1963	60.0	57.5	57.5
Median years in present position (1963)	7.7	5.5	6.3
Average years served as superintendent	11.3	9.5	—
Percentage who hold doctorate	100	50	66
Median age at doctorate	41.0	36.0	38.3

SOURCES: The 1963 survey of twenty urban school chiefs was compiled from *Who's Who,* 1950–1965, *Leaders in Education, 1971;* the AASA survey came from the *Profile of School Superintendents* (Washington: AASA, 1960), pp. 71–126.

[a]The school chiefs were selected from the twenty largest districts in 1966. Atlanta's Ira Jarrell was the only woman who served as an urban top administrator in these years. She served from 1944–1960.

[b]Figures come from 1958 survey results for cities of 500,000.

[c]Figures are means for the three superintendents.

Each, too, eagerly embraced the politics of decision-making in a highly volatile environment without sacrificing his professional ideal of being apolitical in the larger environment.

Yet, with all of these commonalities, definite personal differences in style were apparent among the three. If Willis gloried in whirling through a sixteen-hour day, Spears prided himself on leaving the office daily at 5:30 p.m. and relaxing on weekends. If Hansen could listen patiently to a subordinate with great formality and distance, Willis could dismiss an assistant with an imperious wave of the hand. If Hansen seldom dropped a four-letter word and viewed office air conditioning and deep leather chairs as frills, Spears found both congenial. If Spears enjoyed drawing cartoons for teachers and administrators at Christmas parties, Willis enjoyed visiting possible school sites on Sunday mornings. If Hansen relaxed over a novel or poetry, if Willis unwound by shop-talking at a businessmen luncheon or going fishing, Spears found pleasure in writing or in going to a play or a chatty cocktail party.

Such personal style differences made for interesting individuals but did not submerge the basic commonalities that bound the three together. Were the three boards and school organizations, and their relationships with superintendents, equally alike?

The Boards

According to table 5, the typical board member in our three cities was a white Protestant, middle-aged, college-educated male practicing a profession or managing a business. How closely these boards match comparable ones in other cities can be seen in table 6, which incorporates the results of several studies. Although some divergence can be seen in table 6, the overall figures suggest a rough match.[6]

By definition, the primary function of big-city boards is policymaking. Although they have the final authority over school decisions, more often they mediate conflict and approve their executive's recommendations. Gittell and Cronin found this to be especially true of big-city boards involved in innovation, decentralization, community control, and desegregation issues. So, too, do these functions describe Chicago, San Francisco, and Washington boards.[7]

In determining policy, big city boards leaned heavily upon their professional adviser. Exceptions existed, to be sure, but big city boards with aggressive lay leadership dictating to professional staff have been infrequent departures from the dominant pattern. Studies of New York, Philadelphia, Baltimore, and a dozen other major school systems richly chronicle how schoolmen have effectively used their professional expertise to gain considerable control over policymaking.[8] The chapters on Chicago, Washington, and San Francisco similarly document how Willis, Hansen, and Spears profoundly influenced critical decisions.

Joseph Pois' reflections of his years as a board member during

Table 5   Socioeconomic Traits of Three Boards of Education, 1963–1964

	Number on board	Percentage businessmen or professionals	Percentage college-educated	Percentage black	Percentage white	Percentage female	Percentage male	Average age	Average years served
San Francisco	7	57	67	14	86	29	71	55.5[a]	9.0
Chicago	11	64	80	18	82	18	82	61.0[a]	10.0
Washington	9	77	100	44	56	33.3	66.7	60.0	9.0
Mean for three boards	9	66	82	25	75	27	73	58.8	9.3

SOURCES: Compiled from biographies of members available in each board of education secretary's office.   [a]No information available on one member.

Table 6

Summary: Studies of Socioeconomic Characteristics of Urban School Boards

Source/Year	Median size of board	Percentage businessmen, managers, or professionals	Percentage college-educated	Percentage female	Percentage male	Percentage black	Percentage white	Average age	Average years served
Brown, 1951	N.A.	69	67	14	86	N.A.	N.A.	N.A.	N.A.
Albert, 1958	N.A.	52	72	18	82	N.A.	N.A.	48.6	6.0
NSBA, 1963–1965	7	82	N.A.	20	80	12.5	87.5	N.A.	7.1
Gittell, 1966	9	81.5	80[a]	22	78	23	77	50–55[b]	N.A.
Three boards, 1963 (from table 5)	9	66	82	27	73	25	75	58.8	9.3

SOURCES: R. A. Brown, "Composition of School Boards," *American School Board Journal*, August 1954, pp. 23–24; F. R. Albert, *Selected Characteristics of School Board Members and Their Attitudes toward Certain Criticisms of Public School Education*, originally Ed.D. diss., University of Mississippi (New York: Center for Applied Research, 1964), p. 91; National School Board Association Survey of Forty-Two Cities with 300,000 Population in 1963 reported in *School Management*, Sep-

tember, 1963, pp. 54–57; later survey cited in Carolyn Mullins, "All About the Nation's Big League Boardmen, *American School Board Journal*, September, 1972, pp. 21a2—a124; Marilyn Gittell, *Six Urban Districts* (New York: Praeger, 1967). Above figures exclude Chicago.

[a]Estimate based upon occupation data presented.

[b]"Approximately two-thirds of the board members are over fifty." Gittell, p. 98.

Willis's tenure recorded how the board followed rather than led their chief administrator. The board's dependence—or "submissiveness," as Pois put it—revealed itself most clearly when Dr. Willis resigned in October 1963. Within one week, the board reversed the decision that had provoked the superintendent to resign. He then returned to loud applause from the board majority. Board approval six months later of guidelines governing relations between the board and its administrator was the price for that victorious return. Incorporated into those guidelines was the official administrative view of how boards should operate; Willis found the guidelines satisfactory. In 1966, a few months after Willis finally left Chicago, a management survey drily concluded that "responsibility and authority [in the Chicago schools] are concentrated in a relatively small number of people who administer programs . . . on a highly centralized basis."[9]

In San Francisco there was a similar dependence upon professional expertise. Even at the height of the curriculum controversy when Spears' professional views were under assault, board members persistently deferred to the superintendent's technical skills in curriculum. And when the board finally did contract with outside consultants to evaluate the curriculum, the report they ultimately received from the professors was promptly turned over to Spears for evaluation, the very person whose curricular views had earlier been suspect. In the area of budgeting, the board depended totally upon the superintendent to determine priorities and prepare the budget. Concerned only with how the final sum compared with previous years or whether any of the administration's proposed changes affected the total figure, the board—once satisfied—consistently approved the budgets. Moreover, Spears remembered how he had often persuaded the board to accept tax rate levels he proposed during his tenure.[10]

Carl Hansen's dominant influence upon board policy emerged in his initiating and sustaining two system-wide instructional programs: Tracking and the Amidon Plan. Consider also that the board seldom received the up-coming budget from Dr. Hansen in sufficient time to review it adequately. In most cases, it came to them a few days before the deadline for submission to the city government. Invariably, they hastily skimmed the thick, one-pound document, approving it with few reservations about either the procedure by which it arrived or the content of next year's school program.[11] Save for one board member, no one criticized the superintendent's instructional program or budget process. Not until the influence of professional reformers, federal funds, and antipoverty programs had fermented within the black community did a major anti-Hansen offensive mobilize. A dramatic change in board appointments in 1966 and 1967, replacing Hansen stalwarts with critics, foreshadowed his eventual departure.

Such examples from the three systems illustrate that superintendents often dominated board decision-making in the crucial areas of budget, instruction and curriculum. None of this should be surprising, given the nature of the board member's job, the administrative functions of the superintendent, and the professional orientation of most boards of education.

Consider what big-city school board members have to do. Required by law to authorize every penny spent, from ketchup to paperclips, to approve appointments of personnel, from cooks to assistant superintendents, and to set the direction on the quality and quantity of schooling, board members have to make sense out of multimillion-dollar budgets, percentages of assessed valuation, and technical (if not incomprehensible) prose on instruction. Furthermore, community grievances over alleged obscene library books or rumors of an immoral teacher invariably end up in the lap of the board, which must somehow resolve the problem without angering too many in the community. Faced with suits by parents, teachers, and contractors, board members have to approve complicated legal decisions recommended by the board's counsel. As if this weren't enough, board members must either bargain with union representatives over salaries or approve decisions made by the superintendent with teachers, custodians, and other unions. And this is only a sampling of the enormously complex issues facing the average big-city board member.

Yet these members are unpaid.[12] They serve part-time. They are untrained. Except for the information presented them by the superintendent, or perhaps what they pick up informally, they know little of the underlying issues for the scores of complex decisions requiring their approval at each board meeting. True, big-city board members spend twenty to forty hours a week reading materials, attending committee meetings, visiting with staff, and listening to aggrieved parents and employees. True, as the years pass, individual board members become proficient in particular school matters. And some veteran board members cultivate alternative sources of information. Considering the demanding nature of the job, and the limited time, energy, and information available to board members, it is little wonder that most board members rely upon the superintendent for direction.

Furthermore, the socioeconomic makeup of these big-city boards reveals another subtle pressure tying them to their chief administrator:

there is a high percentage of business managers and professionals on boards. Social origins and occupation seldom determine specific school policies or decisions. What seems to exist, however, is a link between board member status and attitudes toward professional expertise. Since many board members work in professional and managerial positions, they value highly—and, more important, respect—delegated and competent decision-making. Deference to technical skills comes easily to board members. A number of researchers found that higher-status boards (ones with very high percentages of doctors, lawyers, and business executives) incline toward conceding broad decision-making duties to their superintendents. This of course gives boards a professional orientation. Ziegler found that the majority of American school boards "tend to perceive their roles as being consistent with the values of professional educators." Those values, of course, stressed board unity and layman reliance upon professional expertise. Not surprisingly, then, Ziegler found a strong tie between board professionalism and superintendent dominance. The existence of such commonly held values creates filters which determine which issues will surface and which will never see the light of day.[13]

The repertoire of administrative strategies which our three superintendents skillfully used on their boards further explains the boards' dependence. Notice, for example, that big-city superintendents determined what was included in and what was omitted from board agendas. One study found that only 4 percent of all boards in the country independently determined the agenda. In another study, of Baltimore, the researcher found that over a seven-year period almost 90 percent of board agendas concerned hiring or firing employees and school construction programs.[14]

Review of board agendas in the three cities confirms this pattern. Interviews with the three superintendents suggest they carefully planned agendas for what was to be included and excluded; they anticipated board reactions to particular items; and they were content to have boards deal with what they would consider minor issues.[15]

Another administrative strategy was the superintendent's control over the direction and amount of information flowing to the board. Lacking independent staff, board members were compelled to rely upon the executive staff for answers to their questions. Most superintendents frowned upon board members' dipping into the middle of the bureaucracy for information; they wanted all requests for information to come through them. Clear evidence of this control was the dependence of outside evaluators such as Robert Havighurst, Harry Passow, and the eight Bay Area professors upon the cooperation of each superintendent for their data.

By setting the agenda and controlling the flow of information, big-city superintendents defined what the issues were. Wherever possible they would convert complex problems into simpler questions of technical expertise or routine matters. A few studies document how commonly such strategies were used.[16] (A later section of this chapter deals with the three administrators' uses of these strategies.)

Finally, big-city boards ended up being dominated by their superintendent because they perceived themselves less as representatives of the community and more as delegates to approve recommendations of hired professionals. "Superintendents win," Ziegler concluded after a national study, "because boards want them to." More than 90 percent of all school board members felt, in another study, that they should not serve as spokesmen for the community. Pois' harshest condemnation for Chicago schools, for example, fell not upon Willis' head but upon his colleagues for their "cap-in-hand" stance toward their hired executive.[17]

Easy as it is to weave a persuasive explanation for professional dominance over boards of education, a high rate of turnover at the executive level continued to plague the urban superintendency. Board membership changed. Administrators resigned. Flashfloods of community grievances periodically engulfed superintendents, forcing their exit. From time to time, aggressive board committees would sorely tax superintendents by mucking around in the administration. None of this, of course, has ever stopped determined, experienced men from entering (or leaving) the profession, though shaky tenure among urban superintendents remains a volatile topic among schoolmen. The point is that significant influence over board decision-making in no way guaranteed the superintendent a gold watch and a roast beef retirement dinner.

If big-city superintendents were successful in persuading boards to rely upon them, their success was diminished by the expansion of the bureaucracy that accompanied the growth of school population. Consolidation of power within large school bureaucracies proved to be one more arena in which superintendents had to impose their will.

Bureaucracies

Although big-city bureaucracies in the 1960s varied in size, they nonetheless possessed many common traits (see table 7). All were

Table 7   School Bureaucracies in Twenty Big
Cities, 1955–1956

	Number of central officers,[a] supervisors, principals	Number of teachers	Ratio of administrators to teachers
Atlanta	127	3,054	1:24
Boston	159	3,087	1:19
Chicago	572	13,993	1:24
Cincinnati	188	2,349	1:12
Cleveland	330	3,788	1:11
Dallas	157	3,329	1:21
Denver	229	2,681	1:12
Detroit	604	8,840	1:15
Houston	234	4,541	1:19
Indianapolis	173	2,670	1:15
Los Angeles	873	16,097	1:18
Milwaukee	190	3,047	1:16
New Orleans	161	2,635	1:16
New York	1,774	34,852	1:20
Philadelphia	436	7,876	1:18
Portland	130	2,421	1:19
St. Louis	268	3,186	1:24
San Francisco	250	2,959	1:12
Seattle	186	2,982	1:16
Washington, D.C.	270	3,713	1:14

SOURCE: U.S. Biennial Survey of Education, 1954–56, *Statistics of Local School Systems, 1955–1956* (Department of Health, Education and Welfare, 1956), pp. 44–130.

[a]Numbers of administrators in central office are underreported, since school systems reported directors, supervisors, and assistant superintendents.

hierarchical. There were at least a half-dozen administrative layers separating the superintendent from the student. Piled atop one another in carefully printed organizational charts were figures representing teachers, principals, supervisors, directors, coordinators, assistant superintendents and, in the larger cities, associate and deputy superintendents. Solid and broken lines amid arrows on the charts tried to delineate teacher and staff relationships. Arrows and lines notwithstanding, in all of these organizations formal authority flowed downward. In the quest for efficiency, specialization reigned supreme. Divisions for elementary and secondary schools, budget, curriculum, research, guidance, maintenance, and personnel turned up in system after system.

While a number of big cities in the 1960s moved toward decentralizing the organizations of their school systems, Gittell concluded that all of the schemes (including Chicago's) left the district administrator virtually powerless—that is, he had no control over budget or appointment and had no authority to initiate programs.[18] San Francisco had no decentralized effort in these years; Washington's Model School Division can be considered as a modest, if reluctant effort at decentralization. Centralization of decision-making remained in the upper reaches of the bureaucracy. In short, a Weberian bureaucracy model existed on paper.

All big-city systems had thick, multivolume sets of board rules and superintendent regulations. Standard operating procedures covering hiring, budget-making, curriculum development, fire drills, purchasing, grading, corporal punishment, and scores of other subjects guided administrators and teachers in routinizing daily decisions.

All recruitment and promotions of administrators closely followed one pattern. Recruits for the positions of principal and supervisor were drawn mostly from experienced classroom teachers already in the system. Most top central office promotions came from the ranks of principals and supervisors. Merit and seniority procedures froze the pattern into regular grooves. Unsurprisingly, insiders dominated the upward trek through the bureaucracy. Eliminated from this process were noneducators or outsiders, who rarely penetrated the credentials curtain separating the school system from its environment. Interestingly, Willis, Hansen, and Spears were highly mobile career professionals— outsiders—who imported no cadre of loyal colleagues from their previous positions. Instead they accepted the dominant insider pattern, preferring to shift and promote subordinates whom they felt were able.

Marked by hierarchical authority, dominated by rules and routines and embracing rigorous merit and seniority systems in their recruitment and promotion of insiders, Washington, Chicago, and San Francisco bureaucracies differed little from their counterparts across the nation.[19]

Pressure Groups and Responses from the School System

As much as superintendents and bureaucrats would like to deny it, they lived in volatile, churning surroundings. Episodic crises erupted and subsided. Angry factions in the community could weld together a hasty coalition and dump a teacher, program, or superintendent (or all three). Newspaper articles investigating conditions within one school could reverberate throughout the bureaucracy and dominate board discussions for an entire meeting. Throughout the 1950s and early 1960s external groups dissatisfied with how children were taught to read, dissatisfied with inroads of "progressive"educators, dissatisfied with racial imbalance, dissatisfied with levels of popular participation, pressed many big-city school boards for changes. In these years few major cities escaped pressure.

In this study of three cities, two instances of pressure were selected for each city. Altogether, the six incidents include three (one for each city) that were traditionally defined both by schoolmen and laymen as educational issues—for example, curriculum, organizational change, a survey of the school system's needs. The other three instances (again, one in each city) dealt with an issue traditionally defined by schoolmen as non-educational—for example, a social issue such as de facto segregation in which schools should be uninvolved.

In each city external pressure for action on both the educational and social issues struck hard at the superintendent and board. The following sections will describe the origins of these pressures and the strategies used by groups to bring pressure on school officials. We will then compare how these officials initially responded to demands among themselves and contrast their responses with their colleagues across the country.

Social Issue: De Facto Segregation

Pressure for change in the three cities came from formal civil rights organizations and liberal white and black neighborhood groups protesting racial imbalance. Traditional civil rights groups such as the NAACP and the Urban League were joined by activist CORE chapters in each city. Voicing demands for desegregated schooling, they pressed schoolmen to end segregation.

Arising in 1961, pressure against de facto segregation in Chicago was led initially by the NAACP, then the Urban League, and finally CCCO. "Led" is a rather generous term, since leadership shifted often from traditional organizations to ad hoc groups and coalitions of community groups. Often coalitions would fragment, later coalesce, and again splinter, only to reestablish again later. Civil rights leadership, often defined by the press, television, or City Hall, changed hands constantly (as much from internal bickering as anything else, especially when the activist phase occurred).

In San Francisco a similar pattern developed between 1962 and 1965, except neighborhood groups often provided the leadership, time, and energies to fuel pressure upon the school board and administration. Here, too, NAACP, CORE, and an umbrella coalition of civil rights organizations and neighborhood groups surfaced, in no particular, coordinated fashion, the issue of de facto segregation. Here, too, leadership swerved and dodged between and within groups so that board members and Spears would not know with any precision whether last month's demands were still on the agenda when a new face would appear at a conference.[20]

For Washington, where the de facto issue never took hold with the tenacity of Chicago or San Francisco, the Urban League and a handful of activist, integrated neighborhood groups initiated and developed the issue over a period of a year and a half. By 1965, when the specific demands of local groups for boundary changes were met, events rapidly changed, although the larger issues raised by the Urban League remained unmet. By that time the Urban League had moved on to other matters.

In all three cities, political pressure on boards came from established civil rights organizations raising broad policy issues dealing with de facto segregation and from local white and black activist, parent groups, concerned about specific racial composition of their neighborhood schools. What did both want?

In all of these cities, civil rights groups wanted the board of education to concede that segregation existed and then to do something about it. Accompanying this symbolic demand—in effect, a policy statement—in Washington and San Francisco was the specific request for board action to establish a citizens' committee or to take affirmative actions such as initiating open enrollment, busing, pairing of schools, or similar efforts.

All three boards and superintendents initially rejected both the symbolic and specific demands. Spears categorically denied the notion that schools were responsible for de facto segregation. Refusing to take a racial census, he said, in a phrase that came to haunt his subsequent efforts, that as a professional he had "no educationally sound program" for correcting racially imbalanced schools.[21] Hansen, too, rejected outright the Urban League proposals for a citizens group, although he had no quarrel with the board's reaffirming its earlier statement on desegregation. By 1965 standards, however, the 1954 statement of the board was mild: Hansen, of course, knew that the Urban League wanted more. Willis did not initially react publicly to civil rights demands. He had filed an affidavit in the *Webb* case in which he flatly denied that public schools were in any way responsible for de facto segregation. In October 1961 the Chicago school board, after hearing a five-hour string of witnesses demanding an end to segregation, vigorously rebutted NAACP and neighborhood groups' views that racial imbalance resulted from school policies. The first probe by civil rights organizations of the board-superintendent position resulted in a polite listening to grievances with just as polite but firm rejection of demands.

Escalation of protest followed in Chicago and San Francisco but not in Washington. In the District, board consent to Hansen's refusal of Urban League demands—combined with his quietly satisfying neighborhood groups' requests for school boundary changes—effectively squashed the de facto segregation issue. More important was the mounting tracking controversy which diverted civil rights energies into a broader-based campaign against Hansen's policies. The more expressive measures taken by civil rights groups elsewhere, including litigation, boycotts and demonstrations turned up in the tracking fracas during 1965–1967.

Benjamin Willis's refusal to sit down and negotiate with civil rights activists and his vigorous defense of school policies infuriated civil rights and neighborhood groups. Willis maintained that "race is educationally irrelevant. . . . We do not have a problem of segregation, only a complicated problem of education." Moreover, he continued in an interview, "this is not evasion; it is keeping our eye on the educational ball and refusing to be distracted by highly charged emotional issues. Concentrating on racial aspects of a problem only creates more problems."[22]

Protest tactics escalated. The *Webb* suit instigated by the NAACP, Urban League in-depth research rebuttals of Willis statements, "Truth Squads," "Willis Wagon" protests, and CORE's increasing use of direct action traced the growing frustration of citywide and local groups in bargaining with board and superintendent.

While Board President Claire Roddewig negotiated with civil rights and local leaders, it was clear that Willis would have to implement any compromise formula. And Willis's position on civil rights demands (which he considered illegitimate) was evident to the board. Roddewig could bend only so much. With the board's speedy submission after his resignation over a very modest open-enrollment plan, Willis's refusal to concede anything to civil rights groups (i.e., no racial head count, no busing of black children to white schools at public expense to relieve overcrowding, and no comprehensive schemes to end racial imbalance) was, if anything, strengthened after the face-off. With neighborhood groups, Willis and the board often placated them. When citywide publicity occurred, the administration shifted a mobile classroom to another site or slightly redrew district lines to satisfy angry parents.

The impact of Harold Spears' initial rejection of civil rights demands in June 1962 was heightened by the Central Junior High episode. Here liberal white and black parents found citywide support in the NAACP and the newspapers. They pressed Spears to do anything other than open a predominately black school in their community. The two months of jockeying between board, superintendent, and parents produced threats of a lawsuit and boycott from the NAACP. Spears' response pleased the parents. It also got the board off the hook. The decision not to open Central Junior High defused parental pressure and, coming as it did on the heels of Spears' refusal to consider any plan to end racial imbalance, measurably slowed down the momentum of civil rights groups striving for broad, symbolic goals.

When CORE and the NAACP returned to the board in the fall, they again pressed for a policy statement on integration and a citizens' commission. The board responded with their own ad hoc committee, a move Spears felt was wise. Civil rights activities subsided for six months.

With the publication of the ad hoc committee's report, the board went on record that race should be considered as a criterion in making policy. Although the report clearly modified the superintendent's initial response, its main thrust was still toward stronger compensatory programs—a direction Spears had been aggressively pursuing the previous year. Where the report urged that race be taken into account—in effect, partially conceding to one of the symbolic demands of civil rights groups—Spears already privately had leaned in that direction. He felt that none of his principles were being sacrificed. With the release of the ad hoc report, de facto segregation slid out of sight for almost two years.

In all three cities, in the years under study, civil rights efforts failed to achieve fully any of their broadly stated goals. Some neighborhood groups did extract a few short-term gains between 1961 and 1965 in these cities; yet little success materialized in ending racial imbalance or even getting boards and administrators to take substantial affirmative action. Lawsuits, lobbying of board and school officials, well-documented public presentations, noisy demonstrations, sit-ins, boycotts—the complete repertoire of civil rights activism—failed to budge superintendents substantially from their initial position during the remaining years of their tenure.[23]

Responses from superintendents toward civil rights tactics followed a distinct pattern. Their professional gyroscope dictated that school policies must be color-blind and universal in application. Thus, any suggestion to single out one racial group was felt to be undemocratic and discriminatory. Furthermore, schools were for schooling; they were not tools for reshaping society. Finally, they felt that pressure from interest groups pursuing special aims was detrimental to the entire system—especially so if pressure came from laymen lacking professional expertise.

Proceeding from these hard and fast axioms, these superintendents denied the very premises of civil rights groups who, in effect, pushed for symbolic recognition of minority rights. These school chiefs then redefined the issue as noneducational and political, thus rendering it tainted in their eyes and to be avoided by school officials.

Outright rejection of demands, avoidance of the issue, delays, and a dozen other tactics were pursued singly or in groups by administrators, depending upon the degree of influence each carried with the board and how sharp the pressure was. None of the three followed an active bargaining strategy with civil rights groups. They firmly believed they were protecting the schools from outside forces anxious to subvert the schools for illegitimate ends.

How representative were the superintendents' responses on this desegregation issue in these years? Robert Crain and his associates studied eight Northern cities (including San Francisco) experiencing desegregation crises. Of the ten superintendents who served in the eight cities, seven acted independently of their boards in rejecting civil rights demands. In another study of small to large cities, none of the three big systems (including Chicago and San Francisco) met the challenge of desegregation. Describing Willis and Spears as "intransigent" superintendents the authors charitably called St. Louis a "borderline" case. Yet St. Louis superintendent Philip Hickey not only had opposed integrating bused black children into white classrooms but also had condemned open enrollment and any departure from the neighborhood school concept. Hickey's report including these reservations was approved 8–3 by his board. David Rogers and Bert Swanson massively detailed how desegregation policy statements from the New York board of education were buried by a succession of superintendents who either ignored the board, delayed implementation, lacked the will or skill to jolt a stubborn, resistant bureaucracy into action.[24]

Of the nation's fifteen largest cities in 1960, excluding Southern ones, desegregation case studies had been done in twelve. Of these, only two contradicted the response pattern that turned up in Chicago, Washington, and San Francisco.[25]

Educational Issues: School Survey, Structural Change, and Curriculum

External pressure for educational changes in the three cities came from a variety of groups. In Chicago the Citizens Schools Committee, a veteran watchdog organization, and the regional PTA had since the mid-1950s been requesting an independent survey of the board's adminstrative and educational policies. When the board first considered the request in October 1961, Willis interrupted the PTA speaker and snapped: "We do not need a survey to tell us that we could use more teachers." When the board did appoint a committee to plan a survey, Willis publicly responded more favorably, but his basic stance toward outside surveys was evident.[26]

In the next eighteen months the survey of board administrative and educational policies changed into a curriculum study, then shifted to an investigation of de facto segregation, finally crystallizing into the limited form that Robert Havighurst presented to the board in late 1964. Changes resulted from the swift rush of civil rights activism, intense jockeying between board and Dr. Willis, and mounting demands from civic and neighborhood groups for an independent survey. Aggressively, Willis resisted the survey to the point of threatening to resign unless he took an active part in determining the survey's content and scope. The board consented. Havighurst, Willis, and a local dean of education formed a committee overseeing the survey giving Willis the leverage he needed ultimately to discredit the results of the survey as being less than impartial. Moreover, his control over the flow of information placed repeated roadblocks in the way of survey staff. Finally, when the survey and recommendations were accepted by the board, they were turned over to the superintendent. With a solid board majority, Willis could ignore those recommendations that he disliked and accept those he found inconsequential or planned to implement anyway. And this he did.

In Washington, Carl Hansen faced aggressive professional reformers underwritten by federal agencies. Accompanying Washington Action for Youth demands upon the superintendent to establish an experimental subsystem within the District schools were high-pressure tactics aimed at clubbing Hansen into submission. Backed by the White House, Jack Goldberg saw the scenario in simple terms: If Hansen runs the show, either he plays ball with us or out he goes. Ample funds, growing press support, and the rumblings of black activism all were warmly embraced by an Attorney General who visited local schools, wrote to board members, and met with interested people to discuss school reform. Of course, few inside or outside the system forgot that the Attorney General's brother happened to be President of the United States.

After Dallas, of course, the strategy collapsed. Whether Hansen could have continued to weather Jack Goldberg's sledgehammer attacks no one will ever know. What followed, however, became quite manageable for Dr. Hansen. The White House Panel on Educational Research and Development, United Planning Organization, and the Advisory Committee pursued strategies of cooperation mixed with vigorous criticism. Neither worked. Hansen's control over personnel and federal funds and his definition of autonomy for the Model School Division set the limits for the pace and direction of change. He, in short, set the reform agenda. Neither federal agencies nor Advisory Committee could nudge the administration or board from the course the superintendent set.

News of Sputnik hit San Francisco hard. Steady criticism from the local press defined the inferior quality of schooling as a key issue. The debate over "progressivism" vs 3R's focused the controversy in its early months at an abstract level. The independent teacher association, which for some years had been anxious over Spears' policies, entered the fray with a severe indictment of inferior schooling. Pressure from newspapers and teachers was picked up by the board. What transpired over the next year and a half was a sharp battle between board and superintendent over a number of blurred issues.

Critics pursued tactics, often uncoordinated, consisting of polemical blasts followed by sharp volleys of accusations. Newspapers provided the main arena for the battle. Spears responded to the criticism defining the issue in terms of strengthening the existing curriculum and satisfying teacher grievances over student discipline and working conditions. Shrewdly, he included recommendations that embraced the substance of certain key criticisms.

When the board faction established a curriculum committee and eventually contracted with the university professors to do a survey, Spears continued his efforts to toughen up courses. As long as the board accepted Spears' definition of the curriculum problem as a technical matter best left to professionals, and as long as they viewed teacher complaints as a matter to be resolved between staff and administration,

Spears could afford to sit impassively at board meetings, seldom reacting to taunts and barbs from board members or speakers.

The board's heaviest artillery was the professors' survey. For eight academic professors ignorant of public school classrooms to study—in their spare time and on a budget of $10,000—the total curriculum of a system serving over 90,000 children struck Dr. Spears as outrageously funny. As did his fellow superintendents, Spears controlled access to information; so, through the staff, he monitored the professors. Candidly, he admitted that sections of the final report dealing with elementary schools were dismissed simply because the professors lacked expertise. And, Spears confessed, when the board asked him to evaluate the survey recommendations, he called attention only to those recommendations that would cost nothing to implement, that he had planned to do anyway, or that he could undertake without suffering any inconvenience.

In the three cities, then, external pressure groups made few gains in issues they defined as important. Robert Havighurst tallied up what had been undertaken in Chicago two years after he presented his report. Results: six mild, uncontroversial recommendations of twenty-two proposed were in varying stages of implementation. The tough ones had been ignored. The professors' survey produced even less; here, too, Harold Spears accepted what was feasible and rejected out of hand the rest. And the Model School Division, its limits shaped by the hand of Carl Hansen, was a bitter disappointment to its advocates. Labeled a failure by the local press, it nonetheless became an integral part of the school system after Hansen's departure. A decade after its birth, it was virtually indistinguishable in operation from the rest of the school system.[27] Thus, yards of newsprint devoted to criticisms of schools, numerous meetings with superintendents and boards, and countless lobbying efforts all amounted to few tangible returns for the efforts put out by pressure groups.

Superintendent responses had followed a pattern. Civil rights groups were perceived as illegitimate outsiders; federally subsidized reformers and professors were viewed similarly. Worse yet, many of these outsiders lacked professional know-how. The three administrators also responded to pressure by both subtly and openly redefining the problem. Willis took a broad, ambiguous, open-ended outside survey and converted it into one of limited scope. So, too, what began as an experimental, wide-open, innovative subsystem turned into Hansen's Model School Division, which focused on providing urgently needed social and school services to poor children. And Spears took general blasts at "progressive" and mushy schooling and narrowed them to curricular issues and questions of teacher working conditions. The sum total of this process was to reduce very complex—as well as ambiguous —issues into technical and routine matters that both superintendent and bureaucrat could manage.

Another strategy used effectively by Spears and Hansen—less so by Willis in this instance—was co-optation. Commonly used by institutional leaders under pressure—as were most of these strategies—co-optation was a method whereby critics' suggestions were adopted and shaped by the administrators to their specifications. By robbing the critics of their charges, the superintendents were in the position to point proudly to their own flexibility and reform-mindedness while reformers could only wail at the atrocities the superintendent and board had committed upon their ideas. Finally, the superintendents had in their repertoire of strategies the familiar ones used on desegregation demands: they could delay implementation of recommendations, plead lack of money and insufficient man-power, point to other pressing crises, or ignore those segments of the plan that they found objectionable.

Of course, differences among the three cities and their superintendents obviously existed. But this chapter has tried to highlight some of the important similarities among the three cities in environmental pressures, school governance mechanisms, roles of superintendents, and most important, the responses of the three urban school chiefs to external pressure. When these similarities are taken altogether, a number of observations emerge clearly.

First, there is the striking similarity in the responses of the three schoolmen to diverse pressures. All three saw the issue of de facto segregation as a non-school issue. It was political and had to be handled outside of school board–superintendent deliberations. Moreover, they reacted resentfully to suggestions that some children be distinguished racially from others; they saw themselves as color-blind and were proud of it. Feeling this way, the three administrators initially rejected demands of civil rights groups, then either co-opted, avoided, or delayed when the groups persisted in their requests. None of the three school chiefs pursued active negotiations with civil rights leaders. They believed that they were protecting schools from outside pressure groups who were out to undermine public schooling.

When outside pressure came from professional reformers on government payrolls or from university professors, the three schoolmen again redefined the problems of curriculum and inferior education for black children into questions of whether the outsiders had the expertise and professional experience to investigate technical issues of curriculum, survey construction, and the organization of a subsystem. By converting broad educational issues into specific technical questions, the school chiefs could delay, avoid, reject, and co-opt outsiders making surveys and setting up a model subsystem. This strategy of redefining problems into manageable, narrower questions left these administrators in the position of deciding what was proper or improper to pursue—a position of enormous strength that often defused short-term outside pressures.

At the same time, this similarity of response produces a puzzle. Three separate cities with distinctive political cultures, socioeconomic structures, and school systems of varying size had three school chiefs responding to diverse issues in a similar fashion. Why?

Unlocking the Puzzle

The following four models offer plausible explanations for the sequence of events in the three cities and the similarity in superintendent responses. In applying different models to the question, various facets of the possible answer appear.

Model 1: Socioeconomic and Demographic Forces

A rough outline of an argument coming from an advocate of this explanation might run like this. The massive exchange of population in big cities since World War II forced enormous changes upon urban institutions. With increasing numbers of poor, black families making demands on a system which was already hampered by an eroded tax base, city officials resorted to the limited range of responses within their narrow control—lest the city split apart over the twin issues of race and poverty. The 1954 Supreme Court desegregation decision and the subsequent spread of the civil rights movement northward heightened these pressures, which were being felt throughout the nation. The growing self-awareness of underprivileged ethnic groups and the impact of population shifts on the socioeconomic map of each city led to inevitable consequences that severely constrained big-city administrators in what they could or could not do.

Thus, who each superintendent was, what his training had been, which career pattern or tactics he used, and the bureaucracy and decision style of the school board—all mattered little in the larger picture. Like other urban officials, school administrators could do little else than follow the inevitably narrow range of responses left to them.

Imitation might further explain the similarity of responses from urban school chiefs. Caught by forces which they could not manipulate, superintendents learned from one another, copying the more successful of their colleagues. Professional journals, annual and monthly professional meetings, phone calls, and a keen eye on news items from other cities provided paths to learning. Executives desirous of surviving learned quickly which behaviors promised the most staying power on those issues largely beyond their control. Adaptation, not aggressive initiative, was the best they could hope to achieve.

Model 1, then, emphasizes those forces in the larger environment over which individual superintendents had little or no control.

Model 2: Political Bargaining

From the political bargaining model an explanation for similar responses might focus upon how three superintendents, caught up in situations in which boards of education, taxpayers, and community continually made conflicting demands upon them, developed coalitions with those elements in each group that valued the chief resources they possessed: organizational authority and professional expertise. When outside pressure built up, these coalitions of support enabled school bosses to respond the way they did without getting bounced.

Another possible explanation emphasizes how each board of education, under intense pressure from community to make certain changes, listened to and negotiated with those interest groups, ultimately bidding their executive to implement its wishes.

Whereas model 1 stresses the adaptiveness of a schoolman to external forces, model 2 focuses on the interaction between participants in a highly political process. External forces are important in the latter, of course, but only insofar as they introduce new interest groups, coalitions, and different actors to be accommodated within the decision-making process.

Model 3: Organizational Decision-Making

An advocate of this model might underscore the organizational commonalities in big-city school systems. Emphasis would be placed on bureaucratic procedures that reduced budget-making and curricular and instructional decision-making to formulas. The superintendent dealing with a large, unwieldy system might be likened to a helmsman who must depend on a gyroscope to navigate his steamer through fog. Since there was a lack of control over the organization, decisions were more or less automatic, with the school chiefs usually following the traditional ways of reacting to outside pressure. In effect, the three superintendents' responses to demands were system solutions for which each large organization had already developed programmed procedures.

This model may also be used to sketch out a system which works efficiently and effectively because it has carefully thought-out procedures for dealing with crises. This scenario accepts organizational decision-making as flowing from the powerful inner drive of the system but assumes that the process is manageable and subject to sensitive calibration by efficient administrators. From this view, similar responses of our superintendents resulted from rational men choosing among the various standard operating procedures that most closely approximated this situation.

Finally, another variation of this explanation would focus upon how the organization required the superintendent to play prescribed roles. Three administrators besieged by external pressures had to play out certain behaviors expected of them by their immediate staff, teachers, principals, and boards of education—not to mention their professional colleagues around the country—if they wished to survive. Expected to behave professionally, the superintendents would refuse to buckle in to what they saw as vested interests intent upon subverting public schools for special ends.

This model emphasizes the internal workings of the organization as a dominant factor in superintendent behavior. Organizational decision-making patterns, managerial control of the process, and the demands on leadership become key factors in explaining common responses of organizational leaders.

Model 4: Individual Leader

Explicit to this model of explanation is the belief that decisions are made by individuals responsible for their own actions. The quality of a person's decision is influenced by his or her intelligence, training, and experience.

If the individual actor is crucial to this explanatory model, how do we account for three different individuals arriving at roughly the same responses? The key here would be to emphasize the factors that reduced the leaders' range of responses. For example, one might stress the professional training, experience, and career line which the three had in common. Taught to be professional, each superintendent had to define the problem, study it, weigh alternatives, and choose the one that maximized the organization's goal; such learned behavior sharply limits the range of the three superintendents' responses to particular, traditional problems.

Another interpretation would underscore the role each of the three played as superintendent. While each brought distinct, unique personal traits to the role, the pressures of role expectations were sufficiently powerful that, given these demands, top administrators could only respond in certain well-defined ways.

By focusing upon the individual, this model shifts emphasis to factors neglected in previous explanations. While larger environmental forces, political bargaining, and the organization are important, the quality of an individual professional ultimately determines the outcomes of an event.

A plausible case can be made with any one of the four models. Yet none by itself can explain all the data satisfactorily. Nor are these models mutually exclusive, for they overlap in several areas. One is tempted to weave a reasonable explanation by using all of these models. Yet before succumbing to that impulse, let us consider the history of the urban superintendency to explore what the past offers as an explanation.

5 The Vulnerable Superintendent: Insecure Expert

If, indeed, past is prologue, an inquiry into the history of the urban superintendency might be able to suggest important clues to explaining the similar responses of these big-city administrators. A significant part of the answer to their behavior may lie in their conception of leadership roles: how did they view themselves as educational leaders?[1] To answer that question, we will need to examine historically the ideologies and functions of urban superintendents over the past century in an effort to discover the range of leadership roles which developed over time.

Origins

For most cities in the mid-nineteenth century, state legislatures and city councils had local school boards which were chartered to hire teachers, buy books, build schools, and supervise instruction. When cities were no more than oversized villages, the unpaid, popularly elected (or politically appointed) part-time trustees proved workable. With swelling city populations and soaring numbers of children, however, these unpaid, part-time board members found it increasingly burdensome to perform all their mandated duties while working full-time elsewhere. So as early as 1837 (in Buffalo) city boards began hiring superintendents to ease their official burdens.

The office of superintendent, then, did not evolve from the classroom, although many of the early appointees were drawn from the ranks of teachers. Rather, as one former schoolman reminded his readers, the first superintendent's duties ''originated in the delegation to him of powers every one of which belonged to the board and that the board still often exercises.'"[2] Child of the school board, the superintendency would mature, struggle with its parent endlessly, and never escape that fact of ancestry.

Most mid-nineteenth–century superintendents busied themselves with inspecting classes, examining applicants for teaching positions, conducting faculty meetings, helping to select textbooks, determining which pupils would be promoted, suspending incorrigible children, and keeping late office hours to meet with parents and teachers. Some schoolmen, in addition to these tasks, took minutes at board meetings, filed all reports and board records, made out bills for school expenses, and inspected furnaces and toilet facilities.[3]

Hiring and firing of teachers, letting of contracts, purchasing of books—all potent sources of political and economic influence within the community—remained the privileged domain of school trustees. Some boards asked their superintendents for advice in these areas; most did not. By the 1880s, with the superintendency barely a generation old, supervision of pupils and teachers was a mainstay of the job.

A local paper remembered long-time Brooklyn superintendent J. W. Bulkley, who industriously visited classes daily for his eighteen years in this way.

> There are members of the board who are ranged as old members who try in vain to remember ever having heard any suggestion from the superintendent touching public school management. Of the merits of the school books, the construction of school buildings, the grading of school studies . . . . The board never thought of consulting its superintendent and the superintendent never hazarded his own peace by troubling the board on such matters.[4]

Not all schoolmen, of course, were like Bulkley. William T. Harris in St. Louis (1868–80), James W. Greenwood in Kansas City (1874–1914), Aaron Gove in Denver (1874–1904), and John Philbrick (1856–78) actively worked with their boards to bring order out of the chaos of mushrooming school populations layered onto archaic forms of governance designed for village schools.

But most superintendents lacked the skills, charisma, or good fortune of these veterans to serve such long tenures. An urban schoolman who offered unsolicited advice or implemented a pet idea without gaining full board approval often found himself unemployed. Most superintendents at this time served under one-year contracts and went about their supervisory duties circumspectly, hoping to win reelection at year's end.

An Emerging Profession and Governance Reform

In the last two decades of the nineteenth century, when captains of corporations were shaking down their organizational behemoths into trimmer, more efficient operations and when evangelical faith in scientific rationality gripped the intellectual community, a loosely allied coalition of corporate-minded reformers, university professors, and concerned superintendents found urban schools slothful, inefficient, and hopelessly mired in corrupt politics. These reformers criticized the mindless order in factory-like city schools presided over by drill-sergeant superintendents; they felt that thirty- and forty-member school boards with standing committees were cumbersome and grossly inefficient. School trustees elected by ward were vulnerable to political chicanery and boondoggling. Office was sought by ''patientless doctors and clientless lawyers.''[5]

To reformers the source of the problem was how schools were governed. Boards of education, for example, should be smaller and drawn from upper class gentlemen interested in politics. Rather than the twenty-six board members in Cleveland or forty-two in Philadelphia there should be five or seven successful businessmen and professionals transacting school affairs. Smaller, city-wide (rather than ward-based) boards composed of the ''better'' classes would, they felt, eliminate the ''depth of cupidity and cold-blooded selfishness manifested by the partisan politicians.''[6]

The other half of the governance problem, according to reformers, was persistent lay interference in a superintendent's business. Board members haggled over which grammar book to use, whether to mandate a sloping or vertical method of penmanship, whether the board president's uncle would sell his lot for a new school building, or whether the new desks should be maple or oak.[7] Such negotiations, reformers argued, were best left to the experts: the superintendents.

Given their experience and scientific approach to problem-solving, superintendents could deal with each of these matters in a professional manner. ''The most notable examples of marked progress in city schools have been due to the wise commitment of their management to a superintendent selected because of his known ability, not merely to 'run the schools' but to devise, organize, direct and make successful a rational system of instruction,''[8] declared three schoolmen in an 1890 report to their colleagues.

Small, centralized boards under expert leadership, reformers concluded, would insulate school operations from corrupt politics leaving sufficient flexibility to professional schoolmen to root out inefficient, archaic practices while installing sound operating procedures. Left to the leadership of superintendents and small boards, business would be calmly transacted through rapid approval of the executive's recommendations.

By 1910 reform efforts had been largely successful. Urban school boards had shrunk from an average of sixteen members in 1895 to nine in 1915. Superintendent reports and annual meetings of the Department of Superintendence within the National Education Association were filled with praise of "expert" leadership, "efficiency-minded" schoolmen, and the rapid development of professional leadership. While the one effort urban schoolmen made to grasp complete independence from school boards in 1895 failed, their determined drive to gain greater authority met with success. A survey of urban superintendents in 1910 found almost half of the top administrators in twenty large cities satisfied with their powers. A handful made no comment, and only three clearly wanted more.[9]

Dominant Conceptions of Leadership 1870–1910

Uncovering what superintendents as a group have conceived leadership to be since 1870 is difficult. Since a conception is not a behavior pattern, what people wrote about is not necessarily what they did (although intentions emerge). In this chapter, attention will be focused on how city superintendents viewed the job of leading a school system. Wherever there is evidence suggesting how schoolmen operated, it will be introduced.

From the speeches, articles, discussions, and actions of urban schoolmen in the decades following 1870, ideal types of leadership roles were abstracted.[10] How these ideal types were derived, the evidence from which they were drawn, and the reasons why these and not other leadership roles developed will be described in the following pages.

First, a word on method. The enormous diversity in cities, in the origin of school boards and superintendencies as well as political cultures, diminishes the number of generalizations that can be made about schoolmen's conceptions of leadership. Such obstacles, however, have seldom stopped historians. When historians plow ahead, the usual procedure is to identify top school chiefs either by virtue of their position within professional ranks or simply by the volume of their writings and speeches. What they said and wrote are read carefully. Then, inductively, conclusions are drawn about what schoolmen conceived superintendent leadership should be.

Another approach would be to analyze carefully the annual proceedings between 1870 and 1950, since the Department of Superintendence (later renamed the American Association of School Administrators) was dominated by urban schoolmen during that period.[11] The speeches, discussions, resolutions, and published yearbooks would be examined to see what patterns, if any, emerged. In other words, because urban superintendents dominated the association, what they wrote, said, resolved, met in committees about, and spent money on might add up to a rough map of their concerns and interests which could be linked to particular leadership conceptions of the superintendency.

Still another procedure would be to identify particular city superintendents between 1870 and 1950 and locate what they wrote in educational journals. Here, again, the notion is that their articles provide evidence from which one can draw inferences about what they conceived the superintendency to be.

In order to present a convincing argument, all three approaches will be used to reach conclusions in this chapter.

From this large body of data, three conceptions of ideal types of superintendent leadership emerge: teacher-scholar, chief administrator, and negotiator-statesman. As with all descriptions of ideal types, no description of individuals is intended. The purpose is to call attention to general traits that characterized a conception of leadership role.

Teacher-Scholar

The view of superintendent as teacher-scholar surfaced early and vigorously.[12] In 1899 St. Louis superintendent W. T. Harris stated that the superintendent was a "specialist in matters of education." The most important job of the urban schoolman, he said, was making "good teachers out of poor ones." Veteran superintendent James W. Greenwood of Kansas City divided a superintendent's job into office work, school work, and outside work. He saw his job clearly: "I do not trouble the members of the board . . . . They watch the business matters and I look after the schools." Between 7:30 and 9:00 each morning, he took care of clerical and administrative work, from "sending out substitutes to readmitting mischievous boys." The bulk of the day was spent "visiting schools and inspecting the work." When schools closed, he returned to his office and remained until 6:00, doing office work and interviewing teachers. "In one sense"—and Greenwood must have sighed as he said it—"I am a sort of mill—grinding out everything."

Horace Tarbell, Providence, Rhode Island, superintendent for almost two decades, feared that a city superintendent might "become a business man, a manager of affairs, rather than continue to maintain the attitude of the scholar and become more and more the teacher." Worse yet, "he may become the politician."

Indianapolis schoolman Lewis Jones felt that the proper function of supervisors and administrators was to study psychology, child study, and methodology with teachers. "If the superintendent," he said to fellow schoolmen, "can come to be the acknowledged leader in such broad consideration of . . . education he will have done much to enlarge the horizons of his teachers."

These superintendents wrote extensively on the history and philosophy of education as well as on how best to teach. The responsibility of the profession was summed up in an 1890 report on the role of the superintendent:

It must be made his recognized duty to train teachers and inspire them with high ideals; to revise the course of study when new light shows that improvement is possible; to see that pupils and teachers are supplied with needed appliances for the best possible work; to devise rational methods of promoting pupils.

Administrative Chief

The man-in-charge image generated an enormous range of analogies and metaphors in schoolmen's speeches in the late 1800s. The superintendent was seen as a "prime minister" and "the helmsman who must consider wind, steam, storm and tide"; he was also "the governor and the fly-wheel of the educational system," its "chief executive officer."[13] Themes of initiative, authority, instruction and curriculum planning, and careful management resonated through speeches and reports of urban schoolmen in these years.

Former superintendent and editor E. E. White chaired a committee that reported to top administrators. The "one essential condition of progress for a city superintendent," the committee said, is that "the taking of the initiative be his right and duty." Andrew Draper campaigned aggressively for a strong superintendency. "I am not in favor of limiting the authority of city superintendents," he argued at one national meeting. "If I could, . . . I would give them almost autocratic powers within their sphere of duty and action and then I would hold them responsible for results." These ideas shaped his committee's report on organizing city school systems: "The superintendent of instruction," it concluded, "should be charged with the responsibility of making that [instruction] professional and scientific and should be given the position and authority to accomplish that end."[14]

One model that schoolmen were asked to copy was the Cleveland Plan, inaugurated in 1892. Under this plan, a small school council hired a director with complete executive authority. The school director appointed a superintendent of instruction who hired and fired all of his assistants and teachers without interference from the council or school director. Andrew S. Draper, superintendent for two years under this structure and the man who dismissed almost a hundred teachers for incompetence (a fact that he often referred to publicly) fervently believed that the superintendent was the expert who directed, planned, and executed school affairs.[15]

In 1895 Cleveland hosted the NEA convention, at which a committee, chaired by Andrew Draper, produced a report urging further centralization of powers into the superintendent's hands. With few reservations, fellow superintendents enthusiastically adopted the Draper Report as well as the phrase that soon became a maxim among urban schoolmen: "bodies legislate and individuals execute." Likewise, veteran superintendent Frank Spaulding gained approving nods from his listeners when he said that "what the school administrator has to do [is] . . . project ideas ahead, then work up to them."

In fact, some saw administration as the primary role of the superintendent, and so the concept of the superintendent as a "man of affairs," economically managing buildings, fiscal affairs, and personnel, emerged early in the profession. Veteran superintendent R. W. Stevenson of Columbus wrote that "the Superintendent is the best manager who can make his schools efficient in training the youth of his city . . . at the least possible expense." A few years later, however, Denver superintendent Aaron Gove vigorously defined the urban schoolman's job as being larger and more important than teaching and supervising teachers.

It may be doubtless true that the professional efforts of superintendents directed only to the teaching side of his duties would result in a greater efficiency in and about the schoolroom, but these advances would be largely checked by neglect of the other business side of a superintendent's duties.

The construction and location of schoolhouses; the relations of the administration to the industrial and commercial communities, especially to expenditures ... the too lavish or too niggardly appropriations for furniture, apparatus and supplies ... are matters ... within the direct duties of the superintendent.

Gove feared that an unqualified superintendent would be "incompetent ... to participate in the business affairs of the corporation whose executive officer he is or should be."[16]

By 1890, disagreement over the nature of the superintendency was expressed in speeches, articles, and heated discussions (conducted, of course, with genteel courtesy). Some argued that the functions of a big-city superintendent should be separated into two distinct jobs (i.e., business manager and superintendent of instruction, the latter a position recommended in the Draper Report); others maintained that the superintendent should simply surrender to the inevitable impact of largeness upon school systems and become an efficient manager.

Former Cleveland superintendent B. A. Hinsdale saw two classes of schoolmen. Leaving out the "nobodies, there are now ... two classes of superintendents, the line of division of which is by no means a hard and fast one, running between business and professional duties." He concluded that superintendents are either "men of the office" or they are "of the schoolroom," a split he had written about as early as 1888. Hinsdale predicted that in large cities the "superintendents will more and more tend to machinery and administration; that he will become even more an office man than he is now."[17]

Little consensus existed, for there were still other educators who agreed with New York Superintendent William Maxwell that the issue was not a matter of whether the superintendency consisted of two separate jobs or whether the school chief should capitulate to managerial duties. There was a third way: the man whom the board of education hires "should be both a schoolman and administrator."[18]

Thus, well before schoolmen had adapted the technology of scientific management to school affairs in the World War I years and later, several competing views on the nature of the superintendency were well established in the thinking of urban educators.

Negotiator-Statesman

Sensitivity to the impact of the community, to the diversity of groups from which schools need both financial and moral support, and to the inherent vulnerability of the superintendent's position led to a third conception of the superintendent: the negotiator-statesman. There was a good deal said about the political side of superintending, though it was cautiously worded, restrained by the knowledge of the taint of corrupt politics, job-grubbing teachers, and venal trustees.

"While every year new men come upon the school board for the sake of keeping in employment certain teachers," observed Baltimore superintendent William Creery in 1873, "it is the part of wisdom for us not to claim power but to create a popular sentiment." Ten years later, one of his brother schoolmen concluded that the "work of a superintendent is also political in its character. He ought to be a politician." But, he quickly assured his listeners, he was not advocating that a superintendent engage in partisan politics or be a politician "in the common acceptation of that term," only "one versed in the science of government." A few decades later, yet another superintendent addressing his colleagues reminded them that

when we can secure the cooperation of a few influential men and women of the community, the support of two or three newspapers to whose opinion the public listens, the influence of clubs—clubs of the gentler sort—the endorsement of a chamber of commerce, perhaps we have taken a long step in the direction of making outside conditions favorable to successful management.

Schoolmen such as Maxwell, Gove, and Harris seldom lost sight of this conception, even though they did not generally share the same views on the superintendent's role. "The superintendent," Maxwell pointed out, "should be not merely a schoolmaster but a statesman who has a definite policy to carry out and who knows how to take advantage of time and opportunity to secure results."

Evidence drawn from speeches and articles of respected big-city superintendents in these decades reinforce the existence of these three conceptions. While various schoolmen said the nature of the superintendency dictated one or another of these leadership roles, others urged combinations. Some, like R. W. Stevenson, coalesced all into an ideal: "As the superintendent of instruction, [he should be] scholarly, judicious, systematic and comprehensive; as the manager of finance, shrewd, economical and liberal; and as a politician, discreet, active, fearless and patriotic."[19]

Persisting Patterns in Conceptions of Leadership, 1870–1970

In exploring ideas about leadership from 1870 to 1970, one must reckon with the work of Raymond Callahan. In one book and a number of related articles, Callahan has developed an historical overview of the superintendency that has influenced other scholars' views of the past century of school administration.[20]

Callahan saw the superintendency between 1865 and 1964 in terms of four dominant conceptions, one succeeding another. Between 1865 and 1900, the prevailing ideal type was the scholarly educator. This was superceded by a business manager conception (1910–1930) which, in turn, was followed by an educational statesman ideal (1930–1954). According to Callahan, the current dominant conception of superintendent is that of an expert in applied social science. Recognizing that there was overlap in these trends and that the dominance of certain ideal types does not exclude mavericks, Callahan has nonetheless been able to lay out a pattern of consecutive succession in ideas about what a superintendent should be.

The view taken in this chapter, however, is that each of the three ideal types of the superintendency presented earlier—all of which are quite similar to Callahan's formulations—did not automatically exit as the other appeared; instead, all three were vigorously present at any point during the last century. Moreover, the dominance of particular ideal types simply was not as clear-cut as Callahan suggests. Other facets of Callahan's work will be dealt with later in this chapter.

The problem with the kind of evidence presented here and in Callahan's work is that the particular strength of what educators said, and their acceptance or rejection among urban schoolmen, cannot be accurately assessed. Drawn from speeches and writings of certain schoolmen, such evidence seldom persuades convincingly since it is—there is no other word—selective. Thus, historians must search carefully for indications of the degree to which these leadership conceptions were accepted.

Between 1870 and 1910 the Department of Superintendence was a gathering place for professors, state and rural schoolmen, and big-city superintendents. Its annual convention served as "a school for superintendents, a clearinghouse where educational ideas are exchanged, where difficult questions are answered." Three to four days of meetings, round-table discussions, and informal evening sessions where scotch and sherry mellowed the cigar smoke, all made annual meetings "a post-graduate course for superintendents who would stand in line for promotion in their professions and who would keep up with the ever-changing ... standards in school work."[21]

Big-city superintendents dominated the organizational machinery of the department. Consider, for example, that in these four decades, 76 percent of the officers were urban superintendents. Moreover, W. T. Harris, Andrew Draper, William Maxwell, not only were presidents of the association but also chaired important committees and authored key resolutions. Kansas City's James Greenwood, Providence's Horace Tarbell, Cincinnati's John Hancock, Columbus's R. W. Stevenson, and Seattle's Frank Cooper were tireless workers within the department. Discussions, resolutions, committee reports, and agendas were permeated by the concerns, interests, fears, and hopes of the officers that led the association. Tastemakers and pacesetters, big-city schoolmen were the apex of the department.

In order to find the prevailing views of these urban educators, 179 superintendents were researched who served between 1870 and 1910 in a total of twenty-four large cities. (In this period, a large city was one with a population of more than 100,000; Dallas, Atlanta, and Seattle were included although they did not meet this criterion until 1920.) Of that number, 59 (33 percent) attended the annual meetings of the Department of Superintendence and delivered prepared presentations to their colleagues there. Their speeches, along with their resolutions, round-table discussion topics, and committee reports, were itemized, grouped, and then tallied. Specific categories under which the results were grouped were used as indicators of a particular trend in conception of leadership; thus, speeches, resolutions, and such that dealt with the categories of curriculum, instruction, supervision of teachers, and pupil services would show a tendency toward the teacher-scholar viewpoint.

Table 8 shows the conceptions, categories, and their change over the years. Table 9 shows the results of grouping the writings of urban superintendents in three influential educational journals. While differences do occur, there is a rough convergence between the two tables. All conceptions of the superintendency were present prior to 1910, with the teacher-scholar leadership conception apparently dominating the thinking of superintendents.[22]

Dominant Conceptions of Leadership 1910–1950

In the next four decades, between 1910 and 1950, shifts in these views occur. Consider table 10, which includes the earlier period. Three conclusions emerge. First, a shift away from the teacher-scholar conception

Table 8   Percentages of Superintendents Holding Three Major Leadership
Conceptions Drawn from the *Proceedings* of the Department of
Superintendence, 1871–1910

	1871–1880	1881–1890	1891–1900	1901–1910
Teacher-scholar (Categories: curriculum, instruction, supervision, pupil services)	60	46	53	63
Chief administrator (Categories: finance, school plant, school district organization, management)	20	13	14	15
Negotiator-statesman (Categories: school board, community, federal and state concerns)	12	14	13	11

SOURCE: NEA, *Journal of Proceedings and Addresses,* 1871–1910.

NOTE: There were two additional categories (Aims and Functions of Education, and Nature of the Superintendency), making a total of thirteen. These two, however, contained diverse items that could not be placed cleanly within a single leadership conception. Thus, the percentages will not add up to 100 percent because of the absence of these two categories.

toward the chief administrator and negotiator-statesman took place between 1900 and 1920. Second, although it was dramatic in a few categories, the shift was a slow, steady drift from one view to the others. Third, by 1950, when Benjamin Willis was superintendent in Buffalo and Carl Hansen and Harold Spears were assistant superintendents—all three members of the American Association of School Administrators—it had become clear that the managerial leadership conceptions were stronger than the others, yet both the teacher-scholar and negotiator-statesman views had survived quite well in schoolmen's thinking. When only the writings of big-city superintendents were examined, results were as shown in table 11.

A number of discrepancies between percentages in tables 10 and 11 raise questions. Some of the conceptions do not show up as strongly as when the evidence was drawn from the Department of Superintendence and AASA. Yet this does not mean that one is accurate and the other is

Table 9	Percentages of Superintendents Holding Three Major Leadership Conceptions, as Drawn from Their Writings in Three Journals, 1881–1910		
	1881–1890	1891–1900	1901–1910
Teacher-scholar	47 (46)	54 (53)	51 (63)
Chief administrator	5 (13)	18 (14)	19 (15)
Negotiator-statesman	0 (12)	15 (14)	11 (13)

SOURCE: Ninety-one articles in *Education, Educational Review,* and the *American School Board Journal* between 1880 and 1910 were used.

NOTE: Percentages in parenthesis are from table 8. As in table 8, the percentages will not total 100.

not or that both are flawed. What does emerge is a coarse similarity between the two tables and, more important, further corroboration of the three conclusions cited previously. Thus there is a rough mapping of urban superintendents' activities within their association which, along with their writings, offers some crude estimates of the particular strength of each leadership conception at different points in time over the last century.

Consider, too, other data drawn from studies that bear on these changing leadership views. The shift from a teacher-scholar to chief administrator can be seen in the trend toward formal appointment of the superintendent as executive officer to the board of education rather than as superintendent of instruction or board secretary. Between 1883 and 1910, fourteen large cities had made the formal change.[23] As school reformers succeeded in their centralization efforts, superintendents gained authority and, probably, a changing view of leadership.

By 1910 many schoolmen felt their powers had increased. Fifty big-city chiefs were surveyed on their feelings about their appointment power, determination of the budget and courses of study, and so on. Almost 90 percent felt that the superintendent's power had definitely increased. Moreover, more than half that answered the question felt that the causes for increased power were either the "appreciation of expert administration," the "necessity of effective administration in a large business," or "the need for expert management."[24]

Table 10 — Percentages of Superintendents Holding Three Major Leadership Conceptions, as drawn from Department of Superintendence and American Association of School Administrators, 1871–1950

	1871–1880	1881–1890	1891–1900	1901–1910	1911–1920	1921–1930	1931–1940	1941–1950
Teacher-scholar	60	46	53	63	32	32	28	27
curriculum	24	19	13	15	12	15	10	5
instruction	12	9	7	5	5	2	2	7
supervision	8	17	25	23	7	13	8	6
pupil services	16	1	8	20	8	2	8	9
Chief administrator	20	13	14	15	27	26	31	34
finance	0	0	0	2	5	7	11	6
school plant	4	0	4	2	2	4	1	6
district organization	4	2	3	5	7	5	1	3
management	12	11	7	6	15	10	18	15
Negotiator-statesman	12	14	13	11	26	19	25	27
school board	0	0	3	2	3	2	2	3
community	0	1	5	3	10	7	14	17
federal and state relations	12	13	5	6	13	10	9	7

SOURCE: National Education Association, *Journal of Proceedings and Addresses*, 1871–1940; American Association of School Administrators, *Official Report*, 1940–1950.

Table 11		Percentages of Superintendents Holding Three Major Leadership Conceptions, as Drawn from the Writings of 251 Big-City Superintendents, 1881–1950					
	1881–1890	1891–1900	1901–1910	1911–1920	1921–1930	1931–1940	1941–1950
Teacher-scholar	47 (46)	48 (53)	43 (63)	29 (32)	44 (32)	28 (28)	33 (27)
Chief administrator	5 (13)	18 (14)	19 (15)	31 (27)	37 (26)	33 (31)	34 (34)
Negotiator-statesman	0 (14)	15 (13)	11 (11)	12 (26)	7 (19)	10 (25)	15 (27)

SOURCES: Articles prior to 1928 come from *Education, Educational Review,* and the *American School Board Journal,* 1880–1910. After 1928, articles were compiled from *Education Index.*

NOTE: Percentages in parenthesis come from table 10.

By 1920 most big-city administrators could appoint and dismiss principals and teachers, determine new programs and policies in both curriculum and instruction, select textbooks, and prepare the budgets. All of these initiatory powers, of course, required board approval for implementation.[25] Still, the power to act had passed from the board room to the superintendent's office.

At the same time that they were gaining power, superintendents were becoming more socially active. By the 1920s and 1930s, more and more school executives had moved into community activities. One study reported that 41 percent of urban superintendents were officers in the local Rotary, Kiwanis, Chamber of Commerce, and similar groups. A decade later, the figure soared to 68 percent.[26]

In a 1950 survey, big-city superintendents reported how they allotted time during their average 62-hour work week: personnel administration, 12 percent; financial administration, 10 percent; school plant management, 8 percent; general planning, 30 percent; instructional leadership, 18 percent; pupil services, 5 percent; public relations, 16 percent. "General planning" probably included curriculum, supervision, and other areas. Apart from this one category, the time which superintendents allotted to their tasks seems to reflect leadership conceptions of the period rather well.[27]

No pat unchallengeable case has been constructed here. Still the emergence of particular leadership conceptions, their existence over the years, and their shifting in importance from decade to decade have now been more firmly established than they were when we had to rely upon selected quotes from particular big-city superintendents.

Why These Conceptions?

A partial answer to this question has already been suggested. The teacher-scholar conception derived directly from the mandate of school boards to their first appointees. Consider further that part-time elected (or appointed) boards of education authorized by law to make policy could hire and fire their superintendents. From the very birth of the superintendency, then, there was a fundamental layman-schoolman split as well as insecurity of tenure.

Job insecurity was a constant worry to schoolmen. Until the early twentieth century the usual practice had been for a board to offer an annual contract to its administrator. Many schoolmen viewed their job as a delicate exercise in satisfying their employer. Diplomatic skills, a bent for negotiation, and a high tolerance for compromise were necessary to survive annual re-election by the board—in other words, the superintendent had to play the role of negotiator-statesman. "Politics," a word that so many urban superintendents detested, described significant aspects of the behavior of superintendents such as Greenwood, Gove, and Philbrick, and others who stretched annual or indefinite contracts into two or more decades of service. Furthermore, city school surveys in the 1920s, the Great Depression, and world wars all affected urban schoolmen. Alert to the necessity of practicing aggressive public relations, they often attended chamber of commerce luncheons and gave speeches to local Rotary Clubs yet avoided any outward appearance of politics.

Reformer efforts between 1890 and 1910 successfully shrank school board size and duties while turning over more and more rule-making authority to professionals. Still veteran schoolmen had reason to feel insecure. When Willard Goslin, an AASA president and a respected superintendent with a sterling record in a number of cities, was summarily booted out of office in Pasadena, California, in 1950, an electric shock crackled through the ranks of school executives. It was no secret that after eight decades, professional schoolmen remained vulnerable and insecure.

If job insecurity helps to explain the growth of the conception of the superintendent as negotiator-statesman, then professional insecurity may also help explain the further development of the teacher-scholar leadership conception and the origins of the chief administrator ideal. Confronted by law boards of education, sensitive to the signals of their constituents, and unable to attend full-time to school affairs, big-city superintendents in the late nineteenth century had only two commodities to offer: a folk wisdom of schooling gained from experience and the time to spend applying that wisdom to their work. What enhanced the superintendent's folk wisdom and availability were sweeping national changes that had profound influence upon the course of the superintendency.

Ballooning populations swelled city schools, forcing organizational changes within school systems. The prevailing progressive reform movement that focused upon municipal improvements embraced the ethic of efficiency and looked to experts employing scientific procedures to solve city problems. This ethos was also embraced by many schoolmen and board members who came to believe that superintendents were the experts capable of scientifically dealing with school issues.

The concept of the superintendent as expert can be found in Department of Superintendence proceedings as early as 1873.[28] By the 1890s the belief was entrenched within the department and was often expressed in writings of urban schoolmen. It was buttressed by a belief system which held up organization, rationality, and efficiency as a new trinity for an emerging profession. If superintendents could convince lay boards of their expertise, professionalism, and the rational approach to decision-making, then few boards could challenge them. In an era of almost unanimous agreement that organizations should be run scientifically and efficiently, schoolmen became experts. Professional expertise gave urban school executives a pedestal upon which they could stand apart from and above the messy politics that invariably occurred within boards of education. Furthermore, it gave them a major resource with which to bargain with the board. In doing so, administrators lessened somewhat their job insecurity.

To put the argument another way, the concept of professional expertness—spreading as it did from the larger progressive movement—was embraced passionately by schoolmen probably as a means of decreasing their vulnerability to lay interference; but it was also adopted out of a sincere belief in scientific rationality as the solution to educational problems. This, of course, is neither the first nor the last time that fervent ideals and occupational self-interest marched to the same tune.

From the image of the professional expert grew the idea of a chief administrator who conducted the school machine like an expert engineer. The chief administrator planned, initiated, and executed decisions with dispatch. The chief was conductor and engineer. Leaning heavily on management skills, the school boss strove for a smoothly humming operation. After 1910 a variety of such school experts developed within the profession.

Graduate schools of education began introducing administration courses. And with the frenetic burst of city school surveys, both movements interacted with the introduction of scientific management à la Frederick Taylor to produce a bewildering variety of professional experts. In the 1920s and 1930s no facet of school administration escaped the scrutiny of education professors, survey teams, and efficiency experts. Everything that moved (and didn't move) was counted, numbered, categorized, and costed out. A superintendent could win the reputation of being an administrative leader, a plant man, good personnel type, solid business administrator, or dependable budget man.

In short, then, three basic leadership conceptions of superintendents were established between 1870 and 1950. Each one waxed and waned as time passed, yet none disappeared. They competed simultaneously; they were durable. They arose from the very nature of the superintendent-board relationship. Competing role demands beset the superintendent. He was to be chief executive, professional expert on education, advisor to the board on the staff, and supervisor. Around these competing demands of the superintendent grew diverse views of the position.

The Callahan Vulnerability Thesis Examined

This interpretation of leadership conceptions differs in a number of respects from the work of Raymond Callahan, whose writings have heavily influenced theory and interpretation about top administrators since the turn of the century.

Apart from arguing that there was a succession of dominant views of the superintendent—a point dealt with earlier in this chapter—Callahan stressed that the vulnerability of the superintendent has been the chief if not the sole factor in changing conceptions. Referring to the shift from scholar-educator to business manager, he pointed out that "the change was a direct result of the impact of powerful social forces on the one side and the institutional weakness of educators, especially the superintendent, . . . on the other." More specifically, the very theme of Callahan's major work, *Education and the Cult of Efficiency,* is that schoolmen embraced the technology of scientific management after 1910 "to defend themselves and to keep their jobs in a business-dominated, efficiency-conscious society." Job insecurity and the "direct influence of business on school administrators" sum up his vulnerability thesis.

Callahan relates this thesis to the growth of graduate education courses in administration after 1910 that better prepared schoolmen to manage public schools. "Just as schoolmen adopted the business and industrial procedures . . . largely to demonstrate efficiency and to maintain themselves thereby," Callahan concluded, "so the attendance at graduate school and the acquisition of credits and degrees served the same purpose."[29]

Rather than agree or disagree with his strongly stated value positions (he calls, for example, the capitulation of schoolmen to business values "an American Tragedy") or analyze his use of sources, it might be useful to pose a series of propositions based upon the assumption that Callahan is correct in his vulnerability thesis.[30] Consider, for example, the following:

1. If vulnerability to external pressure is true, then massive changes in school population should, over time, lead to demands for more schools, demands for more funds, shifts in board membership, and ultimately an increased turnover of superintendents. ("The Changing Conceptions of the Superintendency," p. 7)

2. If the business-managerial image was fastened upon the superintendency, then during the Great Depression when that image was tarnished and Americans began losing faith in businessmen and their values, there should have been an increase in superintendent turnover. (*Education and the Cult of Efficiency,* p. 47)

3. If superintendents were successful in embracing efficiency technology after 1918 and thereby protecting their jobs until the 1960s, superintendent turnover should have been much higher prior to that year and steadily decreased in subsequent decades until 1960. (Ibid., pp. 110, 248–55)

4. If superintendents were successful in embracing efficiency technology after 1918, their contracts, as a rule, should have been shorter prior to that date and longer afterwards. (Ibid., p. 110)

5. If superintendents protected their jobs by going to graduate school and obtaining credentials, more education among superintendents should lead to decreased turnover. (Ibid., p. 208)

To test these propositions one type of school administrator, the big-city superintendent, was chosen. Over 250 school chiefs from twenty-four cities between 1870 and 1970 were identified, both in the years that

they were appointed and the years in which they left the superintendency. If the thesis has any explanatory power, it should apply to this
group. Figure 1 plots the peaks and valleys on the average number of

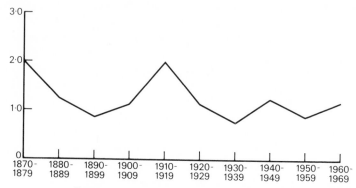

FIG. 1. Mean number of superintendents appointed per decade for
twenty-four cities, 1870–1970

SOURCES: No listing of superintendents by city for this period exists.
Statistics on schoolmen in each city over the past century were compiled by going through annual reports city by city to get approximate
dates of tenure. For statistics between 1940 and 1970 the following
were used: U.S. Office of Education, *Directory,* 1941–1968; *Who's
Who,* 1952–1972.

superintendent appointments in the twenty-four cities over the last century. The graph charts superintendent turnover. The second graph (fig.
2) charts the increases and decreases in school population over the same
period of time in the same twenty-four cities. A number of studies have
stressed the powerful impact of accelerating population on school operations. Table 12 is drawn from a study of urban superintendents in
nineteen cities before 1900.

A close examination of each graph and of table 12 will show that for
the first three propositions the thesis doesn't hold. While for some
decades there does appear to be a relationship between swelling numbers of students and an increased number of appointments (1900–1920),
for other decades an inverse relationship seems to exist (1920–1960)—
even allowing for a decade's lag. For proposition two, figure 2 shows
that instead of increased turnover during the 1930s as predicted, the
superintendency was more stable than it had been in large cities up to
that point in this century. The third statement predicted a turning point
in superintendent appointments around World War I. While that decade
yielded the second highest departure rate in the century and while there

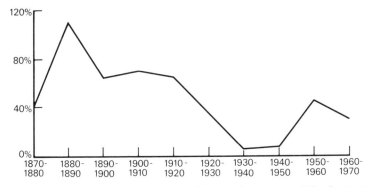

Fig. 2. Mean percentage of increase in school population for twenty-four large cities, 1870–1970

Sources: United States Office of Education, *Biennial Survey of Education,* 1911, vol. 2, pp. 715–26; ibid., 1920–22, vol. 2, pp. 94–101; ibid., 1939–40, vol. 2, pp. 44–51; U.S. Commissioner of Education, *Report,* 1890–91, pp. 1164–81; ibid., 1880, pp. 414–20; ibid., 1871, pp. 574–79; National Education Association, *Research Report,* December 1961, pp. 10–20.

was a decrease in turnover for the following two decades, the peaks and valleys pattern reasserts itself. Of more importance is table 12, which reveals that turnover fluctuated broadly from city to city before 1900 and suggests that the political culture or other factors explain broad diversity in appointment patterns.

The fourth proposition is at least partly supported by table 12. Although the pattern of longer contracts had developed by 1900 (probably as a result of the centralization reforms), well before the efficiency spasm shook the schools, after 1920 contracts do lengthen, as predicted.

For the fifth statement, consider these figures: in 1921 63 percent of big-city superintendents had masters degrees and Ph.D.'s; in 1931, 60 percent; in 1950, 76 percent; and in 1970, 81 percent.[31] Given this information, the graph of superintendent appointments (figure 2) suggests some positive relationships between graduate degrees and turnover between 1920 and 1940, but none after that. Moreover, before 1920, when most big-city superintendents lacked even graduate level work, no relationship is apparent.

Testing Callahan's point of view against a large sample of big-city superintendents raises further doubts as to whether his conceptualizations and conclusions are justified, for another question arising from Callahan's thesis remains. After 1910 was there a sudden dramatic assault by efficiency-intent critics on vulnerable schoolmen that led to

Table 12.   Rate of Turnover among Urban
              Superintendents, from Year of
              Origin to 1900

	Total from inception to 1900	Shortest period served	Longest period served	Avg. years served (mean)
Atlanta	2	8	21	14
Baltimore	4	2	18	9
Boston	4	2	22	12
Chicago	7	2	13	7
Cincinnati	9	1	12	5
Cleveland	8	2	15	6
Denver	3	1	26	10
Detroit	6	1	11	6
Indianapolis	9	1	10	5
Los Angeles	23	1	8	2
Milwaukee	13	1	9	3
New Orleans	13	1	13	4
New York	4	3	21	12
Philadelphia	2	8	9	8
Pittsburgh	2	1	31	16
St. Louis	12	1	15	5
San Francisco	20	1	4	2
Seattle	3	2	10	6
Washington, D.C.	4	1	15	8

SOURCE: Adapted from Theodore Reller, *The Development of the City Superintendency of Schools* (privately published, 1935), pp. 126–27.

massive departures of superintendents, as Callahan's thesis suggests? In short, was there a crisis? Or was this a shift of leadership conceptions that came as the cumulative result of interacting factors—such as the sizeable growth of large city systems, the impact of business ideology, and results from the concerted efforts of earlier progressive school reformers—which combined with the historic vulnerability of superintendents?

Because Callahan links his thesis to the increased departure rate which began in 1912, perhaps an examination of urban superintendents who left office may shed light on this issue. From 1910 to 1919 there were forty-three big-city schoolmen who left positions in twenty-six cities. All were identified by name, and their reasons for leaving were investigated.

Fourteen (32 percent) exited prior to 1912, the year Callahan marked as the onset of the scientific management crisis. Of the remaining twenty-nine, six (14 percent) had died in office or had retired without controversy after at least three decades of public school service. Five (12 percent) moved on to larger cities or other major posts—these were interpreted as promotions or voluntary moves by the superintendent. Three (7 percent) exited due to strictly internal struggles with boards of education that had had long histories prior to the entrance of Frederick Taylor. Thus, 65 percent of superintendent departures can be accounted for without reference to Callahan's assertion that the onslaught of efficiency-minded critics began in 1912.

Of the remaining fifteen administrators, three (7 percent) appeared to have left as a result of city surveys. These surveys were normally conducted by college professors and superintendents imbued with a passion for scientific management. One investigator, however, who examined all the city surveys undertaken between 1910 and 1927 cautioned his readers that there "is no relationship between time at which the surveys are made and the term of office of the superintendent."[32] The three who did leave office can be accounted for as a direct or indirect result of surveys in their city, but no overall pattern exists.

For the final twelve superintendents (28 percent) who exited, no data could be found. They may have retired, resigned for reasons unrelated to efficiency matters, left for better jobs, or indeed could have been nudged out as a result of a concern for scientific management. In view of this data, it would seem overzealous to link the efficiency movement in schools directly to superintendent turnover.

A final aspect of Callahan's vulnerability thesis is that the products of the efficiency movement—that is, business values and management skills—pervaded graduate training programs for administrators. In subsequent decades, these schools cranked out business managers. Callahan stresses repeatedly the impact of educational administration texts, curricula, and professors upon the shaping of the superintendent as business manager.[33] The captains of education, he stresses, were not superintendents; they were professors Elwood Cubberley, George Strayer, E. C. Elliot, Franklin Bobbitt, and brethren. They wrote, taught, and directed research at Stanford, Teachers College, University of Chicago, Wisconsin, and other large institutions. But knowing how many Cubberley texts were sold, how many students Strayer taught, how many speeches Bobbitt gave, or the types of administration courses at Ohio State still leaves the basic question of impact unanswered. Perhaps impact of training in day-to-day administration cannot be assessed with any degree of precision. If that is so, then exaggerating the influence of professional training programs upon the thinking and performance of superintendents would be as grievous as dismissing it.

Some facts may help. Graduate education in administration was just getting underway after 1910. In 1921, most big-city superintendents had masters degrees (63 percent), but few of these degrees were in education. Furthermore, 80 percent had had their last training course in education five or more years earlier. The heyday of educational administration with a pronounced bias toward business management occurred during the 1920s and 1930s. Between 1910 and 1933 almost 300 dissertations in school administration were submitted for doctoral degrees. Not one candidate ever became a big-city superintendent. When Callahan studied forty-three careers of those awarded doctorates, he found that seven (16 percent) were suburban and small-city superintendents at one time or another in their career. More striking was his finding that 77 percent became full-time education professors.[34]

Urban superintendents were queried in 1950 about their preparation in administration. Only 12 percent found courses in financial administration helpful. Moreover, over 30 percent found their training in school plant management, personnel administration, and fiscal affairs least helpful. Over 50 percent of the superintendents reported that their courses in instructional leadership were most helpful.[35]

Self reports are subject to error. Still, when one considers the diversity of topics on which big-city superintendents were writing and speaking to colleagues at professional meetings, then one begins to question whether universities really did manage to stamp out graduate school administration students from the same mold—as some historians claim.

Over the course of his career, an urban superintendent responded to many signals—day-to-day experiences within a large, complex organization, professional contacts, external pressures, and professional education curricula. Graduate training was only one of many experiences that, as the years passed, probably receded into the background. Based upon evidence that the three leadership conceptions existed well before the efficiency mania struck, and based upon the data examining various facets of Callahan's vulnerability thesis, serious doubts arise about the persuasiveness of a single-factor explanation. A more plausible interpretation would stress interacting factors such as growing school systems, impact of business ideology, and influence of earlier progressive school reformers as they combined to cause the historic insecurity of urban schoolmen.

It would be mistaken, however, to dismiss the thesis of vulnerability altogether. Few knowledgeable observers would seriously question the statement that superintendents were vulnerable to lay boards of education or that powerful, cross-cutting pressures from the business community and other interest groups penetrated and influenced both board and superintendent actions. To what extent and in what ways this was so, and what the consequences were, are complicated questions that resist simple, single cause-effect explanations. The problem lies in using Callahan's thesis to explain specific superintendent behavior at a certain point in time rather than seeing the school chief's historic vulnerability and conflicting role expectations as the sources for the differing leadership conceptions that schoolmen shaped to their own personalities and operating styles.

Because Callahan views vulnerability only in terms of external penetration, he leaves the impression that schoolmen were unable to defend themselves. This chapter suggests that though superintendents have been vulnerable—both before and after "efficiency management" became a catch phrase—they found ways of coping with ever-threatening, turbulent surroundings. The development of different conceptions of superintendent leadership among them can be seen as one kind of survival device to stake out a protective perimeter within which they could function. These conceptions gained prominence in particular periods, sometimes overlapping and even combining within the same person, depending upon—and this seems to be the crucial variable—external pressures.

The environment (specific economic, political, and demographic pressures in the community) seems to act as a massive, crude sorter determining the larger set of circumstances in which particular leadership conceptions can effectively (or ineffectively) function. While the sorting process is rough-hewn and often turbulent, it has some give. What seems to be happening is akin to a draw poker game, with each player going for the best possible play, given the cards he is dealt and the ones he exchanges with the dealer if he can find him. While this metaphor certainly cannot be pushed too far, it does underline the importance of the environment and account for the survival of multiple conceptions, each varying in strength over time.

Development of Codes of Ethics:
Serviceable Myths

What seems more to the point is that the need of school chiefs to survive in a job beset by conflicting demands both outside and within a complex organization has been constantly felt in this century. Each generation of schoolmen developed defenses and patterned responses to external pressure. From experience grew a folk wisdom worn smooth and polished into principles, and from these principles grew accepted practices. Some may call these principles and accepted practices the core of professionalism; others may call the very same things myths.[36] Whatever the label, past experiences of big-city superintendents cannot be ignored.

Thus, in order to explain why Willis, Spears, and Hansen vigorously resisted any external involvement from a community interest group that might, in any degree, influence their decisions, one should examine the immediate context. In doing so, there is an irresistible temptation to conclude that pronouncements from the three about lay interference and professionalism were simply self-serving. Yet to do so would be to ignore the traditions—ones that the three superintendents honored— behind the leadership role patterns that they were playing out. Consider, for example, an 1895 resolution passed by the Department of Superintendence.

The public schools should be absolutely free from the domination of those who would prostitute them to political or personal ends. The management of the schools should be in the hands of educational experts clothed with adequate power, protected in their tenure of office and held responsible for results.[37]

Almost two decades later, another resolution condemned the investigation of school systems by outsiders "whose obvious purposes are to debase the system or exalt the investigators." In the late 1920s an annual convention commended school superintendents who were called upon "to take a stand for what they know to be right and necessary for education in the face of hostile political and partisan activity." And in 1940 another resolution warned superintendents that from "innumerable groups come demands that the educational program serve some special or selfish interest." The assembled schoolmen resolved to "defend the integrity of our schools and keep them free from the control of all special interest groups." What must guide educators is the "soundest available scientific thought and usage."[38]

Resolutions such as the ones quoted above are representative of the well-established views on the issue of external participation which greeted our three school chiefs when they entered the ranks of administrators and professional associations in the 1930s and 1940s. (Using resolutions as evidence does not, of course, suggest that such statements guided behavior—only that resolutions often summed up consensus positions held by influential administrators.) By the time Hansen, Willis, and Spears had moved into the superintendent's office, they were quite familiar with what were legitimate and illegitimate forms of external involvement in school affairs.

Similarly, in other areas, such as their views on change, conflict, and equality of educational opportunity, traditional positions had emerged within professional associations, graduate institutions, and educational journals. While there was criticism of these positions, while counter-positions arose and fell, and while these views modified over the decades, still a prevailing wisdom of the profession permeated particular issues.

By the time our three superintendents assumed office, this wisdom had become embedded in standard operating procedures of their big-city school systems. The network of rules that characterized the bureaucratic operations of large school systems expressed the philosophy of the tradition. Heavy reliance upon impartiality in application of rules and the emphasis upon merit procedures which were already encased in formal rules had derived from schoolmen's experiences with partisan politics decades earlier. The emphasis on rationality and deliberate, purposeful change was expressed in detailed directions to planners of new programs. Fear of internal conflict was carried within rules defining what was to occur when and who was to perform the task. Job functions were carved out in specific detail so that spheres of influence were clearly marked. If conflict did occur, routines for handling it developed. Even lower-level decision-making was routinized for specific areas in order for teachers, principals, and administrators to make few or no choices on certain decisions. Thus, the historical lessons learned by schoolmen in their organizations were often distilled into rules in which the system operated.

So, too, by the time these three big-city school administrators assumed office, much of the folk wisdom and accepted practices had been elevated into ethical principles. The American Association of School Administrators' *Code of Ethics* adopted in 1962 laid out specific examples of ethical and unethical conduct for superintendents. That some of the key principles and practices from schoolmen's past should be considered essential enough to be graven into Thou Shalt Not's indicates the strength such traditions had attained in the profession.

These ethical rules and organizational routines are cited to suggest that superintendents saw themselves as acting in the best traditions of the organization and the highest ideals of their profession. When the three chiefs were attacked by press, professors, civil rights activists, and outraged parents for what they did or didn't do, a keen sense of injustice rankled them. They were being attacked not only for acting in what they saw as the best interests of children but also for staying within the framework of ethical principles of a proud profession.

Consider outside participation. Communications from PTAs, unstructured groups of citizens, parent associations, and the usual Rotary, Kiwanis, chamber of commerce groups were, of course, acceptable. But, in the case of other groups, the *Code of Ethics* prescribed that the "ideals of his profession require a school administrator to resist ideological pressures that would contravene the fundamental principles of public education." Furthermore, the ethical administrator "resists all attempts by vested interests to infringe upon the school's program as a means of promoting their selfish purposes."[39] In other words, what a civil rights representative saw as the rightful participation of his group in a public enterprise, a Hansen or Willis may have seen the seeking of private gain by interest groups at public expense.

In the case of conflict within the organization, an ethical administrator "has an obligation to support publicly the school board" if either the school board or superintendent is accused. Nor should he "permit himself to become involved publicly in personal criticism of board or staff members." Nor may he "make derogatory statements" about a colleague or a school system "unless compelled to under oath." If the board adopted policies that the schoolman opposed, it is "not just cause for refusal by the administrator to support and execute them." However, if there was a rule which the superintendent felt was bad, he should not avoid controversy; rather, he should work to revise or repeal it. Unity was inscribed as the ethic. Conflict, especially if it came to public notice, was proscribed.

Equality, too, is an important consideration in the *Code*. Superintendents must be "impartial in the execution of school policies." It is unethical to "give preferential consideration to any individual or group because of their special status or position in the school system or community." Yet the ethical administrator "recognizes that equal educational opportunities for all pupils may require greater or different resources for some than for others." Compensatory programs for disadvantaged children are in the highest ethical tradition of schoolmen, but a racial census or transfer of children to achieve racial balance would be, within the superintendent's view, contrary to the ethics of his profession.

These rules for professional conduct end with the statement that "what happens in and to the public schools of America happens to America." Thus, in less than a century and a half, the superintendent—who began as something of a hired hand to supervise teachers in frail buildings and to examine pupils for promotion—had become, in the profession's eyes, the linchpin for the rise or decline of a nation.

The history of the urban superintendency reveals the strength and durability of three leadership conceptions in the imagination and behavior of superintendents. The origins of these conceptions were traced to the vulnerability of schoolmen bound to a board of education that must represent popular will. Conflicting expectations of what a superintendent is and what he should be have been present since the late nineteenth century. Not completely helpless, urban superintendents adopted diverse philosophies to help them cope with an unpredictable environment; some conceptions proved more durable than others at certain times, but none disappeared, for they were inherent to the nature of the job.

The knowledge and experience that big-city superintendents compiled over the decades was sorted out, refined, and preserved in organizational rules and somber ethical principles that professionals used to guide their behavior. This incremental learning, deposited finally into standard operating procedures and an ethical code, partially explains the content of many responses made by superintendents Willis, Hansen, and Spears when they came under pressure from outside groups.

Models, Leadership Roles, and Superintendents

In earlier chapters of this book various models were used to sketch possible explanations for the similarity of our three superintendents' responses to six different situations; in chapter 5 historical analysis of the urban superintendency produced still another candidate. Yet the puzzle remains. Which explanation or combination of explanations provides the most persuasive answer to this question? What criterion should be used?

Obviously, one criterion for the construction of our answer is the data themselves: do they match or differ with one or more of the models? Does a pattern emerge from the information which has been gathered? It can—and, for some researchers, it does, although too often the implicit explanatory models in a writer's mind will color his interpretation of the data.

Another criterion is the writer's experience. Powerful hold that it has, prior teaching and administrative experience can easily be a factor in particular interpretations. Probably the most important is the writer's intuition about which models offer the most persuasive explanations of the data. That criterion is intensely personal and vulnerable to attack but, in the last analysis, is the essence of even the most sophisticated studies.

There is, however, another tack which can be taken without dismissing any of these criteria. The various models in chapters 4 and 5 indirectly define the limits of leadership. Perhaps a careful examination of what leadership roles are implied in each of these models could make the choice a shade easier.

Theories and Implied Leadership Roles
for Superintendents

Each of the four models (socioeconomic forces, political bargaining, organization decision-making, and individual leadership) suggests dominant leadership roles for the superintendent. As we have seen, particular roles derived from these models have emerged from the literature on the superintendency over the last century, specifically, the teacher-scholar, chief administrator, and negotiator-statesman. These three ideal-types will be integrated into the following discussion.

In the socioeconomic forces model, the superintendent is a highly vulnerable leader. The role assumes that regardless of the leadership traits or managerial skills, no schoolman could manipulate or control the tidal forces at work in society which ultimately and inevitably shape schools. In effect, the role is one of impotence. Perhaps, if the vulnerable superintendent came to understand his position, a marginal leadership role might emerge by his adjusting to these forces. He could administer the organization in a way that would follow, not obstruct, these trends. Another possibility might be the superintendent who understands how constrained he is yet acts as if he controlled the situation. For the most part, however, the vulnerable administrator figures meagerly in leadership as it is conventionally defined.

The political bargaining model suggests a negotiator role. Within this theory, the organization and its environment are viewed as whirling, ever-shifting sets of conflicting interests that a leader juggles and strives to reconcile. Coalitions, compromise, mediation, bargaining, and agreement comprise the decision-making vocabulary of such leaders. Because of the historically strong taboo against schoolmen indulging in overt political bargaining with nonschool-interest groups, a tame but nonetheless faithful version of this role emerged during the last century.

The negotiator-statesman role has had a powerful hold on schoolmen's imagination. The statesman sees policymaking as a huge arena encompassing many groups. Shepherded by a school chief who encourages and assists others to participate, teachers, principals, and community are all involved in the process of decision-making. The administrator's job is to work calmly and democratically with each group, releasing their creative capacities; moreover he is expected to enter the community, unaggressively but firmly, to mobilize its educational resources in behalf of improved schools. Rather than being the expert who incessantly plugs his pet ideas, the superintendent actively seeks personal and group growth both within schools and community. Such is the statesman's role.

The organization decision-making model suggests the corporate administrator who, while dealing with a large bureaucracy, moves to fulfill organizational goals. Here leadership demands skills in coordination, fiscal management, human relations, and delegation of authority; it demands, most of all, rigorous efficiency and effectiveness in operations. Less interested in modifying, dropping, or substituting organizational goals, the corporate administrator is more concerned with scientifically managing a smoothly running system. Historical evidence suggests that the origins of this role are early in the superintendency.

The individual leader model yields at least two roles, both rooted in historical experience. The rational school chief is the classic version of a decision-maker. Problems are identified, alternatives produced—each with probable positive and negative consequences—and finally choices are made to maximize the goals of the organization. While information flows upward through the system, while kinks develop, and while unpredictable events and people intrude, the school chief still commands an organization that moves smoothly from one step to another producing the essential raw material for him to make the best decision. One is reminded here of the ideal of the chief administrator of the early 1900s.

To be sure, the negotiator-statesman and corporate administrator use rational problem-solving techniques, but the rational school chief has refined the process to a science. What distinguishes him from other types is that he tries to shape, build, and change both the organization and environment in which schools function.

Tied closely to the historical experience of superintendents over the last century, the teacher-scholar role represents another variation of the individual leader model. To the teacher-scholar superintendent, a school system is one large classroom. Confident in his knowledge of what is educationally best for children, teachers, and the community, the teacher-scholar instructs the board of education, teachers, and parents on the proper function of education. Particular instructional techniques, curriculum, and school organization are areas of fervent belief and determined action for the teacher-scholar. He teaches staff how they should carry out their principal or classroom duties. Secure in an authority derived from experience, study, professional skills, and certitude, he alone makes key decisions.

While particular leadership roles flow from the models and historical literature on the urban superintendency, there obviously are additional ones as well as numerous variations of each type. This listing is not meant to capture the gamut of possible roles; it only suggests those that roughly embrace a range available to big-city superintendents in the 1960s.

Willis, Hansen, and Spears played out most of those roles (except for the vulnerable administrator) at one time or another, depending upon the issue and circumstances. Particular ones, however, persistently turned up. The corporate administrator, negotiator-statesman, rational school chief, and teacher-scholar appeared with varying degrees in each administrator. Yet certain configurations of these roles consistently assembled in each man. When welded to their views on instruction and curriculum and to their unique personality, particular leadership roles emerged from these configurations. The deep philosophical splits between ''progressive'' and ''basic education'' views among the three men should not blur clear role patterns in each superintendent. Nor should the varying personal styles obscure configurations. Each man had a center. What was it?

Attaching labels to roles and then tagging them onto people (for example, Hansen—rational school chief) implies a level of objective precision that is missing here. Indeed, such categorizing seems presumptuous. Trying to capture dense, infinitely complex attitudes and behaviors in a simple label is bold, at best, given the available evidence. Yet on the basis of a careful scrutiny of their published writings, speeches, and interviews, and pieces of their on-the-job behavior, labels were applied to these men.

Not every speech, comment at a board meeting, or interview with newspaper reporters was available. As with all historical analysis of a question, total documentation or complete data is an ideal seldom reached. What was available, however, were all the books written by each administrator, journal articles, speeches made at national professional meetings, certain extended comments made at board meetings on topics dealt with here, scattered memos, correspondence, official reports, directives, testimony taken at certain federal and state investigations, and personal interviews. These sources cover the last two decades of each superintendent's career.

Still gaps remain. No data from monitoring of each executive's daily work habits were available. Complete files of memos, interoffice memoranda, correspondence, and appointment calendars were unavailable. What each man actually did each day can only be approximately reconstructed. Thus the data that were gathered become suspect since they might be biased. Add, also, the issue of selectivity: which speeches, which articles, which parts of books, which ideas should be analyzed? Finally, there is the difficulty of sorting out each superintendent-author's ideas and perceptions in their original form.

For centuries historians have wrestled with such problems which accompany incomplete written data. Historians learned from Freud that ideas and the written word may well spring from the unconscious and childhood fantasies. They have learned further from Marx that ideas may only serve class interests. Hence, one cannot always trust that what men say is a predictor of what they will do. The solutions of historians to these problems have scarcely satisfied themselves or critics.

Nevertheless, even though what men write is an imperfect guide to their behavior, it remains to some degree an indicator of their intentions. I have used the following approach in interpreting such material:

1. Categorized all available verbal and written statements of each superintendent about leadership, administration of schools, organizational change and conflict, relationships with the board and outside interest groups, and the functions of schooling.

2. Analyzed the actions which each of the superintendents defined as both important and worthwhile, and analyzed the main operating assumptions undergirding those actions.

The first step produced rough groupings of viewpoints that resembled the particular roles described earlier. The second step either corroborated or contradicted the first one by comparing what administrators said and wrote with what they did. If the data of the second step corroborated that of the first (allowing, of course, for slippage from the inevitable ambiguity, irony, and paradox that mark human behavior), then the prevalent role pattern was confirmed within the limits of what was available. If the data of the second step was substantially contradicted, again making a similar allowance, then the behavior, not the words, of the superintendents determined which role was applied to him.

Carl Hansen

While a number of leadership roles characterized Carl Hansen's superintendency, two in particular seemed to dominate: the rational school chief and the teacher-scholar.

We weren't mere shopkeepers. We just didn't react to crises. We initiated.[1]

For Carl Hansen major decision-making on a question proceeded smoothly through several stages: first, advice was gathered from teachers and parents, mainly through formal advisory committees; then some of his staff was set to work looking for more information and alternative ways of dealing with the problem; by the time the problem reached the superintendent's desk, it was neatly packaged and ready for him to mull over before making his decision.

According to Hansen, this description, based upon published sources, records, and interviews, captures the process fairly well. On some occasions, especially those dealing with major instructional matters (e.g., the Amidon Plan and the Four Track Curriculum), there was little doubt that Dr. Hansen defined the problem, chose the solutions, and set staff to work out implementation. While he spoke admiringly of "democratic administration" numerous times, analysis of his remarks reveal that his meaning of the phrase implied cooperation and unity within the administration. It meant an open-door policy on his part; that teachers could freely go to their principal or their superintendent for satisfaction of grievances. It meant that the school administrator could consult with staff, listen to their complaints, and meet with parents and civic groups. But on issues that he defined as essential, the decision was clearly his to make; he could ignore all advice. Listening to people and gathering opinions encompassed the scope of democratic administration.[2]

On what was right and wrong in schooling children Hansen held firm views. "Leadership in public education," he wrote, "is not a pink-tea affair. Any superintendent should conduct a no-holds barred attack against ignorance, prejudice, . . . and professional smugness." Over the years he lived up to his words, and his convictions aroused a storm of criticism. The abuse, said Hansen, was a response to

my unwillingness to play footsie with the politicians in the local and national poverty programs, my stubbornness in maintaining that the schools must be independent of outside controls, . . . my unwillingness to take orders from the Washington *Post* in regard to the track system and my adherence to the principle that children learn best if they are disciplined in selected and demanding subject matter.

The job of the superintendent, he concluded, is to recommend to the board policy changes in accord "with what he believes in and if necessary accept the onus of unpopular action, rather than expect the board to do so." A superintendent who prided himself on his "stubbornness" and "uncompromising" stands on his principles, Dr. Hansen stated consistently throughout his career that his duty to the children of Washington was to give them the "toughest, most demanding and most fundamental schooling that they could absorb."[3]

Take a school chief "who develops his own ideas about education through independent thinking," add determination and confidence in the rightness of his views, and, finally, join both to an unshakeable conviction that the schoolman must be the one who defines the task. What emerges is a vigorous, inner-directed superintendent who leaves an indelible mark on organizational decision-making.

Not surprisingly, Carl Hansen held clear-cut convictions on who should and should not participate in school system decision-making. He drew a line between permissible and impermissible involvement. On one side of the line there were legitimate outside groups—such as PTAs, certain civic association representatives, municipal officials, and, of course, congressmen—that deserved (and got) a receptive ear. In speech after speech before the District PTA Congress, he warmly applauded PTA efforts to join hands with the administration in improving public education. Prompt answers went back to inquiries from commissioners and congressmen. Polite refusals met requests that the superintendent deemed unreasonable. He believed in listening to grievances, answering requests, and diplomatically accepting advice from the right group. When Dr. Hansen spoke or wrote of consultation with outside organizations, he invariably meant these groups. And even with these groups, he insisted repeatedly that "the role of the professional educator, his perspectives, judgment, skills of analysis of educational problems cannot be supplied by . . . lay groups." Never meaning to exclude outside participation, he defined the limits of organizational "input."[4]

On the other side of the line were groups which Hansen felt were pursuing selfish goals that could destroy public schools. Among the illegitimate outsiders he included federal bureaucrats from the Office of Economic Opportunity, the U. S. Office of Education, and the Department of Health, Education and Welfare; "social activists" such as Julius Hobson (who sued the superintendent and board) and his civil rights coterie; the Washington *Post;* and Washington Teachers Union, once it became the bargaining agent for all teachers.[5]

Especially after 1963, when Hansen was forced to absorb volley after volley of criticism, the superintendent turned more and more to counter-attacking "professional cry-babies and perpetual pessimists" intent upon destroying the school system. "Political Policemen," "Roaming Innovators," and "Poverty Politicians" (i.e., federal officials, local anti-poverty executives, and professional reformers) drew scorn from the superintendent. In the records of discussions on the tracking system, Model School Division, and the Hobson suit, the word "political" crops up repeatedly. That word seemed to express Dr. Hansen's disgust with such forms of external participation. "I was determined," he wrote, "to fight off the aggression, to protect the schools against political intervention." To this day, he feels that these outsiders that he vainly struggled against engineered his resignation.[6]

What these outside groups provoked was disturbance. They were "constantly critical of the establishment, the school system"; they agitated parents to attack the educational system and "to participate in the social revolution," thus separating schools from their natural allies. Dr. Hansen abhorred this kind of conflict. He wanted unity, cooperation, and a constructive partnership between members of the professional family.[7]

It appears paradoxical that a man who prided himself in battling enemies and standing up for his principles should avoid conflict. Conflict from within the family, grievances from teachers, principals, or PTA, he could handle. It was the externally induced strife which he found intensely distasteful.

For instance, his anger spilled over during the election for a bargaining agent to go between the union and the local affiliate of the National Education Association. Union attacks upon the administration to gain teacher votes, according to Hansen, destroyed the "partnership principle, made a team effort unlikely, created suspicion where mutual confidence ought to exist and as an end result impaired services to children." Similarly, Hansen saw "political cunning" behind the deliberate move of anti-poverty officials in their "pitting of parents against teachers and principals by community workers supported by public funds." Subsequent bickering drove a hateful wedge between parents, PTAs, and schools, splintering a unity that had brought progress to the schools.[8]

Shortly before he resigned, the superintendent lashed out at those within the system who relished conflict and fractured unity.

Time servers, cynics, professional cry-babies, perpetual pessimists within the school organization—these imperil the future of public education in our city. Washington must have the enthusiastic support of the 10,000 school employees of the school system.... To any school employee whose purpose and behavior are destructive: Leave the school system. Be courageous enough to attack openly from outside the organization.[9]

To Carl Hansen, productive change for children did not emerge from conflict. His view of organizational change depended upon a spirit of cooperation between members of the school family. "The best and most pervasive of changes in the public schools," he wrote, "have been internal as a product of staff effort." Moreover, the formula for change requires that the superintendent "discover strength and then build on that, rather than focus on weakness." Careful planning by professionals is necessary.[10]

External changes forced upon schoolmen drew Hansen's censure. "The people who develop strategies for change in the public schools should inform themselves as to current practices," he stated. "Lacking depth in scholarship," he continued, "the change strategist often finds himself following the clock hand around to its starting point."[11]

Yet the superintendent conceded that at times he acted arbitrarily, although not irrationally, in ordering changes to occur. He recounted an incident when a group of high school principals openly disagreed with his position of support for an important salary bill in Congress. He called the group of principals into his office and gave them ten minutes to write a statement concurring with his position. "Within the time I gave them," he recalled, "they concluded to do the right thing." In establishing Amidon and the multitrack curriculum, he decried "the arbitrary imposition of a school philosophy upon a school staff," although he did favor "compliant followership now and then." He preferred to think of these plans as a "nudge in the right direction that American education must take."[12]

Many of the changes Hansen initiated were, according to him, aimed at equalizing opportunities for all children. In all of his writings and interviews the theme of equality emerges repeatedly. Children, he says, are in school to learn. "No matter what the state of his purse is, what the color of his skin or his place of residence, the child's basic wants are universal." The time will come when it will be "natural to think of educational needs as those of children, not of Negroes and whites." And when poor, culturally isolated children come to school, "systematic, aggressive and fully supported education is one of the best means for the permanent correction of such deficiencies and should be pursued without consciousness of race."[13]

Both the Tracking and Amidon Plans he viewed as means to achieve equal opportunity. "The purpose of ability grouping," he wrote, "is to provide equal opportunity." Thus instruction, as he conceived it, focused upon developing programs equal to pupils' abilities.[14]

Hansen's firm belief in equality of opportunity was matched by his fierce adherence to the merit principle in hiring and promoting employees. After years under a segregated system where race was the chief criterion, Hanson fervently wrote that "merit, not expedience, not political advantage, not racist aims" was the polestar to follow. Anecdotes dot his writings on how he relied upon merit procedures and how they ultimately benefited blacks. While he lost a battle or two on the issue of equal pay for equal work (another guiding axiom), he steadfastly defended the principle in fighting for revisions in teacher and principal salary bills.[15]

Now, in what ways does this map of ideas emerging from Hansen's writings and interviews mesh with what he did? Consider three actions that involved much of his emotional fervor: Track Plan (1958), Amidon (1960), and resignation (1967).

The ideas of tracking came out of early experiences with desegregation, according to Dr. Hansen. As assistant superintendent of secondary schools, he installed in 1956 the multitrack curriculum in all high schools. After becoming superintendent in 1958, tracking was put into all junior high schools. Here the evidence from experience at the upper level justified the expansion. Similarly, in 1960, as a demonstration of his ideas on basic education at the elementary level, he initiated the Amidon Plan at one school. While he avoided the word "experiment," the establishment of a pilot effort at one school was intended to demonstrate whether or not the ideas worked. Based upon what he felt were positive results drawn from a few years of operation, he ordered the Amidon Plan into all District elementary schools. A few years later he appointed the principal of the Amidon School to be assistant superintendent of elementary schools. Here, then, are two examples of planned change under Carl Hansen.

Hansen fathered both programs. He aggressively preached the merits of both plans before principal associations, faculty meetings, civic groups, and PTAs—any organization that wanted to hear about his ideas. With board approval and much staff work, details of each plan were spelled out in directives, charts, and numerous bulletins for principals and teachers to read and follow. They were expected to comply. Planned by the superintendent and his immediate staff, initiated on a small scale and then expanded city-wide, the direction of change was from the top downward, the process was seen as rational.

Both programs were highly detailed efforts to organize instruction and curriculum. Both demanded that teachers plan carefully and focus upon the intellectual domain. Curriculum was divided up into small, neat compartments, one joined to another and, in its totality, making up a sequential, rational whole.

Administratively, both efforts demanded the creation of common standards, routines, and practices. Inevitably, uniformity became at least one by-product of these plans. From the chaos of electives emerged order. From the messiness of having the classroom re-create society sprang efficient instruction and standards that moved children from one point to another in orderly progression.

Assumptions built into each program led also to efforts at offering equal education. Built upon theories that all children were basically the same in psychological and physical needs although differing in intellectual capacity, and harnessed to a conviction that schools must develop the mind, both the Amidon Plan and the Four-Track Curriculum contained written and implicit concerns for equal treatment and equal opportunity, as defined by Dr. Hansen. Of high importance in the implementation of the superintendent's programs and his concept of equality was the use of budgetary formulas such as $1.00 per child for textbooks, or one teacher per thirty children.

Hansen's pride in his plans was evident in the articles, speeches, and books he produced. However, after 1963, when public favor began to curdle, his continual efforts to persuade others of the correctness of this form of education turned increasingly to vigorous defenses of his programs. By 1966 tracking had become the number-one educational issue in Washington. Efforts to soften Hansen's stand on this program had come from WAY, UPO, friendly board members, teacher and principal critics, and the influential *Post*. All to no avail. With the gradual replacement of congenial board members with critics of tracking, and with the Hobson litigation, Carl Hansen's public stand hardened. Outside critics, he charged, were "dilettantes" unfamiliar with the complexities of public schooling. With Judge Skelly Wright's decision in on *Hobson v. Hansen* in June 1967 came a decree ordering the end of tracking, instituting a color-conscious teacher placement policy, and busing black children to predominantly white schools—orders that Hansen felt violated every principle he held dear. The superintendent resigned.

Benjamin Willis

Like Carl Hansen, Benjamin Willis played a number of leadership roles but showed a tendency toward two in particular, this time the rational school chief and the corporate administrator, which merged with his personality to create a unique pattern.

Strong convictions stamped Dr. Willis' prose. Unflagging in his passion for what education could achieve, he believed that schools "must serve all the people so that their skills, their abilities, and their individual characteristics can be developed.'' Equality in schooling, then, meant ''to bring to each child the education needed by each to reach his potential.'' When the superintendent said every child, he meant just that. Professionals and laymen, he felt, must be ''dedicated to all the children of all the people—the gifted, the mentally handicapped, the mischievious and the somber.''[16]

Yet the superintendent knew that concern for all children and for developing each's potential did not mean that all children received the same resources.

With some children, the school must assume extra responsibility, and if the school sees its role as supplying what is needed for each child for an educational experience of high quality, this extra effort becomes a natural response to individual need. Theoretically, the education of the child has a four-sided base—home, church, community and school, but it is open knowledge that today the child from the disadvantaged home and neighborhood is unduly dependent upon the school to break the cultural barriers that have confined his family to inherited poverty and disadvantages required to compensate for historic deprivation.[17]

So quality education, as Willis defined it, for the ''culturally deprived'' child may bear only the vaguest resemblance to quality education ''for the privileged child of an affluent suburb.'' The goal, Dr. Willis wrote in one annual report, was ''to continue to seek the great American Dream of universal public education of making it possible for each to become all that he can become.''[18]

Willis believed just as firmly that community involvement was essential if the educational system was to perform its mission of providing quality and equality in schooling. In an article for a national magazine, Dr. Willis scored schoolmen for ignoring outside participants. ''In some ways,'' he wrote, ''it is in this area that . . . we have had our greatest failures.'' Schoolmen know how important ''parents and civic leaders are in marshalling support for public education,'' but they ''have failed to be sensitive to the opportunity available to encourage them to participate in the planning of education.'' No success will occur unless schoolmen take ''parents with [them] step by step along the way.''[19]

He wrote repeatedly of involving parents in planning new school buildings. In his doctoral dissertation describing his Yonkers, New York superintendency, he wrote without reservation that ''everyone should be consulted in order to have the best possible facility for carrying on an education program." (This theme emerges in his early Chicago annual reports but virtually disappears by the mid-1960s in his writings.) Who was to be involved and to what extent, Willis answered clearly. He saw three groups basically involved in education: professionals, tax-payers, and parents. On other occasions, he mentioned civic leaders, businessmen, and industrial leaders, a segment of the taxpaying community to which Willis often turned for financial support for school-building bond campaigns.[20]

However, in none of his writings or published interviews did the concept of active, outside participation in school decision-making emerge. He did mention "planning" a great deal; probably participation meant "consultation," another word he used often. Furthermore, the facet of outside participation he viewed as crucial was parental, civic, and business support for increased financial backing of the schools.[21]

The concept he pushed consistently was teamwork. Professionals must work cooperatively with "responsible" community groups. "America," he once wrote, "cannot afford to have education dominated by a group of educational experts who claim infallibility" or by parents who insist they know what's best. Yet professionals or boards of education cannot "surrender their responsibility and attempt to give to the community what some group has demanded without regard to the total enterprise." In the last analysis, it was the board and administration who had to decide.[22]

Beyond consultation and financial support, external participation in decision-making was suspect. On state intervention or federal aid, Willis was adamant. Dollars, yes; control, no. Political involvement or any infringements of the merit principle were unthinkable. While he rarely expressed publicly how he felt about civil rights activists, he privately felt many of them were outsiders seeking personal gain.[23]

Although Dr. Willis accepted criticism as a necessary ingredient to the administration of public schools, and although he acknowledged the inevitability of external conflict penetrating public schools, he worked diligently to contain its effects. Conflict within the system and between the organization and its environment was, in the short or long run, unproductive. In his dissertation, "Staffing a City School System," which he wrote while he was superintendent in Yonkers, he flatly stated that "internal conflicts ... certainly operate against the best interests of the children and society." Over and over again throughout his career, Dr. Willis called for peace and a common resolve between the professional family and the community.[24] Even talk about conflict corrosively damaged team effort. In one interview, an irritated Willis said:

I don't see why people talk about the flight of the white. Nothing but trouble results from talking about conflicts, prejudices and racial problems. People reading it and talking about it just get more stirred up, and that makes the real problem harder to solve. The real problem, the one we are working on all the time is the best possible education of all children.[25]

There was little question in the superintendent's mind that social problems spilled over onto schools. Annual reports, addresses to the AASA, and published interviews documented his belief that population shifts, increasing urbanization, and technological change have forced schoolmen to deal with tensions and conflicts. And he didn't like it.[26]

Why was it detrimental to have large numbers of "culturally deprived" children? Because, answered Willis, it made "assimilation and the oneness of mankind" difficult [though not impossible] to achieve." Such a condition spawns all sorts of nasty conflicts. Parents of deprived children come to distrust the local school; criticism unfairly falls upon the system; and the real issue—educating all the children well—is obscured. To focus upon race was irrelevant, in Willis's opinion. "We do not have a problem of segregation. . . . Concentrating on racial aspects of a problem only creates more problems." In his final resignation letter, the superintendent, with perhaps a tinge of regret, wrote that "Chicago is a great city, but its present greatness is only a shadow of the stature it can achieve if it will put people above polity and education above controversy."[27]

Too much conflict disturbed carefully designed plans for change. And planned, measured change was an ideal for which Dr. Willis reached throughout his career. Construction of school buildings, curriculum development, instructional change—any effort to modify existing procedures or programs—were scrutinized and planned for. His thirteen annual reports were paeans to the methodical transformation of school plant and program. In curriculum, periodic review of courses of study became standard operating procedure. Consider, too, his approach to school construction.

We believe that based upon population trend surveys and other sound and continuous sources of statistical data, planning can be done long before the need of a school building is a matter of pressing concern. We plan that there shall be: first, the development of over-all long-range plans on a city-wide level; second, the careful development of plans for each school plant to be built.

For this and other educational activities, Dr. Willis doggedly pursued one principle: "A continuous and formal cyclical review of all of our program and operations as the basis for improvement toward excellence for all."[28]

How decisions about change were to be made, however, and who should make them were questions to which Willis provided blurred answers. On key decisions, Willis wrote repeatedly that board and staff should operate as a team. Except for his abortive resignation in late 1963 when Willis forced the board to accept his definition of how a board and its executive should operate, the concept of who was to decide what, as it emerges in his writings, was ambiguous. On various occasions, for instance, he wrote eloquently about the necessity of administrators being humane, listening, sharing, and so forth, with board and subordinate staff. Democratic planning in decision-making was a frequent theme in his early writings.[29] Yet after 1960 scarcely a word appeared on this topic. Moreover, a careful scrutiny of his articles and published interviews fails to yield any precise formula for what policy issues boards were to deal with and what administrators were to do.

Still there was little question in Willis's mind that the board had the final word. Moreover, the process was clear: superintendent recommends; board approves. Of course, "we" appears throughout his writings, and a careful reader is not sure whether the "we" refers to board and administration or only to the top administrator. But on one point Dr. Willis spoke clearly: professional leadership was crucial to effective decision-making. At the height of the pressure on public schools during the Sputnik controversy, Willis asked: "Shall we be errand boys or leaders? Are we only to *respond* to trends and pressures or are we to help *set* the trends and exert professional pressures of our own? I know of no patient who, upon entering the hospital, dictates to his physician concerning the program of medication."[30]

How closely do Willis's ideas and views match what he did as superintendent? One way to assess convergence of word and deed is to look at what Dr. Willis defined as his achievements. In 1963 he listed twenty-six accomplishments ranging from "the assimilation of a population explosion," through "decentralization of the administrative organization," to an increase in sick leave benefits for teachers. Running through these achievements is a persistent theme of growth and expansion. It is no accident that Willis's first annual report was christened "We Build," a title he kept for every single report thereafter.[31]

In the 1958 report devoted to school construction there were thirty-six pages, thirty-one of which contained a total of 136 photos of school buildings. Five years later, the 1963 report recorded a decade's progress. A six-page insert map showing where all new buildings and additions had been erected was followed by 236 2″ x 2″ snapshots of the buildings, row after row, on a three-page foldout. Twenty-two large quarter- to half-page bar graphs, pie charts, and tables in two colors dramatically showed the system's growth and expansion under Dr. Willis's aegis. And a decade later, Willis proudly observed that those "schools still looked as if they went up yesterday."[32]

During Willis's superintendency more than one-quarter of a billion dollars had been spent on new classrooms and more seats for children. During his tenure the budget increased from $160 million to over a third of a billion dollars for 1966. In 1955, 1957, and 1959 school building bond issues were approved; Willis had worked hard to gain business and community support for them. And he was pleased with all the expansion those dollars financed.[33]

Managing physical growth of a school system demands careful planning and concern for efficient use of public funds. Construction, maintenance, purchasing, and so forth, offered tangible, measurable outcomes in the business of schooling. If planning and evaluation ever play any significant role in school system decision-making, it is probably in this area. Careful, measured rationality must direct the process of assessing a need through examination of population trend data, then developing city-wide, long-range plans, and, finally, surveying potential sites which will meet the local need (a task Willis enjoyed doing on Sundays) and working with school architects to plan the particular building. Evidence is clear that Willis actively participated in this process. He passionately pursued details, relished making decisions, and immensely enjoyed saving a dollar.[34]

The passion for growth and expansion realized Dr. Willis's belief in a color-blind equality. All the children, regardless of race, had to be served—but served only where they lived. By 1963 the double-shift had been eliminated; average class size had dropped from 39 to 32. Yet some children required more than just equitable resources, so the superintendent established dropout programs, compensatory efforts, and stronger vocational training for low-income minorities—years before such programs became fashionable, according to Willis—but seldom to the degree demanded by later critics. Moreover, he was one of the founders in 1956, and chairman for a decade, of the Great Cities Research Council, an organization established by fourteen large cities to define problems and to gather and disseminate information.

Willis's passion for equality, however, scarcely embraced receptivity to civil rights groups or their demands. When he would meet with them, silence was often his policy; on many occasions, he would avoid them. Nor did his view of equality embrace deliberate mixing of different races—a process that would, in his judgment, destroy the neighborhood school, the very symbol, he felt, of equal treatment.[35]

Outside participation or criticism with the potential for generating conflict within the schools was resisted vigorously by the superintendent. The formal complaint Willis filed against the Urban League has already been described in chapter 1, as has his strenuous opposition to an independent evaluation headed by outsider Robert Havighurst. When an untenured teacher marched in a 1961 picket line outside a school, Willis summarily fired her. Finally, when U.S. Commissioner of Education Francis Keppel threatened a cut-off of all federal funds to Chicago schools, Willis's counterthreats and stormy words were carried to Washington by Mayor Daley, whose clout, according to observers, caused the commissioner to reverse his stance.[36]

By now, the direct influence of Superintendent Willis upon decision-making should be clear. Although it was known that Willis was a strong believer in staff work and team efforts, there was little doubt among subordinates as to who was boss and where the buck stopped. Photographs taken at staff meetings and Moraine Conferences (retreats for the administration) showed ·Willis in the center, usually with most eyes on him. Evelyn Carlson, Willis's close associate for the thirteen years, put it most directly: "He leads; we follow."[37] His close monitoring of the building program; his passion for detail, and, as criticism over his policies increased in the early 1960s, intensified surveillance of whatever went before the board, suggest an active, encompassing role in school decision-making.

With his resignation in October 1963 the fact of his dominance over the decision-making machinery became even more evident. One month after the school year had begun, when the board reversed a portion of his recommended transfer plan, he resigned. His letter of resignation, brief departure, and victorious return upon the heels of the board's submission to his demands, illustrated at the least how much the board relied upon the superintendent to operate the system. This was not the first time that he had threatened to resign, nor was it the last; but it signaled how dearly Willis protected his professional prerogatives as school chief.

Harold Spears

One good thing about San Francisco is that a devilish lot of people take interest in education. Lots of groups all over town. And it is comforting when an issue comes up to have so many diverse opinions from the floor. You're not just fighting the public on something or fighting one group.[38]

On many viewpoints, Dr. Spears stood as one with colleagues Hansen and Willis. On the concept of equality little separated Spears from his fellow administrators. "The basic principle of the American school system," Spears said in his AASA presidential address, "is equality of educational opportunity, and [the] necessary corollary is compensatory education." Both themes repeatedly turn up in his writings.[39]

And, just as vehemently as his colleagues, he opposed taking a racial census. Again and again he stressed that "racial accounting serves nothing but the dangers of putting it to ill use."[40] Committed to a color-blind version of equality, yet dedicated "to providing extra help where necessary to compensate for the cultural shortages of children," Spears shared his brother schoolmen's conviction about equality.[41]

Similar, too, were Spears' views on decision-making. In his writings, speeches, and published interviews, the San Francisco superintendent plainly saw, as his colleges did, the separation of professional from lay participation in decision-making. When eight academicians surveyed, among other things, the elementary curriculum in 1960, the superintendent responded to their recommendations bluntly: "their lack of training and proficiency in elementary education has prevented them from being of major assistance at this level." A decade later, he dismissed their report with "they were out of their field." "What's more," he added, "you didn't want somebody to inject into a school system practices in education that had no foundation whatsoever."[42]

So, too, with the board of education, the difference was plain. "There ought to be a clear distinction," Spears said with obvious feeling, "between the board and superintendent; they're the laymen." Educational matters such as choosing a course of study or determining the competence of the teacher "are professional matters that the superintendent has to come in strong on." Shortly before Spears left his position, the board by-passed the candidate whom he had recommended for a position, and had appointed its own candidate. This was the only time it had occurred in his twelve-year tenure, and it stung him. "Hell," Spears exploded, "that wasn't the board's business. That was my business. The board doesn't make appointments."[43] Spears was the professional; he was supposed to make educational decisions.

Most of the time, professional decision-making demanded that the board be managed carefully by the superintendent if his recommendations were to be approved. Spears' careful preparation of the agenda, his assembly of appropriate information on particular topics, and his prior meeting with the board president and, later, with his own staff set the stage for ultimate approval. "The effective superintendent," Spears wrote, "draws a clear distinction between administrative action and board business, never passing on to the Board matters he and his staff should dispose of in routine manner." Just as a good teacher prepared detailed lesson plans (a metaphor Dr. Spears used often in articles and interviews) "so it is today with the superintendent—he'd better not go to class unprepared."[44]

Were Willis and Hansen listening, they would probably nod their heads in agreement. Nor would the two disagree with Spears' beliefs that major decisions had to be made by the top administrator and that the chain of command should be pursued up as well as down insofar as responsibility and authority were concerned. Sharing the same beliefs as his brother schoolmen on teamwork and "democratic school administration" (another theme that reappears consistently in his writings throughout his career), Spears still felt that superintendents had to make snap decisions on many occasions. "You can't always wait to call in a group," he said; "you've got to move"—even if those decisions broke the chain.[45]

On change within an organization, Spears, in both spoken and written word, showed a deep belief in gradual, planned change managed efficiently by professional educators. "School operation is not a catch-as-catch-can affair," he wrote, "but one of principle and planned procedure." Chapters in his textbooks for educators were devoted to persuading teachers and administrators that problems in supervision, curricular development, and classroom instruction should be diagnosed objectively, modifications introduced systematically, and results scrutinized closely before giving them broader application.[46]

Always sensitive to careful use of tax dollars, Spears harnessed his drive for planned change to more efficient ways of doing familiar things. Democratic administration, the "human touch" in staff relations, and core curriculum were rationalized in a framework of doing a more effective job at less cost. Spears viewed efficiency as a "basic feature of the mandate of public education the citizenry passes on to the professional workers."[47]

No efforts at improving efficiency in the classroom or broad-scale program changes, however, could be mandated from downtown. On this issue Spears was unequivocal. Change "cannot be ordered, it must be accepted as promising by those who teach—the masters of the classroom." Differing somewhat from his brother school chiefs, Spears considered it his job to protect the system, and especially the teacher, from "willy-nilly attempts of administrators to change the course of the school each time a new suggestion comes in."[48]

In the two areas of external participation in decision-making and conflict, Dr. Spears showed at least some similarity of opinion with his fellow superintendents. He saw the school universe divided into the same compartments as his colleagues did. These groups—parents, taxpayers, board members, and staff—had to be coordinated by the superintendent. Thus, PTAs, civic groups, and economy-minded taxpayer groups had a legitimate interest in how the schools were run. Again, like his professional colleagues across the country, he had reservations about federal or state intervention, civil rights activists, professors, and other outsiders. His AASA presidential speech catalogued the continuing impact of outsiders upon local education. "We recognize," he said before the assembled superintendents, "that both the state legislators and the Congress in dispensing school funds so often package the stuff . . . [like] druggists handling prescriptions, each shipment indicating the specific patient and the dosage." Ruefully he added, "we carry out the directions." He, too, questioned the motives of activists. Admitting that "many of them were sincere," he still saw "some tag on to civil rights; they were ready for any cause, these people." His views of professors poking into school affairs have already been detailed. Such external participation led to conflict and, like his fellow schoolmen, Spears preferred harmony, unity, and teamwork. He generously praised the work of PTAs in bridging the gap between school and home and creating "mutual understanding and cooperation." He saw the top administrator's job as reducing competition and disunity between staff, board, parents, and taxpayers.[49]

Yet, even with these similarities in views, what emerges from Spears' writings and interviews more than from the words of Willis and Hansen is a begrudging, positive acceptance of conflict and outside participation as "part of the game that you have to play." Spears fondly remembered how professionals used to be insulated from external strife and participation. Then, around 1955, "the quiet committee room lost its status as the source of instructional planning, and the activity was moved into the public marketplace." Professionals had to move over. "The citizen committees and the public participation that we had courted in our youth," he continued, "now moved in with all of their relatives." A new pattern of decision-making emerged.[50]

The pushing and shoving of diverse groups, "private interests, the give and take of society," all now had to be taken into consideration in planning for the school system. Sure, remarked Spears, conflict erupted; but conflict doesn't mean "you get your fists up against the other fellow all the time; the other fellow has his point of view and you learn it by experience on the job."[51]

Spears felt that something positive could come out of a process involving conflict between divergent values, a process where superintendents had to compromise, negotiate, and decide. He saw San Francisco as a city where it was natural to balance interests, much as the city's mayor did when he appointed two Catholics, two Jews, and three Protestants to the board of education. One conclusion Spears drew from his experience as superintendent was that one should "keep the controversy in the board room and education in the classroom." He felt that "the good that comes from this outside give-and-take will eventually seep down and be implemented in the schools. When there are explosive issues facing the system, open discussion and negotiation are crucial—and he used the desegregation fray as an example—for the formation of sound policy.[52]

Thus, while Spears questioned the motives of some civil rights activists, he understood that civil rights groups in San Francisco had only the schools to agitate against, since, as he observed, other institutions were less vulnerable. Conflict couldn't be taken personally. It was part of the system in a "live and let live city, a give and take city [where] you play the game." After all, he observed, the city area is small, the central office is located downtown—"a twenty minute trolley ride gets you there from any part of town"—and "we're handy." Given these conditions, the superintendency becomes a "mobile operation, in and out of public groups.... More than ever, both the citizens and the teachers demand a superintendent who is visible. He can't go into his office and close the door and be hard to reach."[53]

From this cataloguing of Harold Spears' intellectual map on education, some contradictions emerge. For example, his views on handling conflict and making decisions seem to clash. Let us turn, then, to what Spears did.

The superintendent pursued a determined course of action when it came to equality. Believing race to be irrelevant to education, he candidly, if not bluntly, informed the board and the community in his June

1962 report that he, as a professional, had no sound program to eliminate racial imbalance. Resolutely, he turned aside every effort for the
school system to make a racial census. And after he had quietly ordered
the count taken, for three years he steadfastly refused to release figures
on the racial make-up of the schools. Only in 1965, when San Francisco
schools were under multiple investigations, each demanding racial data,
did Spears reluctantly ask the board for permission to release the
figures.

Spears' view of equality showed up in his vigorous efforts to initiate
compensatory education for "culturally handicapped" children. He and
board member Claire Matzger had visited a number of big cities across
the country seeking more information on innovative programs in this
area.[54] Then, building upon an earlier Ford Foundation grant, he
initiated in 1962 the Superintendent's Compensatory Education Program, which expanded pilot efforts in this direction.

Interestingly enough, what Spears was most proud of concerning
equality in these years had nothing to do with race. The superintendent
got the U.S. Army to reverse its postion on the Reserve Officers Training Program. The Pentagon had announced that federally subsidized
ROTC programs would not be extended to any new high schools. Convinced that the program could be of considerable help to those
youngsters who, coming from certain backgrounds, were not helped as
much by other parts of the school program, Spears felt that the with-
drawal of ROTC programs from newly constructed high schools was a
denial of equal educational opportunity to the youth involved. He contacted other superintendents and coordinated a campaign to expand
ROTC to new high schools. The campaign was successful, and the
Army reversed its decision. When Spears retired, the local unit
presented him with a distinguished service award, a gesture he remembered fondly and proudly.

Spears was also proud of his efficient management of change within
the system. He rearranged his immediate staff by cutting out five positions and creating two new ones; he decreased heavy overtime expenditures racked up by his predecessor; and he assumed responsibility for
planning the building program—a task previously contracted out to
architectural firms. All of this occurred during a 14 percent increase in
school population.[55]

Believing firmly in teacher involvement in any curricular change, he
appointed teachers to committees. Teachers were moved downtown to
help create courses of study; they were hired over summers to develop
lessons and units. During the curriculum controversy, Spears came
under strong pressure from board members, teacher organizations, and

the press to order some dramatic curricular change within the schools. Convinced that central office directives do little more than fill wastebaskets, Spears refused to initiate any crash program. He took a great deal of heat but moved deliberately, involving individual school staffs, teacher representatives, and central office administrators at every step of the way.

Plainly, all change within the system did not occur in a careful, managed fashion. Nor did all decision-making neatly emerge from democratic planning sessions. Often, circumstances demanded quick, unilateral decisions by the superintendent. It was on his own initiative that Spears recommended to the Board his fifteen-point program to put starch in the curriculum. It established a framework for change to occur. Similarly, the decision not to open Central Junior High School was Spears' all the way. Of course, much planning and decision-making did come out of his Monday morning cabinet meetings, for Spears was committed to close, personal relations with immediate staff. Still, major decisions were made by the superintendent and he then made the recommendation to the board.

Mention already has been made of how diligently Dr. Spears prepared for board meetings. This meticulous preparation at least partially explains why his recommendations met with few reversals from boards that changed throughout his twelve-year tenure.

Spears recognized that many of his decisions were responses to outside pressure and that much change in the system was externally induced. Dealing with an environment pregnant with conflict required a superintendent to move around, get an enormous amount of information, and possess a high threshold for noise. Thus, Spears was a mixer and visitor. With unvarnished delight, he told interviewers and audiences that he visited most San Francisco schools each year, in some years hitting all 135. And he said he knew what was going on at most of them. These were more than ceremonial occasions. Information was assiduously gathered; information was just as assiduously given. He sipped cocktails at parties with teachers critical of his policies; he attended special Masses for Catholic teachers, a powerful group in the city; he went to wakes to pay his respects; he spoke at PTA meetings in Pacific Heights and broke bread with businessmen at downtown restaurants; he judged Chinese-American beauty contests and listened to Junior League women discuss school problems. In all of these activities, he shook hands, listened, and shared information.

While he had strong feelings about what was right and wrong about education, these convictions did not prevent him from meeting with, negotiating, and compromising with interest groups on those issues that did not crack the inner core of his principles (i.e., moving children around on the basis of their race to effect racial balance, establishing a lay committee to make decisions on educational matters, etc.). He compromised on setting the level of the tax rate. His Central Junior High decision was, in effect, a compromise decision with the Grattan parents, NAACP, and CORE, who he knew would (and did) breathe a sigh of relief when the school did not open. He actively negotiated with the NAACP to gain their support for a school bond referendum. And he got it. So, too, with angry teacher groups, his office was open to their representatives. His Council of Professional Organizations was a vehicle for listening, raising issues, and so on. Spears knew he could not end conflict; it was as natural as a humid Indiana summer; but he felt he could manage its level and influence its consequences.

It should come as no surprise, then, that of the three superintendents, only Spears, somewhat scarred and bowed, retired with the usual testimonials and awards. Willis and Hansen resigned.

The San Francisco superintendent clearly played out a number of leadership roles during his twelve years as top administrator. Yet, as with the others, particular ones combined with his distinct personality to create a dominant style. Spears' management of decision-making and the change process—his awareness of how external forces shape internal events, his involvement with various interest groups, his negotiating with them, and, indirectly their impact upon his decision-making—suggests that the superintendent played out at least two roles: the rational school chief and the negotiator-statesman.

Our four leadership conceptions—teacher-scholar, negotiator-statesman, corporate administrator, and rational school chief—drawn from historical data and explanatory models, describe one range of roles acted out by three big-city superintendents. Does knowing about these conceptions explain the similarity of schoolmen's responses to outside pressure? I think so.

If chapter five produced a historical residue of common beliefs and behaviors that partially explained certain responses of the three school chiefs, this analysis extends further our understanding of the common content to their responses. Dominant leadership patterns do help explain, in part, why they responded as they did. By tracing out the intellectual terrain of beliefs on organizational conflict, decision-making, equality, and the like common to a particular leadership role, and then by linking the configuration to each superintendent's beliefs and behavior, a richer, far more complex picture emerges. Taken together, then, chapters 5 and 6 complement each other in their explanations of why three big-city superintendents responded in a similar fashion to external pressures.

Conclusion

This study began with two basic questions. First, how did big-city superintendents respond to outside pressure? This question was covered in the initial four chapters, in which we saw that superintendents Willis, Hansen, and Spears showed similar patterns of response to critical incidents. The larger and more difficult question was how to explain the similarity in responses. By focusing on ideal types and conceptions of leadership, chapters 5 and 6 produced a number of possible explanations, each in its way quite plausible but not totally satisfying. Why, then, did these three schoolmen respond to external pressure in the manner they did?

In explaining the response patterns of our three school chiefs, three interacting contexts must be considered. Each context can be seen as narrowing the range of responses so that their cumulative effect became an irreducible core of patterns, a particular configuration, available to big-city administrators in these years.

Historical Residue of Beliefs and Practices

The origin and growth of the superintendent, it was argued, accounted for the fundamental insecurity of the position. From the very birth of the job there were competing role demands upon the superintendent, and these have continued unabated to the present. Historically vulnerable to outside pressure, urban schoolmen created conceptions of leadership which crystallized around these expectations. These views nourished beliefs that superintendents were experts possessing the special competence necessary to manage public schools.

Around these leadership role conceptions grew practices and beliefs that seemed to work in terms of increasing prestige, salary, and tenure. Each generation of urban schoolmen reinforced these practices and beliefs through its professional associations, educational journals, and periodic meetings, and gradually it was understood that such traditions were essential for professional conduct and survival. In other words, a series of norms developed around the position of the superintendency. Refined and polished by experience, these norms formed the core of a professional ideology firmly embedded in historical experience of vulnerable schoolmen trying very hard to survive a most complex, demanding job.

The ideology was deposited in codes of ethics, in organizational structure and rules within each large school system, and in an intricate web of professional expectations of colleagues and board of education members. Even had they willed it, few big-city superintendents could have escaped the embrace of this pervasive professional ideology. Carl Hansen, Benjamin Willis, and Harold Spears, accepting the main tenets of professional beliefs, were no exceptions.

Individual Socialization within the Institution

Few organizations normally require their professionals to have been clients of the organization for at least twelve years and then to have served an apprenticeship for at least a decade before being permitted to practice. But this is the process required for becoming a superintendent. Few who have not already been teachers or principals ever move into the superintendent's office. The career route is clearly staked out, with time spent in the classroom and principal's office. As students, teachers, principals, and central office administrators, our three school chiefs each spent an average of twenty-eight years in public schools. If basic elementary and high school education, college, and graduate school are included, each man spent all but the first six years of his life either attending or working in schools prior to his first superintendency! Save for the total environment of a religious order, few professions can match such a long, intense, preparation for practice.

The potency of schooling as a socializing force can only be guessed; and we can but estimate the impact of the many years which the three superintendents spent as teachers and principals, playing out certain organizational roles. Willis, readers will recall, served twelve years as a teacher and principal; Hansen, twenty; and Spears, seventeen. Evidence suggests that rationality, impartiality, acceptance of authority and hierarchy, emotional restraint are but a few of the organizational traits acquired in the process of schooling, teaching, and administering.[1]

Conflicting Organizational Role Demands

Consider also the conflicting demands of large organizations upon their top executives. For example, in 1963 Willis headed an organization of 1,000 administrators and 20,000 teachers. He was responsible to an eleven-member board of education. He took an oath to obey the laws of Illinois and offered public pledges to serve the educational interest of millions of parents and children and to heed the concerns of taxpayers. While he headed this system, much went on that he had little direct control or influence over—various board members entering and exiting their positions, interest groups putting demands upon the organization, central office managers or principals ignoring or sabotaging mandated programs.

For all three superintendents there was a perpetual crossfire of expectations, requests, and demands from board members, middle-level administrators, principals, teachers, students, and different civic groups. With crises breaking daily and enormous demands placed upon the chief's limited time, schoolmen were often forced to adopt those traditional stances and strategies that had helped predecessors and colleagues to avoid conflict while trying hard to maximize consensus within the organization. Such cross-cutting pressures upon executives shoved them into playing out roles (each historically defined) that would gain and retain support without sacrificing their claim to expertness. The superintendent is not unlike a juggler who, in order to keep a dozen objects in the air on a windy day, must constantly move about, keeping his eyes roving; he may be very uncertain that he has the whole dozen, but he doesn't dare stop to find out!

So, the combination of the historic vulnerability of superintendents, the long process of socialization, and the demanding organizational role that each schoolman must play, explain, in my judgment, the similarity in our three superintendents' responses to outside pressure. Of course, this still does not explain why two of the three resigned under fire and one retired, or, for that matter, why a few big-city superintendents seemingly sailed through the 1960s without forced resignation or early retirement. The substantial influence of the larger environment may help to explain this.

The impact of the larger environment is a critical element in explaining why superintendents survived or departed. "Larger environment" refers to the dominant socioeconomic trends, intellectual climate, and political movements that marked particular periods of time and created a local context within which large urban school systems could operate.

The 1950s were years of national political conservatism, population shifts from farm to city and from city to suburb, the reassertion of humanitarian concern for racial minorities, and the expansion of schooling. The 1960s seemed to be different. Even if the Kennedy years were not as left of center as they were initially thought to be, active federal concern for social issues, the rising tide of popular protest against racial injustice, continual economic prosperity, and the explosion of Great Society programs following the death of John F. Kennedy—all brought different actors, different interest groups, different expectations, and, most important for our three school chiefs, different demands to the urban classroom.

Save for the Sputnik controversy, which lasted only a few years (1958–60), the perspective of the 1950s cast schools as an expanding, essential operation highly regarded by most urbanites. There was criticism, of course, but the general view of urban schools was positive, still accepting beliefs that schooling was the path to national greatness and personal success. Typical criticism was that of the highly respected James Conant, who issued sober reports to the nation on education. His reports pointed out the weaknesses, but he mirrored the nation's affirmative beliefs in the recommendations that he offered on how to strengthen the schools—and many of these were fervently embraced by schoolmen.

In the early 1960s, however, the situation in urban schools became increasingly defined as critical. Whether city schools had declined in quality between 1955 and 1967, as critics claimed, is hard to assess. Certainly more information was available; more groups, especially in civil rights, were making more demands than before. "Integration," "culturally deprived," "slum schools," "de facto segregation" became the new magic phrases. Once the situation was defined as a crisis by writers and the media and had seeped into the public mind, then the effects became quite real. This larger environment—especially the subjective, public view of schools—shifted. Old belief systems came under attack, and the idea of education as the "great equalizer" or vehicle for individual success was increasingly questioned. If James Conant's studies reflected the faith of the 50s in schools, Ivan Illich's *Deschooling Society* harvested the growing despair with education that grew throughout the 1960s.

Superintendents such as Hansen, Willis, and Spears had to face unfamiliar demands, expectations, and groups. The world seemed to have changed on them. What worked for them in the 1950s seemingly failed a decade later. Carl Hansen, darling of the liberal, integrationist community in the 1950s, was tagged as a racist a decade later. Unsurprisingly, superintendent attrition rates in big cities reflected the shift. In twenty-five cities during the 1950s, six cities had superintendents that lasted the decade; only two made it through the 1960s. Three cities lost two or more executives in the 1950s, compared to seven cities in the following ten years.

As new crises erupted, as external pressures escalated, our three superintendents responded in familiar ways that had worked perfectly well previously—ways they had learned through experience and shared with colleagues; ways they believed in. But their responses seemed inappropriate now and were often misinterpreted, criticized sharply. When Spears and Willis rejected demands from civil rights activists that a racial census be taken—a shocking denial of equality, from the two superintendents' frame of reference—passions were further inflamed rather than defused. It was as though the schoolmen were saying what had previously been the right things and were pulling what had always been the right levers, but the expected responses just weren't turning up. In their terms, the world had gone awry.

Hansen's choice of the word "dinosaur" to describe himself and his brother schoolmen; the open bitterness of Willis toward the personal abuse he had received after all the buildings, programs, and effort he had made in behalf of minorities; and Spears' sense of unfairness (muted as it was) toward attacks on his policies and actions—all of these mirror the superintendents' belief that they had played the game properly but that somehow someone had changed the rules and had neglected to tell them. In a way, they were like those desperate Japanese soldiers who continued fighting for the honor of Nippon years after World War II ended.

Such an interpretation to explain the similarity in superintendent responses to outside pressure suggests that individual administrators, regardless of personal style or taste, had little room to initiate innovative moves or to depart sharply from norms. Circumscribed as he was by the complex organizational role of superintendent, the historical vulnerability of the position, the socialization process of becoming an executive, and, finally, by the particular set of larger environmental forces impinging upon the local school system, the schoolman was in a position in which his personality, intelligence, and style apparently bore little influence upon what ultimately happened.

While that, indeed, is the explanation offered, it is not to argue that big-city chiefs were wholly programmed by experience and current situations to play out a sequence of moves that were preordained. Nor is it meant to argue that what did happen *had* to occur. This is not a scenario for a Greek tragedy—even one without gods. Personal styles, leadership roles, or other factors may well have made a difference in response patterns and survival ratios. After all, even if Willis and Hansen were coerced into resigning, Spears was not. Moreover, a few big-city superintendents somehow went through the 1960s without suffering reversals. Some margin for the ambiguous quality of leadership remains. How large that margin is, whether it is flexible or rigid, continues to taunt researchers.

One variable which may explain Spears' ability to last, and which perhaps applies to other school executives, is that in times when sharp external pressure strikes the schools, especially pressure from well-organized interest groups, and in times when public opinion of school leadership becomes increasingly skeptical—in such times (1910–19, 1960s, early 1970s), the dominant leadership pattern that seems to have some survival power is that of negotiator-statesman.

The rational school chief conception is bound to ideals, norms, and strategies that minimize conflict; it sees all problems as solvable. When conflict escalates, especially when it comes from outside the organization, superintendent efforts to minimize and eliminate it may seriously misjudge and underestimate the sources and direction of that conflict. The negotiator-statesman approach at least embraces the notion that either external or organizational conflict is inevitable, indeed, basic, to human affairs. Different interest groups are legitimate and somehow must be dealt with. It seems that for the 1960s in big cities, this leadership role had more survival power than other ones. In other periods, when public confidence in school leadership is unshaken, when criticism of schools is unorganized and sporadic, other leadership conceptions seem to have made a better match with the climate of the times— although one could just as easily argue that under those conditions any conception of leadership would work.

A superintendent, then, is not likely to be a man for all seasons. Respected professionals to friends and stubborn autocrats to critics, Carl Hansen, Benjamin Willis, and Harold Spears could not easily adjust to the radical changes which confronted them—although there were differences in adjustment among the three. The times, the local political context, and the dominant conception of leadership may well determine whether a schoolman can do an effective job or not. There are fall, summer, spring, and winter superintendents—but none for all seasons.

Studying these big-city school chiefs leaves one with a reduced sense of the heroic in superintending. The Superman image summoned up by the AASA literature and boards of education search committees testifies more to aspiration than to reality. More modesty, surer sense of humility about the claims for superintendent leadership seem to be in order.

None of this, of course, means that urban administrators were helpless pieces of driftwood tossed onto various shores by a high surf. As superintendents, these men played out numerous roles. The limits on their leadership roles have been carefully examined. But schoolmen did manage to exercise enormous organizational influence through such roles as figurehead of the organization, spokesman of the system, resource allocator, negotiator, crisis-handler, and disseminator of information. The case studies of Hansen, Willis, and Spears clearly illustrate their substantive influence on the course of events. But influence does not mean control, nor does it necessarily even imply leadership.

While it would seem in order to hold more modest, perhaps even humble, views of what a big-city superintendent can achieve as a leader of a school system, the chances are slim that this attitude will become popular. An increasingly critical public whose satisfaction in schooling has eroded in the last decade and a profession which is still anxious to minimize its historic vulnerability seem unlikely to reduce their high expectations. Both the public and the profession seem to need heroic leaders.

Those big-city superintendents who are aware of the narrow margin of leadership available to them as executives of massive organizations may well be able to parlay the multiple, conflicting roles into a leadership constellation that delivers both symbolic and real gains. Such an accomplishment would be, in a word often favored by schoolmen, a challenge.

Appendix 1

Summary Profile of Big-City Superintendents 1953–1971

	1953[a]	1963[b]	1971[c]
Percentage coming from rural or small town background	67	60	60
Percentage with previous experience as teacher	91	81	87
Percentage with previous experience as principal	82	80	87
Percentage holding first teaching position in small town or rural area	61	55	60
Percentage holding Ph.D. or Ed.D.	50	50	80
Percentage appointed as superintendent from outside current system	46	40	72
Median number years as teacher, principal, and supervisor	9.0	10.5	11.0
Median age at first superintendency	29.0	43.0	38.5
Median age now	58.0	57.5	50.5
Average number years in current position	6.5	5.5	4.1

SOURCES: Compiled from vita received from school systems;

Who's Who in America, 1945–1973; Jacques Cattell, ed., *Leaders in Education,* 1st and 4th editions, 1948, 1971.

[a]Information available on 24 of 25 superintendents from largest school systems (selected in 1966).

[b]Information available on 22 of 25 superintendents.

[c]Information available on 24 of 25 superintendents.

Appendix 2

List of Superintendents in Twenty-five Largest School Systems, 1870–1973

Atlanta

Bernard Mallon	1871–1877	Ira Jarrel	1944–1960
W. F. Slaton	1878–1911	John Letson	1960–1972
?		Alonzo Crim	1972–

Baltimore

William Creery	1871–1875	David Weglein	1924–1946
Henry Shepherd	1875–1884	William Lemmel	1946–1953
Henry A. Wise	1884–1900	John Fisher	1953–1958
James Van Sickle	1900–1911	Lawrence Pacquin	1966–1968
Francis Soper	1911–1915	Thomas Sheldon	1968–1971
Charles Koch	1916–1920	Roland Patterson	1972–
Henry S. West	1920–1924		

Boston

John Philbrick	1856–1878	Pat Campbell	1931–1937
Edwin Seaver	1878–1900	Arthur Gould	1937–1948
George Conley	1900–1906	Dennis Haley	1948–1960
Stratton Brooks	1906–1912	Fred Gillis	1960–1963
F. B. Dyer	1913–1919	Wm. Ohrenberger	1963–1972
Frank Thompson	1919–1922	William Leary	1972–
Jeremiah Burke	1922–1930		

Chicago

Josiah Pickard	1871–1877	C. E. Chadsey	1919
Duane Doty	1877–1880	P. A. Mortenson	1919–1924
George Howland	1880–1891	William McAndrew	1924–1928
A. G. Lane	1891–1898	William Bogan	1928–1935
E. B. Andrews	1898–1900	William Johnson	1935–1946
E. G. Cooley	1900–1909	Herold Hunt	1947–1953
Ella F. Young	1909–1915	Benjamin Willis	1953–1966
J. D. Schoop	1915–1918	James Redmond	1966–

Cincinnati

John Hancock	1869–1874	Randall Condon	1913–1927
John Peaslee	1874–1886	?	1927–1929
E. E. White	1886–1889	Edward Roberts	1929–1937
William Morgan	1889–1900	C. V. Courter	1937–1959
R. Boone	1900–1903	Wendell Pierce	1959–1967
F. B. Dyer	1903–1913	Paul Miller	1967–1972

Cleveland

A. J. Rickoff	1867–1882	J. M. Frederick	1912–1917
B. A. Hinsdale	1882–1886	Frank Spaulding	1917–1920
L. H. Day	1886–1892	R. G. Jones	1920–1933
A. S. Draper	1892–1894	Charles Lake	1933–1947
L. H. Jones	1894–1902	Mark Shinnerer	1947–1961
E. F. Moulton	1902—?	William Levenson	1961–1964
Stratton Brooks	1906	Paul Briggs	1965–
W. H. Elson	1906–1912		

Columbus

W. Mitchel	1871–1872	G. E. Roudebush	1937–1949
R. W. Stevenson	1872–1889	N. Fawcett	1949–1956
J. A. Shawan	1889–1916	Harold Eibling	1956–1971
J. H. Francis	1916–1920	John Ellis	1971–
J. G. Collicot	1920–1937		

Dallas

J. T. Hand	1888–1889	Justin Kimball	1915–1922
T. G. Harris	1889–1891	N. R. Crozier	1924–1940
J. L. Long	1891–1908	Julius Dorsey	1941–1945
Arthur Lefevre	1908–1910	W. T. White	1945–1968
J. A. Brooks	1910– ?	Nolan Estes	1968–

Denver

H. Carver	1871–1872	A. L. Threlkeld	1927–1937
F. Garbutt	1872–1874	A. J. Stoddard	1937–1939
Aaron Gove	1874–1904	Charles Greene	1939–1947
Lewis C. Greenlee	1904–1907	K. Oberholzer	1947–1967
Charles Chadsey	1907–1912	Robert Gilberts	1967–1970
William Smiley	1912–1915	Howard Johnson	1970–1973
Carlos Cole	1915–1920	Louis Kishkunas	1973–
Jesse Newlon	1920–1927		

Detroit

Duane Doty	1871–1875	Warren E. Bow	1942–1945
J. M. B. Sill	1875–1887	Arthur Dondineau	1945–1956
W. E. Robinson	1887–1897	Samuel Brownell	1956–1966
W. Martindale	1897–1911	Norman Drachler	1967–1971
Frank Chadsey	1912–1919	Charles Wolfe	1972–
Frank Cody	1919–1942		

Houston

Henry Cline	1873–1875	P. W. Horn	1904–1922
Ashbel Smith	1877	A. B. Cousins	1922–1924
H. H. Smith	1877–1879	E. E. Oberholtzer	1924–1945
E. N. Clopper	1879–1884	W. E. Moreland	1945–1957
W. H. Foute	1884–1885	John McFarland	1958–1966
J. E. Dow	1885–1886	Glenn Fletcher	1967–1969
T. S. Sutton	1886–1896	George Garver	1970–
W. Barnett	1900–1904		

Indianapolis

A. C. Shortridge	1871–1874	E. N. Graff	1917–1929
G. P. Brown	1874–1878	Paul Stetson	1929–1936
H. S. Tarbell	1878–1884	DeWitt Morgan	1936–1943
Lewis Jones	1884–1892	Virgil Stinebaugh	1943–1950
D. K. Goss	1892–1900	Herman Shibler	1950–1959
Calvin Kendall	1900–1911	George Ostheimer	1959–1969
?		Stanley Campbell	1969–1972
J. G. Collicot	1915–1917		

Los Angeles

William Lucky	1873–1876	Albert Shiels	1917–1922
C. H. Kimball	1876–1880	Susan Dorsey	1922–1929

C. B. Jones (Mrs.)	1880–1881	Frank Bouelle	1929–1935
J. M. Guinn	1881–1883	Verlin Kersey	1937–1948
L. D. Smith	1883–1885	A. J. Stoddard	1948–1954
William Friesner	1885–1893	Claude Reeves	1954–1956
William Search	1894	Ellis Jarvis	1956–1962
James Foshay	1895–1906	Jack Crowther	1962–1970
E. C. Moore	1906–1910	William Johnston	1971–
J. H. Francis	1910–1916		

Memphis

H. C. Slaughter	1871–1873	L. E. Wolfe	1912–1915
A. Pickett	1873–1875	A. A. Kincannon	1915–1919
J. T. Leath	1876–1878	W. S. Jones	1919–1923
W. H. Fouter	1878–1880	R. L. Jones	1923–1935
C. Collier	1880–1892	E. C. Ball	1935–1957
George Gordon	1892–1906	E. C. Stimbert	1957–1971
I. C. McNeill	1906–1910	John Freeman	1971–
T. P. Bailey	1910		

Milwaukee

F. C. Law	1871–1875	H. O. R. Siefert	1895–1904
James McAllister	1875–1878	C. G. Pearse	1904–1914
J. J. Somers	1878–1879	Milton Potter	1914–1944
James McAllister	1879–1881	Lowell Goodrich	1944–1950
William Anderson	1882–1889	Harold Vincent	1950–1968
G. W. Peckham	1889–1895	R. P. Gousha	1968–

New Orleans

J. B. Carter	1871–1873	Auguste J. Tete	1941–1946
Charles Boothby	1873–1876	L. J. Bourgeois	1946–1952
William Rogers	1877–1883	James Redmond	1953–1961
V. Bettison	1884–1886	O. Perry Walker	1961–1965
Warren Easton	1887–1906	Carl Dolce	1965–1970
J. M. Gwinn	1910–1923	Gene A. Geisert	1971–
N. Bauer	1923–1941		

New York

Henry Kiddle	1871–1879	William Jansen	1947–1958
John Jasper	1879–1898	John Theobald	1958–1962
William Maxwell	1898–1918	Calvin Gross	1963–1965
William Ettinger	1918–1924	Bernard Donovan	1965–1970
Harold Campbell	1924–1940	Harvey Scribner	1970–1973
John Wade	1940–1946		

Philadelphia

James McAllister	1883–1890	L. P. Hoyer	1946–1955
Edward Brooks	1891–1906	Allan Wetter	1955–1964
James Brumbaugh	1906–1914	Taylor Whittier	1964–1967
John P. Garber	1914–1920	Mark Shedd	1967–1971
Edwin Broome	1921–1939	Matthew Costanza	1972–
A. J. Stoddard	1939–1946		

Pittsburgh

G. J. Luckey	1868–1899	Earl Dimmock	1945–1958
Samuel Andrews	1899–1911	Calvin Gross	1958–1963
S. L. Heeter	1911–1913	Sidney Marland	1963–1968
Wm. Davidson	1913–1930	B. McCormack	1968–1970
Ben Graham	1930–1942	Louis Kishkunas	1970–1973
Henry Hill	1942–1945		

Portland

S. W. King	1873–1877	Charles Rice	1926–1937
T. H. Crawford	1877–1888	R. Dugdale	1937–1943
Ella Sabin	1888–1891	?	1943–1946
I. W. Pratt	1891–1896	Paul Rehmus	1946–1952
Frank Rigler	1896–1913	J. W. Edwards	1953–1961
L. R. Alderman	1913–1916	Melvin Barnes	1961–1970
D. A. Grout	1917–1926	R. W. Blanchard	1970–

Saint Louis

W. T. Harris	1868–1880	Henry Gerlin	1929–1939
E. H. Long	1880–1895	Homer Anderson	1940–1942
Louis Soldan	1895–1908	Philip Hickey	1942–1964
Ben Blewett	1908–1916	Wm. Kottmeyer	1964–1970
John Withers	1917–1921	Clyde Miller	1971–
John J. Maddox	1921–1929		

San Diego

F. W. Pauly	1876– ?	?	
?		H. C. Johnson	1919–1926
E. DeBurn	1888–1894	W. P. Hepner	1927–1934
E. Cubberley	1894–1896	W. C. Crawford	1934–1954
F. P. Davidson	1897–1904	Ralph Dailard	1954–1969
W. S. Small	1904–1906	Jack Hornback	1969–1971
D. Mackinnon	1906– ?	Thomas Goodman	1971–

San Francisco

J. Widber	1870–1873	A. Roncovieri	1906–1923
James Benman	1873–1876	A. J. Cloud	1923
H. Bolander	1876–1877	J. Gwinn	1923–1933
A. Mann	1877–1880	E. Lee	1933–1936
J. W. Taylor	1880–1883	J. Nourse	1936–1943
A. Moulder	1883–1887	Curtis Warren	1943–1947
J. Anderson	1887–1891	Herbert Clish	1947–1955
John Swett	1891–1895	Harold Spears	1955–1967
A. Moulder	1895	Robert Jenkins	1967–1970
M. Babcock	1895–1896	Thomas Shaheen	1970–1972
R. Webster	1896–1903	Steven Morena	1972–
W. Langdon	1903–1906		

Seattle

E. Ingraham	1882–1888	Worth McClure	1931–1945
Julia Kennedy	1888–1889	Samuel Fleming	1945–1956
F. J. Barnard	1889–1891	E. Campbell	1956–1965
Frank B. Cooper	1891–1922	Forbes Bottomley	1965–
Thomas Cole	1923–1931		

Washington, D.C.

Zalmon Richards	1869–1870	Ernest Thurston	1914–1920
J. O. Wilson	1870–1885	Frank Ballou	1920–1943
Edward Paul	1885	Robert Haycock	1943–1946
William Powell	1885–1900	Hobart Corning	1946–1958
Alexander Stuart	1900–1906	Carl Hansen	1958–1967
Wm. Chancellor	1906–1908	William Manning	1967–1968
Alexander Stuart	1908–1911	Hugh Scott	1970–1973
William Davidson	1911–1913		

SOURCES: U.S. Office of Education, *Educational Directory,* 1941–1968; *Report of the Commissioner of Education* (Washington, D.C.: G.P.O.), 1898–1910; *Who's Who in America,* 1945–1973; information on superintendents supplied by individual cities.

NOTE: The dates are approximate. Often interim superintendents served while a search took place; also, dates can indicate either when a person took office or when he or she was appointed.

Notes

Introduction

1. Few women have been superintendent between 1870 and 1970. In twenty-five big cities during these years, six women (3 percent) have been superintendent. In 1973 June Marr found .2 percent of the superintendents to be women. These, for the most part, were located in small, nonmetropolitan districts. See June Marr, "Survey of Women Superintendents" (unpublished seminar paper, Stanford University, January 1974).

2. Ray Callahan, "The Fight to Control Policy," in *Struggle for Power in Education,* ed. Frank Lutz and Joseph Azzarelli (New York: The Center for Applied Research in Education, 1965), p. 29.

3. Joseph Cronin, "The Superintendent in the Crucible of Urban Politics," in *Toward Improved Urban Education,* ed. Frank Lutz (Worthington, Ohio: Charles A. Jones Co., 1970), pp. 146–47; Luvern Cunningham, "Community Power: Implications for Education," in *The Politics of Education in the Local Community,* ed. Robert S. Cahill and Stephen P. Henchley (Danville, Ill.: Interstate Printers and Publishers, Inc., 1964), p. 47.

4. Of the few that have been done, the following are most recent. Donald J. McCarty and Charles E. Ramsey, *The School Managers* (Westport, Conn.: Greenwood Publishing Corp., 1971); Richard Carlson, *The Superintendents* (Columbus, Ohio: Charles Merrill Co., 1973); Joseph Cronin, *Control of Urban Schools* (New York: Free Press, 1973); Robert L. Crain, *The Politics of School Desegregation* (Chicago: Aldine Publishing Co., 1968).

5. Educational Policies Commission, *The Unique Role of the Superintendent of Schools* (Washington, D.C.: National Educational Association, 1965), p. 1.

6. In Henry Mintzberg's study of five executives pursuing their daily activities, one of the subjects was the administrator of a large suburban school—a case study seldom found in school professional literature. We have much data on what superintendents say they do, but the literature on executives is rich with examples of discrepancies between reported and actual behavior. See Henry Mintzberg, *The Nature of Managerial Work* (New York: Harper and Row, 1973), chapter 2 and Appendix A.

7. Roald Campbell, "Is the School Superintendent Obsolete?" Phi Delta *Kappan*, October 1966, p. 53.

8. See the studies mentioned in note 4 above. Each does see a pattern, but little similarity in patterns is found from one study to another.

9. Between 1970 and 1973, twenty new school superintendents were appointed in the twenty-five largest cities.

10. American Association of School Administrators, *School Administration* 20 (September 1971): 2.

Chapter 1

1. Interview with Benjamin C. Willis, June 28, 1973.

2. *Chicago Daily News,* July 3, 1963. Chicago Public Schools, *We Build: Annual Report of the Chicago Public Schools, 1953–1963*, p. 7.

3. "A Philosophy for Administration: Interview with Benjamin Willis," *Nation's Schools,* April 1961, p. 72. Interview with Willis, June 28, 1973.

4. *Chicago Daily News,* July 2, 1962.

5. See "The Schoolmaster 1960," *Newsweek* 67 (November 12, 1967): 97; Jack Star, "Chicago's Troubled Schools," *Look* 29 (May 4, 1965): 59–61; Stewart Alsop, "The Brookses and the Gowsters," *Saturday Evening Post* 238 (December 4, 1965): 10; J. C. Furnas, "He Runs Everything Except Tugboats," *Nation's Business* 39 (May 1951): 43–44, 78–79; Robert Liston, "Pugnacious Planner of America's Future," *True,* May 1965; "Benjamin Willis," *Saturday Review* 43 (September 17, 1960): 74; *Time* 78 (September 15, 1961): 52–53.

6. B. J. Chandler, Dean of College of Education, Northwestern University, quoted by Liston, p. 26.

7. *Chicago Tribune,* October 5, 1963.

8. Interview with Willis, June 28, 1973.

9. Furnas, pp. 78–79. Liston, p. 26. Interview with Willis, June 28, 1973.

10. This is a reconstruction of a typical day, as drawn from interviews and descriptions of Willis's schedule.

11. "Philosophy for Administration," p. 72.

12. Joseph Pois, *The School Board Crisis* (Chicago: Educational Methods, Inc., 1964), p. 45.

13. Furnas, p. 42. "Benjamin Willis," p. 93. *Chicago Daily News,* July 2, 1962.

14. Evelyn Carlson quoted in Liston, p. 26. *Chicago Daily News,* July 2, 1962.

15. Letter from R. J. Spaeth to other board members, April 29, 1963, p. 3. More than half of the board members who served in these years were either on record in the official *Proceedings* or quoted by the press as being firmly behind and appreciative of Willis's efforts.

16. *Saturday Evening Post* 236 (October 9, 1963): 26. Interview with Warren Bacon, June 28, 1973.

17. Pois, pp. 210–12. *Official Report of the Proceedings of the Board of Education,* July 12, 1961, p. 27.

18. *Chicago Daily News,* July 9, 1962.

19. Stephen London, "Business and the Chicago Public School System, 1890–1966," Ph.D. diss., University of Chicago, 1968, p. 150; ibid., pp. 146–73.

20. Edward C. Banfield, *Political Influence* (New York: The Free Press, 1961), pp. 252–53.

21. *Chicago Tribune,* October 5, 1963. See also Mike Royko, *Boss* (New York: New American Library, 1971), p. 147.

22. *Time*, September 15, 1961, p. 52. *Chicago Daily News,* August 19, 1961; *Chicago Sun Times,* August 19, 1961.

23. From 492,000 blacks, or 13.6 percent of Chicago's population, in 1950, to 812,637, or 23.6 percent of the city's population, in 1960.

24. See Mary Herrick, *The Chicago Schools: A Social and Political History* (Los Angeles: Sage Publications, 1971), p. 304.

25. Chicago Public Schools, *Ten Years of Growing,* p. 3.

26. A charge constantly leveled at Willis by community groups, the Urban League, and the Coordinating Council of Community Organizations (CCCO) was that there were more children in the schools during 1931–32 than in any subsequent year including 1961–63. In other words, because of the suburban exodus,

space was available to relieve overcrowding in other areas. Willis, they argued, had in effect manipulated the data presented to the board and the public in order to create the image of overcrowding in black areas so that bond issues would be passed for more buildings; thus he could avoid moving students to closer, available classrooms in other neighborhoods.

The point is valid only if one accepts either that the superintendent had racist motives or that the board and administration operated on the premise of the neighborhood school, or both. Seen through the eyes of these officials, parts of the city were sorely in need of buildings, additions, and mobile units. Without this neighborhood school policy, they probably would not have perceived a serious space shortage. Moreover, as will be pointed out later, the ideology of neighborhood schools was bound up with professionalism. For documentation of the charge, see *Handbook of Chicago School Segregation 1963,* pp. 10–17.

27. Ibid., p. 4. John Coons, "Chicago," in *Civil Rights U.S.A.: Public Schools,* 1962 (Washington, D.C: U.S. Commission on Civil Rights, 1962), p. 223.

28. *Proceedings,* December 27, 1961, pp. 924–25.

29. "De Facto Segregation in the Chicago Public Schools," *Crisis* 65 (February 1958): 87–93, 126. Protests against segregation, and documented charges, go back to the 1930s and 1940s with the efforts of the Citizens Schools Committee, Urban League, and the Federation of Colored Womens' Clubs.

30. *New York Times,* June 28, 1961. *Webb* v. *Board of Education,* Affidavit in Answer to Affidavit of Paul Zuber, no. 61, C 1569 (U.S. District Court, Northern District, Illinois, 1961), p. 2.

31. "Dr. Willis and Segregation," *Daily Defender,* September 5, 1961. "Resolution by Chicago Urban League Board of Directors Submitted to the Chicago Board of Education," October 13, 1961, p. 4.

32. *Proceedings,* December 27, 1961, p. 924.

33. Urban League, "Unreported Classrooms," December 5, 1961. *Daily Defender,* September 5, 1961.

34. Coons, "Chicago," *Civil Rights U.S.A.,* p. 198.

35. *Proceedings,* December 27, 1961, p. 924. *Chicago Sun Times,* October 13, 1962.

36. *Chicago Daily News,* May 25, 1963. Claire Roddewig, quoted in *Chicago Tribune,* September 1, 1963.

37. Most probably, the introduction of the permissive transfer policy was due to increasing civil rights activity in these months. In January 1962 sixteen parents picketing overcrowded Burnside Elementary were arrested (*Chicago Tribune,* January 17, 1962). A new court suit, *Burroughs* v. *Board of Education,* charging deliberate segregation at the school, came as an aftermath of the protest. In June, "truth squads" of black mothers, mostly from the activist Woodlawn Organization, entered white schools and photographed empty classrooms. Arrests were made for trespassing (Charles Silberman, *Crisis in Black and White* [New York: Random House, 1964], p. 331).

38. *Proceedings,* August 22, 1962, p. 286. What taxed activist black and white parents was that the 40–30 formula was discriminatory. That is, thirty pupils per class had always been an official goal of the school system, whereas here, where black children were concerned, there had to be forty in a class before any were eligible to transfer. See Coons, "Chicago," pp. 191–94.

39. Urban League, "Statement to Board of Education," November 19, 1962. In an effort to halt their criticism of the schools, Willis filed a formal complaint with the welfare council that provided the Urban League with funds. The league documented all their charges, placing them in the context of citizen action. There was a lengthy hearing of the council's board of directors, and the Urban League was cleared of Willis's complaint. Hal Baron, head of the Urban League Research Department and the person who had to document all of the League criticisms said, "At that point, as far as we were concerned, Willis was a son-of-a-bitch and we were ready to go full force on him" (interview with Hal Baron, June 27, 1973).

40. August Meier and Elliot Rudwick, *CORE: A Study in the Civil Rights Movement, 1942–1968* (New York: Oxford University Press, 1973), pp. 109–10, 121, 193.

41. Caples resigned shortly after the picketing. Both Mayor Daley and writer Charles Silberman concluded that the picketing led to the resignation. (*Chicago Tribune,* August 17, 1963. Silberman, p. 331; also see pp. 318–48 for his portrait of TWO).

42. See August Meier and Thomas Kahn, "Recent Trends in the Civil Rights Movement," *New Politics* 3, no. 2 (Spring 1964): 1–20.

43. See, for example, *Chicago Tribune,* July 1963–August 1963.

44. *Chicago Tribune,* July 8, 13, 1963.

45. Ibid., July 12, 1963.

46. *Chicago Daily News,* July 17, 1963. Meier and Rudwick, p. 247.

47. During July and August, Willis was spending a great deal of time, mostly on weekends, but during the week also, in Massachusetts directing a statewide survey he had contracted for in January 1963. See last section of this chapter.

48. *Chicago Tribune,* August 13, August 3, 1963.

49. Ibid., August 15, August 16, 1963.

50. Ibid., August 17, August 21, 1963.

51. Ibid., August 24, 1963. The panel was later named the Hauser Panel after its chairman, Dr. Phillip Hauser of the University of Chicago.

52. For details of these events, see the *Daily Defender, Tribune, Daily News,* and *Sun Times,* September 4–19, 1963.

53. *Chicago Tribune,* September 12, 1963.

54. John Coons, "Chicago" (draft manuscript for report to U.S. Office of Education, 1965), III-17.

55. After the change, CORE chairman Milton Davis said: "He [Willis] yields immediately to protest of white parents while complaints of dozens of Negro groups concerned with education of their children go without any comment from the Superintendent. It is apparent that public protest by Negroes means nothing to Willis.... Negroes have been complaining about overcrowding and poor education for their children for a long time and whenever a token gesture is made to do something about this, Willis buckles under the protest of the white parents" (*Chicago Sun Times,* September 21, 1963).

56. *Chicago Tribune,* September 28, 1963.

57. Ibid., September 30, 1963; Willis's view was expressed in the interview.

58. Rumor had it, as did press reports, that Willis scooted down a side stairwell while the deputy sheriff chased after him. Willis repeatedly denied this. At one meeting, Pasnick repeated the accusation and Willis angrily injected: "I did not run down any back stairs. I would not run from all the people in this room.... You get your facts straight" (*Proceedings,* March 11, 1964).

59. *Chicago Tribune,* October 5, 1963. This was not the first time that Willis talked resignation. Board members Bacon, Friedman, and Pois recalled in interviews and elsewhere numerous instances when Willis threatened in executive session that he

would resign. The last portion of this chapter deals with the Havighurst Report, another instance when he vowed to leave.

60. Ibid.

61. Ibid.

62. Stephen London concluded that this telegram was very influential in the Board's final decision. My interviews confirm London's conclusion.

63. See the *Chicago Sun Times, Daily Defender, Chicago Tribune,* October 5–9.

64. *Chicago Tribune,* October 5, 1963.

65. Interview with Hal Baron, June 27, 1973.

66. *Chicago Tribune,* October 17, 1963.

67. *Proceedings,* November 22, 1961, p. 779.

68. Ibid., January 23, 1963, pp. 1848–51.

69. Ibid., p. 1848. McSwain, quoted in Coons (USOE Report), p. III-4.

70. Letter of Edward Keener to Claire Roddewig, January 16, 1963.

71. Interview with Hal Baron, June 27, 1973. For example of adverse reaction from the media, see the WBBM-TV editorial on the survey, March 13, 1963.

72. See "Education and the Social Problems of the Big City," a speech Havighurst gave to the American Association for the Advancement of Science, December 30, 1962.

73. Interview with Bernard Friedman, June 26, 1973.

74. *Chicago Daily News,* May 2, May 7, May 9, 1963. Letter from R. J. Spaeth to other board members, April 29, 1963.

75. *Chicago American,* May 29, 1963; interviews with Bernard Friedman, June 26, 1973, and Warren Bacon, June 28, 1973.

76. *Proceedings,* May 22, 1963, p. 2234. That Dr. Willis, an outsider, had been appointed the Massachusetts study director did not trouble the superintendent one bit in his criticism of the sub-committee's choice for survey director. He even used his appointment as an example of how state authorities used to make policy prior to his arrival.

77. Ibid., p. 2235.

78. Ibid. *Daily Defender,* May 27, 1963.

79. Interview with Warren Bacon, June 28, 1973. *Chicago American,* May 29, 1963.

80. *Daily Defender,* May 29, 1963. *Chicago Daily News,* May 29, 1963.

81. Letter from Robert Havighurst to Edward Keener, May 30, 1963.

82. *Proceedings,* November 27, 1963, pp. 739–46. *Chicago Tribune,* May 27, 1964. Robert Havighurst, *The Public Schools of Chicago* (Chicago: Board of Education, 1964), p. 7. *Chicago Daily News,* June 3, 1964.

83. Coons (USOE Report), p. III-7.

84. Interview with Bernard Friedman, June 26, 1973; *Chicago Tribune,* November 13, 1964.

85. Havighurst, pp. 28–30.

86. *Chicago Tribune,* November 13, 1964.

87. "Comparison of Survey Recommendations and Dr. Willis' Comments," Memo from Havighurst to CSC, December 29, 1964.

88. "Importance of the Superintendent in the Program for Integration," speech by Havighurst to Chicago Region of Illinois Congress of Parents and Teachers, February 11, 1965, p. 2.

89. *Chicago Daily News,* October 8, 1966.

90. *Proceedings,* May 28, 1965, pp. 2592–97.

91. London, pp. 148, 173; see also his unpublished interviews for doctoral dissertation, Interview 5, p. 1.

92. Interview with Hal Baron, June 27, 1973. Interview with Lloyd Waterloo, June 28, 1973. Interview with Bernard Friedman, June 26, 1975.

Chapter 2

1. Washington, D.C., *Annual Report: Government of the District of Columbia, 1962,* pp. 3-1, 3-2; Harry Passow, *Toward Creating a Model Urban School System* (New York: Columbia University, Teachers College Press, 1967), pp. 84, 173, 181; *Hobson* v. *Hansen* Decision, reprinted in *Congressional Record,* June 21, 1967, pp. H7662–63. A 1906 law directed federal district judges to appoint board members for three-year terms. Between 1906 and 1967, judges appointed three blacks, six whites. Since 1962, a fourth black has been appointed.

2. Carl Hansen, *Danger in Washington* (Nyack, N.Y.: Parker Publishing Company, 1968), pp. 24, 14, 16.

3. Carl Hansen, *Amidon Elementary School* (Englewood Cliffs, N.J.: Prentice-Hall, 1962), pp. 66, 151.

4. Four tracks were introduced in high schools—Honors, College Preparatory, General, and Basic; three in junior high and elementary (College Preparatory was omitted from the lower levels).

5. Notes taken by the author at city-wide Teachers' Conference, October 30, 1965.

6. Interview with Carl Hansen, August 28, 1973.

7. Peter Marris and Martin Rein, *Dilemmas of Social Reform* (New York: Atherton Press, 1967), p. 17.

8. The preceding description of professional reformers is drawn from Marris and Rein, chapter 1; Daniel Moynihan, *Maximum Feasible Misunderstanding* (New York: Free Press, 1970), chapters 3–4; and Stephen Thernstrom, *Poverty, Planning and Politics* (New York: Basic Books, 1969), chapter 1.

9. *Washington Post,* December 27, 1964.

10. President's Committee on Juvenile Delinquency, *Washington Action for Youth,* March, 1965, volume 1, pp. 9, 27, 30–31.

11. Interview with Carl Hansen, August 28, 1973.

12. *Washington Post,* March 27, 1963.

13. Interview with Jack Goldberg, May 3, 1972.

14. Memoranda to Superintendent Carl Hansen from assistants John Koontz, Irene Hypps, John Riecks, et alia, October–December, 1963.

15. Interview with Jack Goldberg, May 3, 1972. Interview with Carl Hansen, August 28, 1973. Board of Education *Minutes,* vol. 111, January 15, 1964, p. 41. Hansen, *Danger in Washington,* p. 130.

16. Sargent Shriver, *Point of the Lance* (New York: Harper and Row, 1964), p. 99.

17. List of participants at seminars appended to "Innovation and Experiment in Education," President's Panel on Educational Research and Development, March 1964.

18. Joseph Turner, *Making New Schools* (New York: David McKay, 1971), p. 175. Interviews with Joseph Turner, March 28 and April 10, 1972.

19. "Innovation and Experiment in Education," p. 37.

20. Interview with Norman Nickens, June 9, 1972; interviews with Joseph Turner, March 28 and April 10, 1972.

21. *Superintendent's Report to Board of Education,* June 11, 1964, p. 1.

22. Hansen, *Danger in Washington,* pp. 128–29.

23. *Washington Post,* August 19, 1964.

24. "Model School System: A Preliminary Report," September 15, 1964, pp. 16–17.

25. "Innovation and Experiment," p. 38; emphasis added.

26. Letter from Carl Hansen to Wesley Williams, August 4, 1964.

27. Gail Saliterman, "Citizen Participation in an Urban School System: The Washington Case," in Barry Passett and Edgar Cahn, eds., *Citizen Participation* (New York Community Training, Inc., 1970), p. 164.

28. Letter from David Bazelon to Wesley Williams, November 20, 1964. Gail Saliterman shaped the first in-service institute for MSD teachers, the subsequent summer in-service training in four curriculum areas, and the imaginative follow-up program. She coordinated the use of consultants, did much of the leg work along with Barbara Hazel, an Assistant Director of the MSD. Her constant negotiations with MSD staff, UPO staff, and outside consultants, however, could not reverse the powerlessness of the committee.

29. Interview with Norman Nickens, June 9, 1972.

30. "Model School System Submission of Education Proposals," November, 1964, p. 3.

31. *Washington Post,* July 19, 1965.

32. Washington *Evening Star,* April 25, 1965.

33. *Washington Post,* September 1, 1965.

34. *Superintendent's Circular—99,* October 1, 1965. Board of Education *Minutes,* Vol. 114, pp. 27–28.

35. Hansen, *Danger in Washington,* p. 129.

36. Interview with Louise Steele, April 14, 1972.

37. "Summary of MSD Per Pupil Expenditures for Elementary and Secondary School Pupils by School Year," 1968, p. 1.

38. From the private journal of Gail Saliterman, October 6, 1965.

39. *Washington Post,* November 1, 1965.

40. They grew up a block apart from each other in Anacostia; they were "good friends" (words both used in interviews). They went to Dunbar High, graduating a year apart. Coincidentally, both chose the same motto—a line from one of Paul Lawrence Dunbar's poems, to summarize their beliefs: "Keep a-pluggin away." (Dunbar *Liber Anni,* 1936, 1937).

41. Interview with James Banks, May 5, 1972; interview with Irene Hypps, April 6, 1972.

42. Interview with Diane Sternberg, UPO education specialist,

April 7, 1972. Memorandum from Cy Rotter to UPO Task Force on Education, March 11, 1966.

43. Hansen, *Danger in Washington*, p. 24.

44. *Time,* vol. 75, February 1, 1960; vol. 76, October 31, 1960 . "Carl Hansen," *Saturday Review,* vol. 44, December 16, 1961.

45. Board of Education *Minutes,* vol. 113, April 22, 1965, p. 7.

46. Interview with Carl Hansen, August 28, 1973.

47. *Minutes,* May 25, 1954, p. 1.

48. This is the title of a pamphlet Hansen authored for the Anti-Defamation League on desegregation in 1957.

49. *Time,* February 1, 1960. *Saturday Review,* December 16, 1961.

50. Hobson v. Hansen (1967) in *Congressional Records,* pp. H7658, H7662–63, H7665, H7669.

51. *Afro-American,* June 29, 1963. *Evening Star,* June 23, 1963.

52. Washington, D.C., Urban League, "Integration and the Public Schools," June 1964, pp. 4, 7, 18.

53. *Minutes,* June 23, 1964, Vol. 111, pp. 97–98.

54. Carl Hansen, "Response of the Superintendent to Urban League Proposals on Desegregation," September 1, 1964, pp. 6, 8, 12, 22. In 1966 testimony before Judge Skelly Wright both Carl Hansen and his Assistant John Koontz admitted that certain boundary changes and creation of optional zones were devices to retain white families in schools they wished to attend (Hobson v. Hansen, pp. H7659–60).

55. Hansen, "Response of the Superintendent...", pp. 30, 31.

56. Hansen, *Danger in Washington*, p. 74.

57. Urban League press release, December 16, 1964, p. 1.

58. *Minutes,* February 17, 1965, Vol. 113.

59. Two black members, West Hamilton and Wesley A. Williams, board president, had been members of the 1954 board and had worked with Hansen closely, admiring his efforts during the last decade.

60. Hansen, *Danger in Washington*, p. 75.

61. "It seems like a contradiction. Here I was the man who put black teachers at previously white Anacostia and Coolidge high schools on the basis of merit and I should be charged with racial prejudice. . . . It is not too difficult to have a sense of injustice about it all" (interview with Carl Hansen, August 28, 1973).

62. Ibid.

Chapter 3

1. Ava Swartz, "Everyone's Favorite City," *California Living,* September 16, 1973, p. 16.

2. Frederick Wirt, "Alioto and the Politics of Hyperpluralism," *Transaction* 7 (April 1970): 50.

3. The Board is appointed for five-year terms but must be approved by the electorate at election time. A gentleman's agreement has the Mayor appointing three Protestants, two Catholics, and two Jews. Of these two must be women, one from the business community and one representing labor. Since 1961, at least one black (usually a Protestant) has been appointed. (Robert Lee, Jr., "Educational Ideology and Decisionmaking in the San Francisco Schools, 1956–1966" [Ph.D. diss., Syracuse University, 1967], p. 47).

4. Interview with Harold Spears, July 18, 1973.

5. San Francisco *Call-Bulletin,* November 18, 1957.

6. San Francisco *Chronicle,* November 30, 1957.

7. *Call-Bulletin,* December 3–12, 1957; San Francisco *Examiner,* December 30, 1957.

8. *Examiner,* December 13, 1957; *News,* December 19, 1957; *Call-Bulletin,* December 5, 1957; *Call-Bulletin,* January 30, 1958.

9. Interview with Harold Spears, July 18, 1973.

10. *Examiner,* February 15, 1958.

11. *Call-Bulletin,* March 4, 1958.

12. *Examiner,* March 15, 1958.

13. *Examiner,* May 5, 1959; May 27, 1958; May 5, 1958.

14. Ibid., March 15, 1958.

15. San Francisco, *Board of Education Transcript,* March 18, 1958, p. 82.

16. *News,* June 5, 1958.

17. Interview with Harold Spears, July 18, 1973.

18. Mortimer Smith, "How to Teach the California Child: Notes from the Never-Never Land," *Atlantic* 202 (September 1958): 34.

19. *Examiner,* September 5, 1958. *San Francisco Progress,* September 9–10, 1958; October 8, 1958.

20. The following accounts of proceedings at various board meetings are based on the *Board of Education Transcript,* October 21, 1958, pp. 49, 51, 59, 60, 61; ibid., November 4, 1958, p. 60; ibid., February 26, 1959, pp. 65–66.

21. Lee, p. 60. Interview with Harold Spears, July 18, 1973. Spears, by his account, seldom met privately with board members to discuss official business. But this was a crucial issue he didn't want to lose. It left such a bad taste in his mouth that he never did it again.

22. *Board of Education Transcript,* June 16, 1959, p. 70.

23. *Curriculum Committee Transcript,* April 15, 1959, p. 56.

24. San Francisco *News,* July 18, 1959.

25. Ibid. Interview with Claire Matzger Lilienthal, July 11, 1973.

26. *Report of the San Francisco Curriculum Survey Committee,* April 1, 1960, p. 7. The following description of recommendations is taken from pp. 7, 54, 35, and 43.

27. Interview with Harold Spears, July 18, 1973.

28. Harold Spears, "Preliminary Reactions to the Report of San Francisco Curriculum Survey Committee," May 13, 1960, pp. 4–5.

29. *Curriculum Committee Transcript,* May 24, 1960, p. 6.

30. Lee, p. 75.

31. Interview with Harold Spears, July 18, 1973.

32. *Examiner,* August 8, 1961. Interview with Harold Spears, July 18, 1973.

33. Lee, p. 131.

34. John Kaplan, "San Francisco," in Roscoe Hill and Malcolm Feely, eds., *Affirmative School Integration* (Los Angeles: Sage Publications, 1967), pp. 64–65. Robert Crain, *The Politics of School Desegregation* (New York: Aldine, 1968), p. 107.

35. *Call-Bulletin,* September 4, 1957.

36. *News,* September 25, 1957. *Call-Bulletin,* September 25, 1957; ibid., October 3, 1957.

37. Lee, p. 134.

38. *Board of Education Transcript,* December 5, 1961, pp. 23–24.

39. Kaplan, p. 66.

40. See *Board of Education Transcript,* January 23, 1962, pp. 46, 51–52, 55, 59–60.

41. Harold Spears cited in Kaplan p. 67.

42. *Examiner,* May 13, 1962.

43. Harold Spears, "The Proper Recognition of a Pupil's Racial Background," June 19, 1962, pp. 6, 7, 14, 23, 24, 25.

44. Interview with Harold Spears, July 18, 1973.

45. *News,* June 20, 1962; *Chronicle,* June 27, 1962.

46. Kaplan, pp. 70, 71.

47. *Examiner,* July 24, 1962. *Board of Education Transcript,* August 7, 1962, p. 111.

48. In the business session prior to speakers on Central, the board approved the superintendent's request for an additional $100,000 to expand the Ford-funded compensatory education program. Having returned from a national tour of big cities, Spears and board member Claire Matzger saw increasing emphasis on compensatory programs in New York, Chicago, and Washington, D.C. While applauding this move, civil rights activists saw it either as a strategic move by the administration to divert attention from de facto segregation or, at best, perceived the two as a related problem. (Interview with Claire Matzger Lilienthal, July 18, 1973; Lee, p. 54; see Dr. Z. Goosby's testimony in *Board of Education Transcript,* September 18, 1962.)

49. *News,* August 16, 1962.

50. *Chronicle,* August 9, 1962. *News,* August 11, 1962.

51. Interview with Harold Spears, July 18, 1973.

52. *Examiner,* August 24, 1962.

53. Ibid., September 28, 1962.

54. *Board of Education Transcript,* September 18, 1962, pp. 176–77. The Ad Hoc Committee consisted of Claire Matzger, chairwoman, Joseph Moore, and James Stratten.

55. Lee, p. 163. *Chronicle,* October 3, 1962.

56. Lee, p. 166. Interview with Claire Matzger Lilienthal, July 18, 1973.

57. *Report of the Ad Hoc Committee of the Board of Education to Study Ethnic Factors in the San Francisco Public Schools,* April 2, 1963, pp. 7–8, 14.

58. Kaplan, p. 73.

59. Ibid., pp. 73–74.

Chapter 4

1. San Francisco politics is the subject of Frederick Wirt's article "Alioto and the Politics of Hyperpluralism," *Transaction* 7 (April 1970): 46–55; In Robert Crain, *The Politics of School Desegregation* (New York: Aldine, 1967), a chapter on the unfolding controversy over de facto school segregation in San Francisco is included. Chicago's pluralist politics is the subject of Edward Banfield's study *Political Influence* (New York:

Free Press, 1961); Stephen London's doctoral dissertation "Business and the Chicago Public School System, 1890–1966" (University of Chicago, 1968) includes material on the political structure.

2. See Constance Green, *The Secret City* (Princeton, N.J.: Princeton University Press, 1967), chapters 9–11; Andrew Kopkind and James Ridgeway, "Washington—The Last Colony," *New Republic,* April 23 and 30, 1966, pp. 13–17, 19–22; Harry Passow, *Toward Creating a Model Urban School System* (New York: Teachers College Press, 1967), chapters 2 and 10.

3. D.C. had a complicated congressional review process of the entire District budget, including the schools. Nonetheless, the school system retained broad decision-making powers relatively free from commissioner and congressional involvement.

4. Dr. Carl Hansen's correspondence file, 1963–1967, is filled with letters from congressmen asking the superintendent to consider certain constituents for a particular job. Often these were not just any congressmen; among those who sent letters to Hansen were John McMillan, Sam Ervin, Strom Thurmond, and Adam Clayton Powell, powerful members of the very House and Senate committees from which Hansen had to gain approval for his budget. Invariably, Hansen's polite reply would express appreciation for the recommendation but remind the legislator that the person would receive equal consideration with all the candidates. When the particular individual did obtain a teaching position or a promotion, Dr. Hansen sent a letter informing the legislator what happened.

5. Interview with Carl Hansen, August 28, 1973.

6. For further comparison with other boards of education, see Crain, *The Politics of School Desegregation,* chapter 12; Keith Goldhammer, *The School Board* (New York: Center for Applied Research, 1964); Frederick Wirt and Michael Kirst, *The Political Web of American Schools* (Boston: Little, Brown and Co., 1972), pp. 79–85.

7. Marilyn Gittell and T. Edward Hollander, *Six Urban School Districts* (New York: Praeger, 1958); Joseph Cronin, *The Control of Urban Schools* (New York: Free Press, 1973).

8. Numerous case studies document reliance upon professionals. See David Rogers, *110 Livingston Street: Politics and Bureaucracy in the New York Schools* (New York: Random House, 1968); Gittell and Hollander, *Six Urban School Districts;* H. Thomas James, et al., *Determinants of Educational Expenditures in Large Cities of the United States* (Stanford:

School of Education, 1963); Peter Shrag, *Village School Downtown* (Boston: Beacon Press, 1967). Interestingly enough, Robert Crain's earlier study, in which he concluded that superintendents played a minor role in the politics of desegregation, has been subsequently revised to their having more influence. See David Kirby et al., *Political Strategies in Northern School Desegregation* (Lexington, Mass.: D. C. Heath, 1973), chapter 6.

9.   Joseph Pois, *The School Board Crisis* (Chicago: Educational Methods, Inc., 1964). Chicago, *Official Report of the Proceedings of the Board of Education,* April 23, 1964. Booz, Allen, and Hamilton management survey of the Chicago schools prepared in 1967 and cited in Morris Janowitz, *Institution Building in Urban Education* (Chicago: University of Chicago Press, 1969), p. 25.

10. H. Gerald Rowe, Jr., "A Taxonomic Analysis of the Budget-Making Structure of the San Francisco Unified School District," (Ph.D. Diss., Stanford University, 1966), pp. 26, 75. Interview with Harold Spears, July 18, 1973.

11. Passow, p. 173.

12. Expenses are usually covered and, in some instances, modest payments are made to board members. Los Angeles and New York board members receive enough compensation and fringe benefits in the form of limosines and such to make the position relatively attractive. Chicago and Washington members were unpaid; San Francisco's received $100 a month in the years of Spears' crises. Robert Bendiner, *The Politics of Schools* (New York: Harper and Row, 1969), p. 24.

13. David Minar, *Educational Decision-Making in Suburban Communities* (Washington, D.C.: U.S. Department of Health, Education and Welfare, 1966), p. 832. Neal Gross, *Who Runs Our Schools?* (New York: John Wiley, 1958), p. 95; T. R. Bowman, "Participation of Superintendents in School Board Decision-Making," *Administrator's Notebook* 11 (January 1963): 1–4. Harmon Zeigler, M. Kent Jennings, and G. Wayne Peak, "Governing American Schools" (unpublished manuscript, 1973), p. 38. Peter Bachrach and Morton Baratz, "The Two Faces of Power," *American Political Science Review* 57 (December 1962): 947–52.

14. Zeigler, p. 34. Eugene R. Smoley, Jr., *Community Participation in Urban School Government,* (Washington, D.C.: U.S. Office of Education, 1965), p. 180.

15. Spears and Hansen suggested but did not say these things directly; inferences come from this writer. Joseph Pois reached these same conclusions about Willis—as, again, did this writer.

16. Crain, pp. 115–117; Irwin Johnson, "Problems Inherent in Big City Boards," (paper presented to Conference of American Educational Research Association), February 18, 1967.

17. Ziegler, p. 39. James Lipham, Russell Gregg, and Richard Rossmiller, "The School Board: Resolver of Conflict?" *Administrator's Notebook* 17 (April 1969). Pois, p. 114.

18. Gittell and Hollander, p. 95.

19. See Gittell and Hollander, chapter 4; Wirt and Kirst, pp. 85–88.

20. Interview with Harold Spears, July 18, 1973.

21. Harold Spears, "The Proper Recognition of a Pupil's Racial Background" (report to the school board), June 19, 1962.

22. "Willis Concentrates on Quality Education for All: An Interview," Phi Delta *Kappan* 46 (December 1964): 160.

23. By mid-1965, Spears did release the results of a racial head count quietly taken the previous year. He did so, however, only after being the target of three separate investigations into racial imbalance and discrimination which were undertaken by state and federal officials. Kirby et alia found that virtually no desegregation had occurred in Chicago and Washington by 1971, although San Francisco, under court order to desegregate, did have a hefty increase in mixed schools. Moreover, Kirby argued that some civil rights strategies did result in change. See pp. 185–87, 102.

24. Crain, pp. 115–16. Roscoe Hill and Malcolm Feely, *Affirmative School Integration* (Beverly Hills, Cal.: Sage Publications, 1967), "St. Louis," pp. 53–60. See Rogers, chapters 7–8; Bert Swanson, *The Struggle for Equality* (New York: Hobbs, Dorman, 1966).

25. Detroit and Pittsburgh were the exceptions. And here the time-bound nature of these studies is self-evident, since now, a few years later, these conclusions of aggressive desegregation practices upon the part of the system would not apply even in those cities.

26. Alan B. Anderson and George Pickering, *The Issue of the Color Line: A View from Chicago* (Chicago: University of Chicago Divinity School, 1973), chapter 3, p. 19, citing the *Chicago Tribune*, October 17, 1961. Letter from R. J. Spaeth to board of education members, April 29, 1963.

27. Interviews with Mrs. Barbara Hazel, Mrs. Marilyn Brown, and Mrs. Anne Pitts, August 28, 1973.

Chapter 5

1. As used here, "leadership" means the power to do things and to get people to do things that the leader, by him- or herself, would not be able to do. Implied in this definition is the link between leader, the led, and the situation. The leader knows how to get the compliance of the led in a particular situation and uses that compliance effectively.

   This view of leadership departs from older theories but is well within the mainstream of current literature on the subject. Over the years there has been a shift from an investigation of personal traits in leaders (determination, intelligence, commitment, etc.) to more of an emphasis upon followers, the situation, and the interplay between all of these factors. Early investigators could only come up with, at best, correlations between certain personality traits and leadership status. Few theorists pursue this line of inquiry now (see R. Stogdill, "Personal Factors Associated with Leadership: A Survey of the Literature," *Journal of Psychology,* vol. 25, pp. 35–71). Emphasis on interaction of leaders and followers has been put forward by a number of researchers. C. Argyris, *Integrating the Individual and the Organization* (New York: John Wiley & Sons, 1964), and E. H. Schein and W. Bennis, *Personal and Organizational Change through Group Methods* (New York: John Wiley & Sons, 1965) are a few representative studies. These theories and studies stress the importance of positive interpersonal relations in effective leadership. Fred Fiedler's works constitute the clearest statement of those investigators who explore the interaction between leader and the situation. See his *Theory of Leadership Effectiveness* (New York: McGraw Hill, 1967) and "Leadership" (General Learning Corporation., 1971).

   "Leadership," of course, is a catch-all term for the superintendent's daily role. He is, for instance, figurehead, spokesman, crisis-handler, negotiator, entrepreneur, resource allocator, disseminator of information. For a fuller discussion of the roles played by superintendents, see Henry Mintzberg, *The Nature of Managerial Work* (New York: Harper and Row, 1973), p. 59. Of the five executives he studied, one was a superintendent of a large school district. The multiple roles school chiefs play are also dealt with in Neal Gross, *Who Runs Our Schools?* (New York: John Wiley & Sons, 1958) and Richard Carlson, *School Superintendents: Careers and Performance* (Columbus, Ohio: Charles Merrill, 1972).

Leader power permeates all of these working roles. As Mintzberg pointed out, clues about what the superintendent will do are communicated to various members of the organization in a variety of ways—encouragement or criticism of a subordinate, a memo sent to an assistant, a quick entry and exit at a department head's office, a brief phone call to pass on information (Mintzberg, p. 61).

The widespread, subtle influence of leader power throughout the organization, then, is acknowledged. The concept of leadership role as used here, however, will refer only to decision-making activities. In addition, "role," as used here, refers to those sets of behaviors accompanying the position of superintendency. Individual personality affects how the role is played out (leadership style—an important consideration), but it does not determine whether the role is performed.

2. B. A. Hinsdale, "The American School Superintendent," *Educational Review* 7 (January 1894): 46; also see chapter 5 in Theodore Reller, *The Development of the City Superintendency of Schools in the United States* (Philadelphia: Published by the author, 1935), and Thomas Gilland, *Origin and Development of the Power and Duties of the City School Superintendent* (Chicago: University of Chicago, 1935), pp. 8–19.

3. Gilland, pp. 39–74.

4. Reller, p. 162, citing the Brooklyn *Daily Eagle*, July 9, 1873.

5. John D. Philbrick, *City School Systems in the United States*, Circular of Information, no. 1 (Washington, D.C.: Government Printing Office, 1885), p. 14. See also David Tyack "City Schools: Centralization of Control at the Turn of the Century," in J. Israel, ed., *Organizational Society* (Free Press, 1972).

6. L. H. Jones, "The Politician and the Public School: Indianapolis and Cleveland," *Atlantic Monthly* 77 (June 1896): 813.

7. For a rich recounting of similar examples see S. A. Wetmore, "Boston School Administration," *Educational Review* 14 (September 1897): 105–17.

8. National Educational Association, *Journal of Proceedings and Addresses, 1890,* "Report of the Committee on City School Systems" (Topeka, Kan.: Kansas Publishing House, 1890), p. 311.

9. Tyack, p. 65. Detailed recounting of the 1895 episode can be found in Raymond Callahan, "The Fight to Control Policy," in Frank Lutz and Joseph Azzarelli, eds., *Struggle for Power in Education* (New York: The Center for Applied Research in

Education, 1965), pp. 22–30. Arthur Chamberlain, "The Growth and Enlargement of the Power of the City School Superintendent," University of California, *Publications* (May 15, 1913): 411; also see appendix.

10. While these ideal types were derived from the rhetoric, writings, and actions of urban schoolmen, top administrators did not consciously use these categories when they spoke and wrote. These types were, in effect, distilled from a huge body of evidence. Could these superintendents have read this study, they might well have recognized the types but the language and phrasing would be unfamiliar to them.

11. Between 1870 and 1950, 78 percent of the officers of the association were big-city superintendents (i.e., those cities defined as large in each period). In the same years, 56 percent of the presidents of the department were urban schoolmen. Urban men led the Association every year between 1908 and 1915. From 1919 to 1937 urban administrators served as president every year but three. Major committee assignments, chairmanships of resolution committees, yearbook assignments, and reporting tasks often went to big-city schoolmen in these years. Compiled from listings of officers in the Department of Superintendence, 1870–1937, and the American Association of School Administrators, 1937–1970, in *Official Report: American Association of School Administrators, 1971–1972* [Washington, D.C.: AASA, 1972], pp. 176–82.)

12. The schoolmen's views of the superintendency quoted in this section are taken from the following issues of the National Educational Association, *Journal of Proceedings and Addresses:* 1882, p. 98; 1899, p. 310; 1880, pp. 519–22; 1890, p. 463; 1897, p. 221; 1890, p. 313.

13. Such phrases were used often; these were taken at random from various volumes of the speeches of urban superintendents between 1873 and 1900. Specifically, see NEA, *Journal of Proceedings and Addresses,* 1873, p. 249; 1890, p. 463; 1895, p. 386.

14. Ibid., 1890, pp. 313, 467, 383.

15. Ibid., 1894, p. 309; Ronald M. Johnson, "Captain of Education: An Intellectual Biography of Andrew S. Draper, 1848–1913," (Ph.D. Diss., University of Illinois, 1870), p. 175. Cleveland hosted the 1895 NEA convention, from which came another report urging further centralization of powers into the superintendent's hands.

16. Johnson, p. 171. Raymond Callahan, *Education and the Cult of Efficiency* (Chicago: University of Chicago, 1962), p. 193. *Journal of Proceedings and Addresses*, 1884, p. 284; 1890, pp. 463–64.

17. Hinsdale, p. 49.

18. *Journal of Proceedings and Addresses*, 1901, p. 26.

19. Ibid., 1873, p. 253; 1904, pp. 272, 264; 1882, p. 292.

20. Callahan's main conclusions on the superintendency are included in *Education and the Cult of Efficiency; The Superintendent of Schools: A Historical Analysis* (Washington, D.C.: Office of Education, 1966); "Historical Change of the Role of the Man in the Organization, 1865–1950," co-authored with Warren Button, in Daniel Griffiths, ed., *Behavioral Science and Educational Administration*, vol. 63, part 2, (Chicago: University of Chicago Press, 1964).

21. Editorial, *American School Board Journal* 20 (February 1915): 30.

22. Raymond Callahan also concluded that the teacher-scholar conception dominated schoolmen's thinking in these years. My point, however, is to show both the continuing presence and relative strength of the other conceptions almost from the origin of the superintendency rather than to view leadership conceptions as appearing and disappearing in some sort of order.

23. Gilland, p. 154.

24. Chamberlain, p. 404; Appendix of Survey Answers.

25. John C. Morrison, *The Legal Status of the City School Superintendent* (Baltimore: Warwick and York, Inc., 1922), p. 88; Bennett C. Douglass, "Professional and Economic Status of the City Superintendent of Schools in the United States" (Ph.D. diss., Columbia University, 1923), pp. 125–39.

26. Douglass, p. 102; Department of Superintendence, *Educational Leadership*, Eleventh Yearbook (Washington, D.C.: National Educational Association, 1933), p. 369.

27. American Association of School Administrators, *The American School Superintendency*, Thirteenth Yearbook, (Washington, D.C.: AASA, 1952), pp. 452–53.

28. NEA, *Journal of Proceedings and Addresses*, 1873, pp. 248–50.

29. Callahan, "Historical Change of the Role of Man in the Organization," p. 77; idem, "The Changing Conceptions of the Superintendency in Public Education, 1865–1964" (undated

speech), p. 6; idem, *Education and the Cult of Efficiency*, pp. 48, 208.

30. One researcher who disagreed with Callahan took issue with the historian's single-minded explanation for penetration of business management techniques. Joseph Cronin traces the various threads within the nation and education that would account for the rapid introduction of scientific management. He pointed to the municipal reform movement which stressed efficient operation and was part of the larger progressive effort that had as its aim social efficiency. Cronin also cited earlier moves to develop a science of education that G. Stanley Hall, William James, and John Dewey pioneered, the efforts by Lewis Terman and Edward Thorndike to develop measurements of achievement and the general trend toward expertness that grew out of centralization reforms in public schools. See Joseph Cronin, *The Control of Urban Schools* (New York: Free Press, 1972), pp. 177–83.

31. Douglass, p. 35; AASA, *The American School Superintendent*, p. 44.

32. Hollis Caswell, *City School Surveys: An Interpretation and Appraisal* (New York: Teachers College, Columbia University, 1929), p. 51.

33. See Callahan, *Education and the Cult of Efficiency*, chapter 8.

34. On education of superintendents, see Douglass, pp. 30–34. On the bias toward business management see Harold Gear, "The Rise of City School Superintendency as an Influence on Educational Policy" (Ed.D. diss., Harvard University, 1950); Joseph Gwinn, "Twentieth Century Developments in City School Administration," in Jesse B. Sears, ed., *School Administration in the Twentieth Century* (Stanford: Stanford University Press, 1934); Elwood P. Cubberley, *Public School Administration* (Boston: Houghton Mifflin Company, 1916), chapter 10.

Statistics on education dissertations and later superintendencies are from Jesse H. Newlon, *Educational Administration as Social Policy* (New York: Charles Scribner's Sons, 1934), p. 260 and Appendix, and Callahan, *Education and the Cult of Efficiency*, p. 249.

35. AASA, *The American School Superintendent*, p. 448. Sixty-four percent had done graduate work in school administration. Since their median age was 56, it can be assumed that they attended school in the 1920s and 1930s.

36. Wallace S. Sayre, "Additional Observations on the Study of Administration," *Teachers College Record* 60 (October 1958): 75.

37. NEA, *Journal of Proceedings and Addresses*, 1895, p. 216.

38. Ibid., 1912, p. 331; 1927, p. 871; 1940, p. 191.

39. American Association of School Administrators, *The AASA Code of Ethics* (Washington, D.C.: AASA, 1966), p. 20; p. 23. The following discussion of the *Code* is based from pages 27, 18, 17, and 34.

Chapter 6

1. Interview with Carl Hansen, August 28, 1973.

2. Carl Hansen, *Danger in Washington* (West Nyack, N.Y.: Parker Publishing Co., 1968), pp. 145–46, 167, 173; Carl Hansen, *Amidon Elementary School* (Englewood Cliffs, N.J.: Prentice-Hall, 1962), ix; interview with Hansen, August 28, 1973.

3. Hansen, *Amidon Elementary School*, p. viii; *Danger in Washington*, pp. 93, 10, 133, 204.

4. Carl Hansen, "More to Come," speech given to D.C. Congress of Parents and Teachers, May 4, 1967; "Period of Danger, Time of Hope," speech given to D.C. Congress of Parents and Teachers, May 3, 1966. Hansen's correspondence file, 1963–1966, abounds with letters to congressmen, answering questions, politely rejecting requests of employment for constituents, and letters graciously responding to a legislator's recommendation. Interview with Hansen, August 28, 1973.

5. "Danger Facing Nation's Schools," interview with Carl Hansen in *U.S. News and World Report*, July 24, 1967, p. 42; Carl Hansen, "The Revolution and Big-City Schools," speech given to Teachers' Institute, October 27, 1965, p. 7.

6. Hansen, "More to Come," p. 5. *Danger in Washington*, pp. 109, 112, 133; "Danger Facing Nation's Schools," pp. 42, 48. *Danger in Washington*, pp. 133, 93; interview with Hansen, August 28, 1973.

7. Hansen, "Period of Danger, Time of Hope," p. 38; "Danger Facing Nation's Schools," p. 42; *Danger in Washington*, pp. 144, 147.

8. Hansen, *Danger in Washington*, pp. 144, 147; "Period of Danger, Time of Hope," pp. 3, 8.

9. Hansen, "More to Come," p. 5.

10. Hansen, *Danger in Washington*, pp. 90, 179; see also Carl Hansen, *Miracle of Adjustment* (New York: Anti-Defamation League, 1957), p. 52, where he admiringly describes how

desegregation was planned by himself and Superintendent Hobart Corning.

11. Hansen, *Danger in Washington,* p. 89.

12. Ibid., p. 177; *Amidon Elementary School,* p. ix.

13. Hansen, *Danger in Washington,* p. 157; *Addendum: A Five Year Report* (New York: Anti-Defamation League, 1960), p. 5, 8.

14. Carl Hansen, *Four Track Curriculum for Today's High Schools* (Englewood Cliffs, N.J.: Prentice-Hall, 1964), pp. 22–23.

15. Hansen, *Danger in Washington,* pp. 104, 177; *Miracle of Adjustment,* p. 54; interview with Hansen, August 28, 1973.

16. "A Philosophy for Administration: Interview with Benjamin Willis," *Nation's Schools,* April 1961, p. 74; Chicago Public Schools, *Annual Report,* 1965–1966, p. 1; Benjamin Willis, "Education, the Partner of Progress," American Association of School Administrators, *Official Report, 1958* (Washington, D.C.: AASA, 1959), p. 138.

17. Benjamin Willis, *Social Problems in Public School Administration* (Pittsburgh: University of Pittsburgh Press, 1967), p. 26.

18. Ibid., p. 27; Chicago Public Schools, *Annual Report,* 1963, p. 2.

19. Benjamin Willis, "Using the Criticism of Public Schools for Constructive Purposes," *Elementary School Journal,* September 1954, p. 20.

20. Benjamin Willis, "A Mid-Century View of Staffing a City School System; (Ed.D. diss., Teachers College, Columbia University, 1950), p. 12. Chicago Public Schools, *Annual Report, 1953,* p. 26; See also *Annual Report, 1963–1966; Social Problems in Public School Administration.* Willis, "Using the Criticism," p. 21.

21. Benjamin Willis, "Preserving Our Way of Life," *The School Executive,* June 1950, p. 54; Willis, "Using the Criticism," p. 14.

22. Willis, "Using the Criticism," p. 21.

23. See interview in *U.S. News and World Report,* November 11, 1965, p. 61; also "A Philosophy for Administration" in *Nation's Schools,* p. 75; Willis, "A Mid-Century View of Staffing," p. 37; and interview with this author on June 28, 1973.

24. Willis, "A Mid-Century View," p. 27. American Association of School Administrators, *Official Report, 1961* (Washington, D.C.: AASA, 1961), pp. 368–69; Willis, "Using the Criticism," p. 20.

25. "Willis Concentrates on Quality Education for All," Phi Delta *Kappan*, December 1964, p. 159.

26. Ibid., pp. 159–60; *Official Report, 1961*, pp. 368–69; Chicago Public Schools, *Annual Report*, 1953–1966.

27. Willis, *Social Problems*, pp. 18, 31. Willis, "Quality Education," pp. 159, 160. Chicago Public Schools, *Annual Report*, 1965–1966, p. 1.

28. *Annual Report*, 1958, pp. 55–56; 1963, p. 16; 1953, p. 24; 1963, p. 52.

29. Willis, *Social Problems*, p. 57; Chicago Public Schools, *Annual Reports*, 1953–1966.

30. Willis, "Preserving Our Way of Life," p. 19; Willis, "A Mid-Century View of Staffing," pp. 28, 35; Willis, *Social Problems*, p. 39; interview with Willis, 1973; Willis, "The Need for Professionalism," p. 276.

31. Chicago Public Schools, *Annual Report*, 1963, p. 52. Superintendent Herold Hunt, Willis's predecessor, published annual reports under various names: "Our Chicago Public Schools, 1950–1951," "A Report to the Stockholders, 1951–1952," and "Let's Teach, 1952–1953." In 1953, Willis' first report focused upon school construction. The phrase "school building" was used seventy-six times in only thirty-two pages. The peak usage of the phrase "we build" was eight times in four paragraphs on just two pages (*Annual Report*, 1953, pp. 30–31).

32. *Annual Report*, 1958; 1963, pp. 22–32; interview with Willis, 1973.

33. Mary Herrick, *The Chicago Schools* (Beverly Hills: Sage Publications, 1970), p. 310.

34. *Chicago Daily News*, July 2 and 7, 1962; interview with Willis, 1973.

35. *Chicago Sun Times*, July 31, 1963; see also chapters 1 and 5 of "The Growth of Direct Action" in Alan B. Anderson and George W. Pickering, *The Issue of the Color Line: A View from Chicago* (Chicago: University of Chicago Divinity School, 1973).

36. Anderson and Pickering, chapter 3, p. 17. Herrick, p. 332.

37. Robert Liston, "Pugnacious Planner of America's Future," *True*, May 1965, p. 26.

38. Interview with Harold Spears, July 18, 1973.

39. Harold Spears, "The Superintendent's Giants and His Windmills," *Official Report, 1966–1967* (Washington, D.C.: AASA, 1967), p. 157; *School Administrator* 23 (March 15,

1966): 1; Harold Spears, *The High School for Today* (New York: American Book Company, 1950), pp. 3, 8–10; Harold Spears, *Improving the Supervision of Instruction* (Englewood Cliffs, N.J.: Prentice-Hall, 1953), pp. 454–55.

40. Harold Spears, "The Proper Recognition of a Pupil's Social Background," speech delivered to the San Francisco Unified School District, June 19, 1962, p. 24; see also pp. 3–4, 24. The concept of equality also embraced his conviction about the equity of a single salary schedule for teachers.

41. Spears, "The Superintendent's Giants and His Windmills," p. 157; San Francisco, *Board of Education Transcript,* March 17, 1959, pp. 34–36; Association for Childhood Education, "Don't Push Me," introduction written by Harold Spears (Washington, D.C.: Association for Childhood Education, 1960), p. 1. Harold Spears, "Preliminary Reactions to the Report of San Francisco Curriculum Survey Committee," May 13, 1960, p. 31.

42. Interview with Spears.

43. Interview with Harold Spears, May 1973, in Phi Delta *Kappan;* see also Spears, *High School,* p. 209. Interview with Spears.

44. Harold Spears, "Why School Board Meetings Go to Pot," *Education Digest,* February 1969, p. 6; Harold Spears, "The Superintendent and Leadership," *American School and University* 37 (October 1964): 52; interview in *Kappan.*

45. Spears interview in *Kappan.* These seemingly contradictory concepts—democratic school administration and chain of command—appear and reappear in all three schoolmen's writings.

46. Spears, "The Superintendent and Leadership," p. 52. Spears, *Improving the Supervision of Instruction,* chapters 4, 7, 13, 16, 20–21; Spears, *High School Today,* chapters 5, 7, 10.

47. See Spears, *Improving Supervision,* pp. 47–48, 93–94, 112–113. See also internal memoranda on budget preparation for 1962–64 found in H. Gerald Rowe, Jr., "A Taxonomic Analysis of the Budget-Making Structure of the San Francisco Unified School District" (Ph.D. diss., Stanford University, 1966), pp. 25–26.

48. Spears, "Preliminary Reactions," p. 47; San Francisco, *Board of Education Transcript,* March 4, 1958, p. 17; Spears, *Improving Supervision,* p. 125; San Francisco *Examiner,* March 15, 1958; interview with Spears. A.C.E., "Don't Push Me," p. 2; *School Administrator,* Summer 1970, p. 12.

49. *Board of Education Transcript,* March 4, 1958, p. 96. Spears, "The Superintendent's Giants and His Windmills," pp. 154, 158. Interview in Phi Delta *Kappan.* Harold Spears, "Rededicate the Bridge between School and Home," *Nation's Schools,* August 1955, p. 38; *Board of Education Transcript,* March 4, 1958, p. 96.

50. Spears, "The Superintendent's Giants and His Windmills," pp. 150–51.

51. Ibid., p. 160; interview in Phi Delta *Kappan.*

52. Interview with Spears, interview in Phi Delta *Kappan.* Spears, "The Superintendent's Giants and His Windmills," p. 147.

53. Interview with Spears, interview in Phi Delta *Kappan.*

54. Interview with Claire Matzger Lilienthal, July 11, 1973; *Board of Education Transcript,* March 17, 1959, pp. 34–36.

55. Office of Superintendent, "1958–1959 Administrative and Supervisory Staff, Compared with 1954–1955" chart prepared for the Board of Education, February 25, 1959.

Conclusion

1. See Robert Crain, *The Politics of Desegregation* (Chicago: Aldine Publishing Co., 1968); Robert Dreeben, *On What Is Learned In School* (Menlo Park: Addison Wesley, 1968); Alex Inkeles, "The Socialization of Competence," *Harvard Educational Review* 36 (Summer 1966); 265–83.

Bibliography

Allison, Graham T. *Essence of Decision*. Boston: Little, Brown and Co., 1971.

American Association of School Administrators. *Official Report*. Washington, D.C.: AASA, 1940–1972.

———. *The American School Superintendent*. Thirtieth Yearbook. Washington, D.C.: AASA, 1952.

———. *The AASA Code of Ethics*. Washington, D.C.: AASA, 1966.

Anderson, Alan B., and Pickering, George. *The Issue of the Color Line: A View from Chicago*. Chicago: University of Chicago Divinity School, 1973.

Banfield, Edward C. *Political Influence*. New York: Free Press, 1961.

Bendiner, Robert. *The Politics of Schools*. New York: Harper and Row, 1969.

Bowman, T. R. *Administrator's Notebook*. Vol. 11 (January, 1963), pp. 1–4.

Callahan, Raymond. "The Changing Conceptions of the Superintendency in Public Education, 1865–1964." Mimeographed, n.d.

———. *Education and the Cult of Efficiency*. Chicago: University of Chicago, 1962.

———. "The Fight to Control Policy." *Struggle for Power in Education*. Edited by Frank Lutz and Joseph Azzarelli. New York: The Center for Applied Research in Education, 1965.

———. *The Superintendent of Schools: A Historical Analysis*. Washington, D.C.: Office of Education, 1966.

Callahan, Raymond, and Button, Warren. "Historical Change of the Role of the Man in the Organization, 1865–1950." *Behavioral Science and Educational Administration*, Vol. 63. Edited by Daniel Griffiths. Chicago: University of Chicago Press, 1964.

Carlson, Richard. *School Superintendents: Careers and Performance.* Columbus, Ohio: Charles Merrill Co., 1972.

Chamberlain, Arthur. "The Growth and Enlargement of the Power of the City School Superintendent." University of California, *Publications,* vol. 3, May 15, 1913.

Charters, W. W., Jr. "Social Class Analysis and the Control of Public Education." *Harvard Educational Review* 23 (Fall 1953): 268–83.

Chicago Daily News. 1961–1965.

Chicago Defender. 1961–1965.

Chicago Public Schools. *Official Report of the Proceedings of the Board of Education.* 1960–1966.

————. *We Build: Annual Reports.* 1953–1966.

Chicago Sun Times. 1961–1965.

Chicago Tribune. 1961–1965.

Chicago Urban League. *Unreported Classrooms.* Chicago. December 5, 1961.

Cohen, Sol. *Progressives and Urban School Reform.* New York: Columbia University, Teachers College, 1964.

Coons, John. "Chicago." In *Civil Rights U.S.A.: Public Schools, 1962.* U.S. Commission on Civil Rights, 1962.

Crain, Robert L. *The Politics of School Desegregation.* Chicago: Aldine Publishing, 1968.

Cronin, Joseph. *The Control of Urban Schools.* New York: Free Press, 1973.

Cubberley, Ellwood P. *Public School Administration.* Boston: Houghton-Mifflin Co., 1916.

"*De Facto* Segregation in the Chicago Public Schools." *Crisis* 65 (February 1958): 87–93.

Department of Superintendence. *Educational Leadership.* Eleventh Yearbook. Washington, D.C.: National Education Association, 1933.

Douglass, Bennett C. "Professional and Economic Status of the City Superintendent of Schools in the United States." Ph.D. dissertation, Columbia University, 1923.

Furnas, J. C. "He Runs Everything Except Tugboats." *Nation's Business,* May 1951, pp. 43–44, 78–79.

Gear, Harold. "The Rise of City School Superintendency as an Influence on Educational Policy." Ed.D. dissertation, Harvard University, 1950.

Gilland, Thomas M. *The Origins and Development of the Powers and Duties of the City-School Superintendent.* Chicago: University of Chicago Press, 1935.

Gittell, Marilyn, and Hollander, Edward T. *Six Urban School Districts.* New York: Praeger, 1968.

Goldhammer, Keith. *The School Board.* New York: Center for Applied Research, 1964.

Green, Constance. *The Secret City*. Princeton, N.J.: Princeton University Press, 1967.

Gross, Neal. *Who Runs Our Schools?* New York: John Wiley, 1958.

Hansen, Carl. *Amidon Elementary School*. Englewood Cliffs, N.J.: Prentice-Hall, 1962.

―――. Correspondence File, 1963-1967.

―――. *Danger in Washington*. West Nyack, N.Y.: Parker Publishing Co., 1968.

―――. *Four Track Curriculum For Today's High School*. Englewood Cliffs, N.J.: Prentice-Hall, 1964.

―――. *Miracle of Adjustment*. New York: Anti-Defamation League, 1957.

―――. "More to Come." Paper presented to D.C. Congress of Parents and Teachers, Washington, D.C., May 4, 1967.

―――. "Period of Danger, Time of Hope." Paper presented to D.C. Congress of Parents and Teachers, Washington, D.C., May 3, 1966.

―――. "Response of the Superintendent to Urban League Proposals on Desegregation." Washington, D.C., September 1, 1964.

―――."The Revolution and Big City Schools." Paper presented to Teachers' Institute, Washington, D.C., October 27, 1965.

―――. "Superintendent's Report to the Board of Education." Washington, D.C., June 11, 1964.

Havighurst, Robert. "Education and the Social Problems of the Big City." Paper presented to the American Association for the Advancement of Science, December 30, 1962.

―――. *The Public Schools of Chicago*. Chicago: Board of Education, 1964.

Herrick, Mary. *Chicago Schools: A Social and Political History*. Beverly Hills: Sage Publications, 1971.

Hill, Roscoe, and Feely, Malcolm. *Affirmative School Integration*. Beverly Hills: Sage Publications, 1967.

Hinsdale, B. A. "The American School Superintendent." *Educational Review* 5 (January 1894): 42–54.

Inkeles, Alex. "The Socialization of Competence." *Harvard Educational Review* 36 (Summer 1966): 265–83.

Janowitz, Morris. *Institution Building in Urban Education*. Chicago: University of Chicago Press, 1969.

Johnson, Ronald W. "Captain of Education: An Intellectual Biography of Andrew S. Draper, 1848–1913." Ph.D. dissertation, University of Illinois, 1970.

Kirst, Michael, and Wirt, Frederick. *The Political Web of American Schools*. Boston: Little, Brown, 1972.

Kopkind, Andrew, and Ridgeway, James. "Washington—The

Last Colony.'' *New Republic,* April 23 and 30, 1966, pp. 13–17, 19–22.

Lee, Robert Jr. ''Educational Ideology and Decision-Making in the San Francisco Schools, 1956–1966.'' Ed.D. dissertation, Syracuse University, 1967.

Liston, Robert. ''Pugnacious Planner of America's Future.'' *True,* May 1965, pp. 71–76.

London, Stephen. ''Business and the Chicago Public School System, 1890–1966.'' Ph.D. dissertation, University of Chicago, 1968.

March, James, and Cohen, Michael. *Leadership and Ambiguity.* New York: McGraw-Hill, 1974.

Marris, Peter, and Rein, Martin. *Dilemmas of Social Reform.* New York: Atherton Press, 1967.

Meier, August, and Rudwick, Elliot. *CORE: A Study in the Civil Rights Movement, 1942–1968.* New York: Oxford University Press, 1973.

Mintzberg, Henry. *The Nature of Managerial Work.* New York: Harper and Row, 1973.

''Model School System: A Preliminary Report.'' Washington, D.C. Public Schools, September 15, 1964.

Morrison, John C. *The Legal Status of the City School Superintendent.* Baltimore: Warwick and York, Inc., 1922.

Moynihan, Daniel. *Maximum Feasible Misunderstanding.* New York: Free Press, 1970.

National Educational Association, *Journal of Proceedings and Addresses.* 1871–1940.

Newlon, Jesse H. *Educational Administration as Social Policy.* New York: Charles Scribner's Sons, 1934.

Nickens, Norman. ''Model School System Submission of Education Proposals.'' Washington, D.C. Public Schools, November, 1964.

Passow, Harry. *Toward Creating a Model Urban School System.* New York: Columbia University, Teachers College, 1967.

Philbrick, John D. *City School Systems in the United States.* Bureau of Education, Circular of Information, no. 1. Washington, D.C.: Government Printing Office, 1885.

''Philosophy for Administration: Interview with Benjamin Willis.'' *Nation's Schools,* April 1961, pp. 71–76.

Pois, Joseph. *The School Board Crisis.* Chicago: Educational Methods, Inc., 1964.

President's Committee on Juvenile Delinquency. *Washington Action for Youth.* Vol.1 (March 1965).

President's Panel on Educational Research and Development. *Innovation and Experiment in Education.* March 1964.

Reller, Theodore. *The Development of the City Superintendency of Schools in the United States.* Philadelphia: Published by author, 1935.

''Report of the *Ad Hoc* Committee of the Board of Education to

Study Ethnic Factors in the San Francisco Public Schools.''
San Francisco Unified School District. April 2, 1963.
Report of the San Francisco Curriculum Survey Committee.
April 1960.
Rogers, David. *110 Livingston Street: Politics and Bureau-
cracy in the New York Schools.* New York: Random House,
1968.
Rowe, Gerald H., Jr. ''A Taxonomic Analysis of the
Budget-Making Structure of the San Francisco Unified
School District.'' Ph.D. dissertation, Stanford University,
1966.
Saliterman, Gail. ''Citizen Participation in an Urban School
System: The Washington Case.'' *Citizen Participation.*
Edited by Barry Passett and Edgar Cahn. New Jersey Com-
munity Training, Inc., 1970.
San Francisco Call-Bulletin. 1957–1965.
San Francisco Chronicle. 1957–1965.
San Francisco Examiner. 1957–1965.
San Francisco News. 1957–1965.
San Francisco Unified School District. *Board of Education
Transcripts.* Selected meetings, 1958–1964.
————. *Curriculum Committee Transcript.* Selected readings,
1959–1960.
Sayre, Wallace. ''Additional Observations on the Study of
Administration.'' *Teacher Record* 60 (October 1958):
73–76.
''The School Master, 1960.'' *Newsweek,* November 12, 1960,
pp. 96–97.
Silberman, Charles. *Crisis in Black and White.* New York:
Random House, 1964.
Smith, Mortimer. ''How to Teach the California Child: Notes
From the Never-Never Land.'' *Atlantic,* September, 1958,
pp. 32–36.
Spears, Harold. *The High School Today.* New York: American
Book Co., 1950.
————. *Improving the Supervision of Instruction.* Englewood
Cliffs, N.J.: Prentice-Hall, Inc., 1953.
————. Interview. Phi Delta *Kappan.* Bloomington, Indiana.
May, 1973.
————. *Preliminary Reactions to the Report of San Fran-
cisco's Curriculum Survey Committee.* San Francisco Unified
School District, 1960.
————. ''Rededicate the Bridge between School and Home,''
Nation's Schools, August 1955, pp. 38–39.
————. ''The Proper Recognition of a Pupil's Racial
Background.'' San Francisco Unified School District, June
19, 1962.
————. ''The Superintendent and Leadership.'' *American
School and University* 37 (October 1964): 51–53.
————. ''The Superintendent's Giants and the Windmills.''

Official Report, 1966–1967. Washington, D.C.: AASA, 1967.

Star, Jack. "Chicago's Troubled Schools." *Look,* May 4, 1965, pp. 59–61.

Tyack, David. "City Schools: Centralization of Control at the Turn of the Century." *Organizational Society.* Edited by J. Israel. New York: Free Press, 1972.

———. *The One Best System.* Cambridge, Mass.: Harvard University Press, 1974.

Turner, Joseph. *Making New Schools.* New York: David McKay, 1971.

United Planning Organization. "Memorandum from Cy Rotter to Task Force." Washington, D.C., March 11, 1966.

"U.S. Appeals Court Judge J. Skelly Wright's Decision on the District of Columbia's Track System." *Congressional Record,* June 21, 1967, pp. H7655–H7702.

Washington Afro-American. 1962–1967.

Washington, D.C. *Annual Report: Government of the District of Columbia.* 1962.

Washington, D.C., Board of Education. *Minutes.* Vols. 110–115, 1963–1968.

Washington, D.C., Model School Division. "Summary of Per Pupil Expenditures for Elementary and Secondary School Pupils by School Year." 1968.

Washington, D.C., Public Schools. *Superintendent Circulars.* 1963–1967.

Washington, D.C., Urban League. "Integration in the Public Schools." June 1964.

Washington Post. 1962–1967.

Washington Star. 1962–1967.

Willis, Benjamin C. "Education, the Partner of Progress." *Official Report.* Washington, D.C.: AASA, 1958.

———. "A Mid-Century View of Staffing a City School System." Ed.D. dissertation, Teachers College, Columbia University, 1950.

———. "The Need for Professionalism in Education Today." *Chicago School Journal.* Vol. 40 (March, 1959), pp. 273–280.

———. "Preserving Our Way of Life." *School Executive,* Vol. 69 (June, 1950), pp. 57–58.

———. *Social Problems in Public School Administration.* Pittsburgh: University of Pittsburgh Press, 1967.

———. "Using the Criticism of Public Schools toward Constructive Purposes." *Elementary School Journal.* Vol. 55 (September, 1954), pp. 13–23.

"Willis Concentrates on Quality Education for All: An interview." Phi Delta *Kappan* 46 (December 1964): 159–161.

Wirt, Frederick. "Alioto and the Politics of Hyperpluralism."
    Transaction 7 (April 1970): 46–55.
Zeigler, Harmon; Jennings, Kent M.; and Peak, Wayne G.
    Governing American Schools. Sciutate, Mass.: Duxbury
    Press, 1974.

Index

AASA (American Association of School Administrators), xi, xii, 2, 59, 63, 80, 115, 122, 137, 157, 159, 171

Ad Hoc Committee to Study Ethnic Factors (San Francisco): appointed by school board, 77–78; denies existence of de facto segregation, 78; findings of, 78–79

Administrative chief (corporate administrator), superintendent as, 116–18, 127–28, 141, 142, 143

Administrative strategies of superintendents, 94–95

AFT (American Federation of Teachers), 71

Amidon Plan (Amidon School, Washington, D.C.), 31, 32, 33, 35, 48, 50, 145, 147, 148, 149, 150

Bacon, Warren, 5

Banks, James, 46–47

Bazelon, David, 42

Boards of Education. *See* School boards

Bureaucracies of big cities, compared, 95–97

Cardozo school area (Washington, D.C.): chosen

by WAY for its experimental project, 36–37; proposed by Hansen for model subsystem, 40; slighted by Hansen in funding, 46

CCCO (Coordinating Council of Community Organizations) (Chicago), 13, 28, 98

Central Junior High School (San Francisco), and desegregation controversy, 74–77, 101, 162, 163

Chicago: action taken by civil rights groups in, 9–28; compared with San Francisco and Washington, D.C., 81–85; Democratic machine politics in, 7; pattern of community in, 83; pattern of segregation in, 8–9; political structure of, 81, 82, 83

Chicago board of education, 2–29 passim; accused by Willis of changing neighborhood school policy, 23; approves Willis's school boundary changes, 14–15; clashes of some members with Willis, 5; dominated by Willis, 5–6, 92; and mobile classroom controversy, 15–16; and "permissive transfer" policy, 18;